C000042665

Higher Education and Police

Colin Rogers • Bernhard Frevel
Editors

Higher Education and Police

An International View

palgrave
macmillan

Editors
Colin Rogers
University of South Wales - Pontypridd
Pontypridd, UK

Bernhard Frevel
Institut für Polizei- & Kriminalwissenschaften
FH für öffentliche Verwaltung NRW
Münster, Nordrhein-Westfalen, Germany

ISBN 978-3-319-64408-0   ISBN 978-3-319-58386-0   (eBook)
DOI 10.1007/978-3-319-58386-0

Library of Congress Control Number: 2017955017

© The Editor(s) (if applicable) and The Author(s) 2018
This work is subject to copyright. All rights are solely and exclusively licensed by the Publisher, whether the whole or part of the material is concerned, specifically the rights of translation, reprinting, reuse of illustrations, recitation, broadcasting, reproduction on microfilms or in any other physical way, and transmission or information storage and retrieval, electronic adaptation, computer software, or by similar or dissimilar methodology now known or hereafter developed.
The use of general descriptive names, registered names, trademarks, service marks, etc. in this publication does not imply, even in the absence of a specific statement, that such names are exempt from the relevant protective laws and regulations and therefore free for general use.
The publisher, the authors and the editors are safe to assume that the advice and information in this book are believed to be true and accurate at the date of publication. Neither the publisher nor the authors or the editors give a warranty, express or implied, with respect to the material contained herein or for any errors or omissions that may have been made. The publisher remains neutral with regard to jurisdictional claims in published maps and institutional affiliations.

Cover illustration: jsmith

Printed on acid-free paper

This Springer imprint is published by Springer Nature
The registered company is Springer International Publishing AG
The registered company address is: Gewerbestrasse 11, 6330 Cham, Switzerland

Acknowledgement

Professor Colin Rogers would like to acknowledge his wife, Alison Rogers, for her support throughout his career and for her encouragement in this work.

Contents

List of Contributors

Aun Hunsager Andresen is a police superintendent in charge of the evaluation of police students attending the second year of their bachelor's degree at the Police University College, Norway. Prior to this, he was a teacher at the Police University College for eight years, and then a patrolling officer. He holds a master's degree in police science from the Norwegian Police University College and has also studied educational guidance and management.

Publications: (2014) *Politiets trening på bruk av fysisk makt.* Oslo: Politihøgskolen. (2008). *Arrestasjonsteknikkens historiske utvikling i norsk politiutdanning.* Oslo: Politihøgskolen.

Zheng Chen is a lecturer at National Police University of China. He studied policing studies at Charles Sturt University, Australia. He researches police culture, community policing, police occupational attitude, police job satisfaction and police education.

Selected publications: 2016. *Measuring police subcultural perceptions: A study of frontline police officers in China*, Springer: Singapore; 2016. An exploratory study of police cynicism in China, Policing: An International Journal of Police Strategies and Management, 39 (1), 175–189; 2016. Measuring police role orientations in China: An exploratory study, *International Journal of Law, Crime and Justice*, 44 (1), 43–67.

Steve Darroch is the head of School Prevention and an acting director training at the Royal New Zealand Police College. He is an inspector of New Zealand Police. He studied psychology and sociology at Victoria University of Wellington

New Zealand; management and business at Massey University Palmerston North New Zealand and criminology and criminal justice at Griffith University Queensland, Australia. He leads training for New Zealand Police in crime prevention, family violence, youth interventions, road policing, intelligence, community policing and problem solving and training for New Zealand Police international deployments into the Pacific and beyond. His research interests include intelligence-led policing, police innovation, police training and the intergenerational transmission of harm.

Selected publications: *Intelligence: The dilemmas of Intelligence and Ethical Police Practice: Policing Terrorism and Managing Covert Human sources in Ethical Police Practice*. Edited by P. A. J. Waddington, John Kleinig, and Martin Wright Oxford (2013). Intelligence-led Policing: A comparative analysis of organizational factors influencing innovation uptake (with Professor Lorraine Mazerolle) *Police Quarterly* March 2013. Intelligence-led Policing A comparative analysis of Community Context influencing innovation uptake (with Professor Lorraine Mazerolle) *Policing an International Journal of Police Strategies and Management*, April 2013.

Bernhard Frevel is Professor of Social Sciences at the Fachhochschule für öffentliche Verwaltung NRW – University of Applied Sciences for Public Administration of North Rhine-Westphalia (Germany). He studied pedagogics, sociology, psychology and political science at the Universities of Siegen, Cologne and Hagen. He researches the security system in Germany, local safety and crime prevention, security governance and police education.

Selected publications: (with Hartmut Aden) 2017. Policing metropolises in a system of cooperative federalism: Berlin and Cologne compared. In Paul Ponsaers, Elke Devroe and Adam Edwards (ed.), *Policing European Metropolises*. Oxon (Taylor & Francis); (with Colin Rogers) 2016. Community Partnerships (UK) vs. Crime Prevention Councils (GER): differences and similarities. In *The Police Journal – Theory, Practice and Principles*, vol. 89 (2), pp. 133–150; 2015. Pluralisation of local policing in Germany. Security between the state's monopoly of force and the market. In *European Journal of Policing Studies*, vol. 2 (3), pp. 267–284.

Anders Green is a Ph. Licentiate in criminology. For the master's degree in social sciences, he studied political science, criminology and sociology at the universities of Lund and Stockholm. He has been working within the Swedish judicial system for approximately 25 years, whereof the major part as a senior lecturer at the former Swedish National Police Academy. Amongst his other employees, one can find the Police Authority and the Swedish Prison and

Probation Service. He is working as a researcher at the Swedish National Council for Crime Prevention. His research CV is versatile and covers long-term prisoners, community policing and domestic violence. The field of research for the postgraduate level was football and hooliganism in England and Scandinavia. (All publications are written in Swedish.)

Tracey Green has 22 years of police experience as a sworn officer in the UK. Serving to the rank of detective inspector, she has extensive experience in the areas of serious and serial criminal investigation, in particular, homicide, drug and police corruption. Since joining Charles Sturt University, Green has been a strong advocate of policing as a profession and has developed a history of collaboration with police and law enforcement agencies ensuring that educational and research opportunities are relevant and aligned to policing. She has also been instrumental in the development of postgraduate courses in the areas of investigation, intelligence, terrorism and police leadership all of which involve research by the practitioner into their own area of professional expertise.

Green has been instrumental in establishing formal partnerships between the university and numerous law enforcement agencies both national and international. She has also been chief investigator for several ARC grants and has delivered numerous papers at industry conferences. Green is engaged in research in relation to Police Education and Investigative Interviewing and recently published her co-authored text book *Investigative Interviewing Explained* (4th edition).

Katja M. Hallenberg is Senior Lecturer in Criminal Psychology, Criminology and Policing, School of Law, Criminal Justice & Computing, Canterbury Christ Church University.

Recent publications: Hallenberg, K. M. & Haddow, C. (2016) 'Beyond Criminal Justice: Connecting Justice and Sustainability', *The Law Teacher,* 50(3), pp. 352–370. Hallenberg, K. M. (2016) 'Benefits and challenges of academic police education'. In Phillips, S. W. & Das, D. K. (eds.), *Change and Reform in Law Enforcement: Old and New Efforts from Across the Globe.* Boca Raton, FL: CRC Press, pp. 3–26. Hallenberg, K. & Tennant, M. (2016) 'Criminology Picks Up the Gauntlet: Responses to the Whole Earth Exhibition'. In Woodfield, K. (ed.), *Inspire – teaching and learning in the Social Sciences.* HEA. Available online at: http://inspiringsocsci.pressbooks.com/chapter/criminology-picks-up-the-gauntlet-responses-to-the-whole-earth-exhibition/

Jan Heinen was a police officer for nearly 20 years in Amsterdam and studied Law (LLM) at the University of Amsterdam. He is Lecturer in Laws at the Police

Academy of the Netherlands, School of Higher Police Education (bachelor and master of policing), and coordinator of the minor Police Science and an international school (Summerschool) with partners in Germany and Wales. Since 2014, he is also the secretary of the Board of Appeals for the Exams on the Police Academy of the Netherlands. He is a member of the advisory board of a high school (Guido) in the city of Amersfoort and a member of the Board of Appeals of the Dutch Football Association (KNVB).

Nina Jon holds a PhD in Criminology from the University of Oslo. She is an associate professor and head of studies master degree at the Norwegian Police University College. Her main professional interests are juvenile delinquency, masculinity, men and gender equality, and crime prevention.

Selected publications: "Transforming Cowboy Masculinity into Appropriate Masculinity" in Ingrid Lander, Signe Ravn and Nina Jon (ed.), *Masculinities in the Criminological Field: Control, Vulnerability and Risk-Taking.* London: Ashgate, 2014; Ericsson, Kjersti og Nina Jon (2006). Gendered social control: "a virtuous girl" and "a proper boy" *Journal of Scandinavian Studies in Criminology and Crime Prevention*, vol. 7, pp. 126–141.

André Konze is working at the European External Action Service within the Civilian Planning Conduct Capability, Brussels. He obtained another part of his international experience as a program manager of the Police and Human Rights Programme within the Council of Europe. On a German national level, he held the positions of head of police precincts, head of the Police Scientific Training, Development and Research at the German Police University, and head of a Training Department. Furthermore, he was involved in CEPOL (Collège Européen de Police) and several other training activities, and in numerous international conferences. He possesses a great experience in exploring foreign organisations. As a distance-learning student with Portsmouth University, he acquainted himself with how to interpret international legislation such as the European Convention on Human Rights and international terrorism countermeasures and dealt with the US legislation after the attacks of 9/11 in his dissertation. Konze is enrolled as a doctoral learner with the University of Phoenix on a DM course on Organizational Management. He was the chair of the ELEES Working Group CEPOL and was also involved in developing and reviewing training handbooks of the OSCE.

Detlef Nogala has been working at the European Union Agency for Law Enforcement Training (CEPOL) in Budapest as Research & Knowledge Management Officer since 2007. He has received university diplomas in organisational psychology and criminology and used to be a lecturer at the University of Hamburg and Police Academy of Hamburg. Before joining CEPOL, he was a scholar at the Max-Planck-Institute for Foreign and International Criminal Law in Freiburg i.Br., Germany.

Selected publications: (co-editor) 2017: "Police science and police practise in Europe". Special Conference Edition No. 2, European Police Science and Research Bulletin (co-editor), 2016: "Policing civil societies in times of economic constraints". Special Conference Edition No. 1, European Police Science and Research Bulletin. Luxembourg: Publications Office of the European Union.

Harry Peeters retired from the Police Academy of the Netherlands as a senior strategic consultant for the executive board, which enabled him to become the architect of the coherent system of Dutch police training from basic educational levels up to master programmes and to get involved in constructing curricula for CEPOL, for example, with regard to a Competency Framework for Senior Police Officers, a 'Policing in Europe' course and the European Joint Master Programme as well as for collaborative projects of Canterbury Christ Church University (CCCU) and the Dutch Police Academy, for example, with regard to a European Diploma in Policing (EDP) and MSc in Policing, of which he was the former programme director on the Dutch side. As a visiting senior research fellow for Canterbury Christ Church University, Peeters teaches a module on European Policing of CCCU's MA in Policing & Criminal Justice. He also acts as a liaison between CCCU, Dutch Universities of Applied Sciences and the Police Academy of the Netherlands. His publications in English refer to reviews for the London MET Police Service on efficiency, culture and branding of the Dutch Police as well as to articles on ways to blend academic learning within professional police training and on constructing internationally comparative competency profiles. He contributed to the publication of Leading Policing in Europe (Caless and Tong) in terms of conducting and translating interviews with Dutch, Belgian and German police leaders. Formerly, he was a director of a Governance & Law Faculty at Saxion University of Applied Sciences in Enschede, the Netherlands. He graduated in political science and specialised in international relations and polemology. He was a councillor for a Pacifist-Socialist Party in the city of Nijmegen.

Colin Rogers is Professor of Police Sciences at the University of South Wales, UK, where he is a senior academic and research lead for the International Centre for Policing and Security. A former police officer with 30 years of service, Rogers studied police studies (BA Hons) and social science research methods (MSc) at the University of Glamorgan. He also undertook his PhD with the same university. He has researched many aspects of policing at a national and an international level including work in countries such as Uruguay, Brunei, and Australia and across Europe. He has taught police officers at all levels of academia and on practitioner courses. He edits three police-related journals.

Selected publications: Rogers, C., (2016) *Plural Policing, Theory, Practice and Principles*, Policy Press, Bristol. (Book), Rogers, C., (2017), Alley gates and domestic burglary: Findings from a longitudinal study in urban South Wales, *Police Journal: Theory, Practice and Principles*, vol. 1, pp. 1–17; Cuerden, G., and Rogers, C., (2017), Exploring Race Hate Crime Reporting in Wales following Brexit, *Review of European Studies*, vol. 9, no.1, Toronto, Canada; Skilling, L. and Rogers, C., (2107), Crime prevention and coping mechanisms in neighbourhoods: Insights from Kibera, Nairobi. *The International Journal of Crime Prevention and Community Safety*, vol. 19, (1); Rogers, C., (2016), Call to Arms, *Police Professional*, issue no. 490, pp. 21–22; Rogers, C., (2016), Slipping under the radar? *Police Professional*, issue no. 497, pp. 18–19; Rogers, C. and Welch, D. (2016). Cultural perceptions. *Police Professional*. June, issue no. 509, pp. 16–17.

José-Vicente Tavares dos Santos Sociologist, Federal University of Rio Grande do Sul, Brasil; Master of Sociology, University of Sao Paulo, Brasil; Docteur d'Etat, University of Paris X, Nanterre. He is Professor of Sociology and Director of the Latin American Institute for Advanced Studies, Federal University of Rio Grande do Sul, Brazil, and a senior researcher at CNPq, National Council of Scientific Development. His researches are about violence, security policies in Latin America, police education and the novels of violence.

Selected publications: (with BARREIRA, César (Eds.). *Paradoxos da Segurança Cidadã*. Porto Alegre, TOMO, 2014 (http://www.clacso.org.ar/ libreria-latinoamericana/inicio.php); with BARREIRA, César; ZULUAGA, Jaime (Eds.). *Control social, conflictos y ciudadanía*. Barranquilla, Colombia: Universidad del Norte Editorial/CLACSO, 2012. (http://www.clacso.org.ar/ libreria-latinoamericana/inicio.php); Violências e Conflitualidades. Porto Alegre: TOMO, 2009, 176 p.; "*Contemporary Latin American Sociology and the Challenges for an International Dialogue*". In: BIALAKOWSKY, Alberto L. et alii (eds.), *Latin American Critical Thought: Theory and Practice*. Buenos Aires: CLACSO, 2012, pp. 237–271. http://bibliotecavirtual.clacso.org.ar/clacso/sur-sur/20120801013201/LatinAmericacriticalthought.pdf

Bethan Smith is a postgraduate student and researcher based at the International Centre for Policing and Security, University of South Wales. She is currently engaged on an outreach work for a local authority and her research interests included police and community interactions, as well as the introduction of the College of Policing.

Stephen Tong is Reader in Policing & Criminal Justice at the School of Law, Criminal Justice & Computing, Canterbury Christ Church University. He is the director of the Canterbury Centre for Policing Research (CCPR), Canterbury Christ Church University, and an adjunct associate professor, Charles Sturt University, Graduate School of Policing & Security.

Selected Publications: (with R. Heaton) (2015). *Evidence-Based Policing: From Effectiveness to Cost-Effectiveness. Policing.* 10. 1–11. 10.1093/police/pav030. (with M. Brunger & Danise Martin (eds.) (2016) *Introduction to policing research. Taking lessons from practice.* Oxon: Routledge. (with Bry Caless) (2017) *Leading policing in Europe. An empirical study of strategic police leadership.* Bristol: Policy Press.

List of Figures

List of Tables

1

Introduction: Higher Police Education— An International Perspective

Colin Rogers and Bernhard Frevel

When considering the future of policing one thing is certain. Policing does not exist in a vacuum. It is impacted upon daily and, in the long term, by changes in the social, political, economic, technological, environmental and legal structures, in whatever country it is practised. It therefore follows that the future structure and activities of policing will be shaped by the future changes within these and other activities.

In particular, policing is a 'people and information' occupation. Therefore, those who are responsible for police education in all countries need to clearly understand how populations alter, responding to strong currents within their society. Further, there is a need to understand how information is gathered, exchanged and utilised, and the consequences of

C. Rogers (✉)
University of South Wales,
Pontypridd, UK

B. Frevel
FH für öffentliche Verwaltung NRW, Institut für Polizei- und Kriminalwissenschaften, Münster, Nordrhein-Westfalen, Germany

© The Author(s) 2018
C. Rogers, B. Frevel (eds.), *Higher Education and Police*,
DOI 10.1007/978-3-319-58386-0_1

1

these activities. Globalisation, and the global economy, is now character-ised by the almost instantaneous flow and exchange of information, capi-tal and cultural communication (Castells 2010). The increasing nature and scope of crime and substantial increases in immigration tend to dem-onstrate that, what happens in one country can have an impact in others. It is in the face of these challenges that most Western-style police agencies are attempting to professionalise their police and, as a major part of this process, are involving their Higher Education (HE) system in some for-mat for educating their police officers. In order to understand why this should be the case, there is a need to briefly consider and understand the different types of challenges that lay ahead for the police.

Future Global Trends

The world's population will reach 8 billion by 2025, up from 6 billion in 2000 (National Intelligence Council 2008). However, this increase will not occur evenly across all countries. Developed countries will see a decline in population whilst those of developing countries will increase, particularly in sub-Saharan Africa and South Asia, which will have extremely youthful populations. Developed countries will witness an age-ing population rise, coupled with declining fertility rates, leading to less individuals of working age to support the population as a whole. Workers have to come from somewhere; as a consequence, we may witness a large expansion in immigration and shifts in population from one country to another. In terms of social changes then, such a population shift – which increases both migration and immigration – will bring with it the atten-dant risk of internal and external change within different societies. For example, the above population shift could bring about an expansion of the 'middle classes' across different countries, which could lead to an expansion of the consumerist society already witnessed in most Western countries to the global stage (Spybey 1996). This in turn could lead to a higher demand from communities for more service-oriented, citizen/consumer-style policing (Clarke et al. 2009), rather than a law enforce-ment model of policing as people come to understand their rights as consumers of private and public services.

Urbanisation is set to grow to about 60% in all countries (National Intelligence Council 2008) which not only will require a concentration of policing services within those areas but may also elicit a decline in social cohesiveness, which is required to support and promote 'self-policing'. This has been part of a continuing responsibilisation strategy for most democratic governments for some time within communities (Garland 2001).

Rapid political changes, coupled with wider social movements, are likely to exist, which might produce serious governance difficulties. There may be wider democratisation, which will lead to greater calls for transparency and accountability in policing agencies across the globe, coupled with greater franchise. This could occur despite the possibility of increased nationalism. Clearly the political landscape will be far more complicated in the future than hitherto.

Perhaps the biggest area of change for international policing will be seen in the greater use and expansion of more and more sophisticated technology on a global stage. Not only will it influence organisational behaviour and crime trends, but it will also impact upon individual and personal lifestyles. Developments in technology will further enhance the potential for greater and swifter communication between groups of people who are able to organise themselves for dealing with such activities as political protest, whilst the potential for global crime, such as terrorism, will increase exponentially. Schafer et al. (2012) suggest the following major challenges for the police in terms of the current trends in technology:

- New types of crime will come into being
- Traditional crime will become enhanced by new technologies
- There will develop a technology gap with the police falling further behind the private sector in understanding and acquiring new technologies.

Whilst new technology provides challenges for police, it can also provide benefits. For example, improvements in data analysis tools, biometrics and less lethal technologies provide enhancements for police activities.

One cannot ignore the fact that increased problems for policing agencies may occur as a result of environmental and climate change. The recent large-scale bush fires in Australia, extensive floods in UK and elsewhere in the world, and severe snow-storms in the USA, may indicate that natural disasters could increase in scale and intensity. Increased opportunities for global travel may increase the possibility of a worldwide pandemic. These potential environmental problems will in turn require different and varied responses at a national and international level, and a greater need and demand for closer cooperation between police agencies with more and wider services across the world.

Possibly more crime prevention activities will need to be in place, with the greater use of surveillance, and situational crime prevention techniques, rather than costly social interventions. The challenge for all policing agencies will be that of providing and stimulating a need for greater social cohesion/community involvement (Rogers 2012; Wedlock 2006) in the delivery of policing services due to the 'thinning out' of previously well-funded police organisations. This enhanced cooperation and partnership approach with communities will be vital in order to maintain the very legitimacy that allows for policing in democracies.

Old Structures Challenged

Like most modern organisations, police agencies in Western countries trace their origins to the country's industrial revolution and, consequently, their structures are similar, with workers being supervised by an overseer within a hierarchical structure that separates front-line officers from strategic policy makers (Hebdon and Kirkpatrick 2006). The paramilitary model of policing does not adapt well to external demands for change or accountability, and there is still a tendency to adhere to historical ideas regarding management practices. Therefore, policing agencies in developed countries are in need of a revolution in their organisation, leadership and management models in order to deal with the future issues that they will have to face. The fundamental tool in achieving this will be the education of police officers. The concept of community policing, whether rhetoric or reality (Green and Mastrofski 1988), is an appealing one for countries seeking to legitimise their policing process, especially when tourism or leisure economics are seen as a way of developing growth and security. However, the very idea of the Western or democratic style and structure of policing is itself in need of enormous change, and therefore international police agencies need to appreciate and understand the potential impact of future trends upon traditional police structures.

In addition, we have seen, particularly in Western-style democracies and police agencies, how the delivery of policing has altered. Previously police organisations were considered experts in their field and were stand-alone agencies who dealt with all crime-related matters. Over the past decade or so, there has been a drive to involve many other agencies in policing, particularly in the field of crime prevention (Rogers 2012). This has meant police officers at all levels of the organisation having to become involved in more and complex partnership working arrangements. In particular, police officers now have to work with many other professionals who are in the main, all degree or higher educationally qualified. The partnership approach to policing means that the police organisation has, in many instances, to improve its performance alongside other professionals. This also encapsulates a different form of thinking about how policing should be carried out with partners. The rise of the Problem-Oriented Policing approach (Goldstein 1990), for example, has introduced sometimes complex theory directly into mainstream policing activities. In support of more focused activities of policing and partnership working, evidence-based policing has gained momentum. Here the utilisation of information and intelligence to focus police and partner agency resources has meant that a deeper and more scientific understanding of the knowledge gathered by police and other groups is required. In many senses police officers and staff are becoming knowledge workers (Harfield et al. 2008), as more complex uses of information and intelligence are developed by the police.

Challenges for Police Organisations

Given the organisational changes to police agencies in the last decade or so, coupled with a more complex manner of dealing with crime and disorder, the way police are educated is of vital importance. Old methods of policing need to be challenged and sometimes to be replaced as societies change. The so-called professionalisation of police agencies across the globe, which includes greater involvement of HE establishments in police education, is seen as one way of dealing with such complexities.

For developing and developed countries alike, the education of their police will need to be adjusted to meet the potential global challenges that are likely to occur. Technology and financial links, coupled with increased travel technology, means that threats and risks are constructed on a global landscape as well as locally, regionally and nationally. An understanding of such, and an appreciation of how structures are connected at the global level, will be an important skill for the police in whatever country they are situated. Further, an ability to manage change at short notice, coupled with complex abilities such as an understanding of research methods, mastering and understanding technological changes and trends will be required. Factors that impact upon national and international law and an ability to integrate strategy, culture and political concerns within the organisation will also be required skills. In particular, as a framework surrounding all of these changes and ideas, police leaders of today need to understand that they were trained in a substantially non-changing, bureaucratic, structured organisation which has resulted in an organisational culture which sometimes displays fixed attitudes, and that this structure will need to be changed in order to meet the challenges of the future.

The Structure of the Book

The first part of this book discusses several aspects of professionalisation and tries to answer the question of how HE not only influences the educated officers but also changes the organisation towards professionalism. Referring to Abbott (1988: 8) 'professions are exclusive occupational groups applying somewhat abstract knowledge to particular cases'. And so the question occur, whether HE builds up this 'abstract knowledge', whether HE- institutes, meant: police academies and universities, develop this knowledge by (police) research and how both effects alter the organisation, the perception of the organisation by the citizens and therefor influences the legitimacy of the police.

In the chapter 'Education and the police professionalisation agenda: a perspective from England and Wales' Steve Tong and Katja Hellenberg (Canterbury Christ Church University) chart the development of police learning and education from historical perspective, starting with the role of police services in providing skills and knowledge for their officers. As a result of the changes to police practice and expectations, police education has gradually moved to the hands of outside providers, particularly HE institutions. The engagement between universities and the police and the different approaches adopted are discussed. The chapter offers an in-depth analysis of the various models of policing-related degrees, discussing the issues relating to professional knowledge, academic knowledge and flexibility of learning. The professionalisation agenda is key to understanding the increasing 'academisation' of police education and discussed here in the context of the introduction of the College of Policing and the code of ethics. Finally, the chapter considers the recent consultation around degree entry requirements for police officers and the consequences of this to serving police officers, future recruits and HE.

Anders Green (Swedish Crime Prevention Council & Swedish National Police Academy) draws the attention to Sweden, where a struggle between vocational and academic police training has been protracted and a political dimension has also developed. The social democrats put reforming police training in the top spot on their criminal political agenda for the election in 2014. During the last decade three governmental investigations have also looked into the necessity and circumstances to make police training academic, which will mean adding a year's training. And the police union is eagerly applauding this professionalisation in progress. Some steps have already been taken towards reforming the police education in an academic direction, even though the National Police Board is deciding the curriculum. But the training is still vocational, as the former conservative government did not consent to developing it into a bachelor degree. Noteworthy is that at the same time police training at one of universities recently has been merited with credits and its own university degree. So, the question is: What will happen next in this educational muddle?

On the other side of the word, in New Zealand, an inconsistent history of engagement between HE and police took place. Steven Darroch (University of Queensland) explains that the relationship has had its good and bad times with police and academics not really understanding each other's world-view or how they might constructively work together. At various points academic qualifications have been in vogue only to fall out of favour in the face of police reasserting hegemony over their own business. More recently the point of HE and academic inquiry has become clearer to police. The introduction of community policing and problem-solving approaches, coupled with the emergence of intelligence-led policing, crime sciences and third-party policing, has shown police the value of research and evidence. This in turn has driven strategic change in terms of police education under the banner of evidence-based policing. Despite this there appears some confusion as to how to weave science literacy and research skills into a qualification and training framework that makes sense. The variability of academic offerings to police has created uncertainty, with the most recent developments seeing the police partner with a polytechnic to support the development of initial training. The more practical, grounded nature of the polytechnic environment—where skills similar to policing such as nursing and social practice are taught—may help bridge the gaps between academe, research and front-line practice when this did not seem entirely achievable up to this point.

The second part of the book searches for the recent trends of innovation of HE. This innovation applies to fundamental changes in the organisation of HE or to new approaches within existing systems.

Colin Rogers and Beth Smith (University of South Wales) give an overview of the impact of the College of Policing in the UK. The relationship between HE and policing in England and Wales has historically been an inconsistent one. The introduction of the College of Policing as an overarching body for police education in 2011 was believed to be an important point in time to consolidate and update this relationship. However, what impact does it appear to have had upon the relationship between HE and policing and what are the possible future implications?

This chapter explores the rise in the College of Policing, its historical precedents, and its aims and objectives. Further it critically examines the expanding role of the college in terms of police research as well as the drive for the so-called professionalisation of policing, including its aim for creating a degree entry profession. As part of this aim, the college's relationship with HE and its impact upon a policing education qualifications framework are discussed.

The next chapter, written by Zheng Chen (National Chinese Police University), provides an overview of the development of police HE in China since the founding of the People's Republic of China. Different from Western countries, police HE in China bears its own characteristics. There are both national police universities and provincial police colleges or academies around the country, providing associate degree, undergraduate degree and postgraduate education. The education in these institutions includes both liberal studies that other universities provide and specialised courses aimed to train a police officer. Most graduates from these institutions will become police officers after attending competitive State Civil Service Examinations. These institutions also provide courses for in-service police training nationally or within a certain province. In addition, some comprehensive universities in China have also set up colleges or schools that offer police studies programmes or forensic studies courses. In this chapter, the author first introduces the history of police HE in China, with an emphasis on the development after the adoption of the reform and opening-up policy in 1978. The author also illustrates the police education and training system in China and introduces the main police universities, police colleges and police academies together with the main education and training programmes they offer.

Many countries in Late Modernity have introduced reforms in police academies, mainly to counter the public dissatisfaction with the policing model and the efficiency of law enforcement agencies. José-Vicente Tavares dos Santos (Federal University of Rio Grande do Sul, Porto Alegre) discusses the dilemmas of police education in Latin America and specifically Brazil, analysing both the issue of police education and the models of policing practices that are embedded in the Police HE system. In Brazil, there are two types of police in each state: the Patrol Police and the Judiciary Police. So, each one has their own Police Academy, divided into two blocks: one for the police officers, the other to the upper level of the hierarchy. The sociological question could be stated as follows: do the effects of social inequalities and the culture of violence in Brazil shape the dominant political culture in Police Academies? Are the Police Academies preparing aspiring officers to enforce the law, while respecting the limits imposed by the Constitutional State to ensure citizen's rights? Or else, are aspiring police officers being entrusted with repressive social control functions in contemporary Brazil? In this research, the key issue is that of the flow of information across nations, and the diffusion of concepts about institutions and organisations in a connected society. The Public Universities have been an important actor in this process, as a lot of institutions have provided graduate courses to police officers, supported by the Ministry of Justice. The main conclusions state a dilemma between 'training' and 'education' in police academies: this conceptual tension is between a narrow definition of the Police work and a more larger vision of the Police role in a democratic society.

With a comparative look on the developments of Higher Police Education in Europe Detlef Nogala (CEPOL) and Andre Konze (European External Action Service) finish this part of the book. In November 2013 the Governing Board of the European Police College (CEPOL) established the 'working group for the updating of the survey on the european law enforcement education systems (ELEES WG)'. ELEES followed previous CEPOL surveys. The purpose of the ELEES WG was to develop and to implement an online survey aiming at gathering data of and from institutions responsible for the training of law enforcement officials in the Member and Associate States of the European Union (MS/AS). ELEES covered 28 MS of the European Union, plus Iceland, Switzerland and Norway. For the data collection, an online questionnaire was sent to a network of respondents in the various countries. The data covered a wide range such as the status and internal organisation of law enforcement training institutions, the attribution/non-attribution of ECTS (European Credit Transfer and Accumulation System; measures the workload of students in HE), the involvement in Erasmus type programmes and/or in other European or international-level law enforcement training activities. The chapter is based on this unique set of pan-European empirical data on the structure and trends of law enforcement training and education in the European Union. In reference to earlier similar surveys in 2008 and 2011, actual developments and trends are highlighted.

Part three of this book presents some applications of Higher Police Education in Europe. Similarities and differences will show up and it becomes clearer that the specific programmes in Norway, Germany and the Netherlands not only give insight into the didactic of police education but also highlight the underlying 'police philosophies'.

Nina Jon introduces the Master programmes at the Norwegian Police University College and discusses how they respond to needs of higher analytical competence in the police. When the Norwegian Police University College offered its first 'Master in Police Science'-programme (120 ECTS) in 2006, it was an answer to a perceived need in the police for more analytical skills and competencies among its staff. Knowledge-based methods of policing required such competencies. The purpose of the Master's degree in police science is enhancing analytical and research expertise within the police. The programme will help strengthen the police's competence in a knowledge-based policing. It qualifies for various national and international assignments for the police such as analysis, project management and strategic management. There has been an increased demand for higher levels of education in criminal investigation, in particular because of several cases of failed investigations and errors of justice. Investigation is one of the police core tasks with stated requirements for rapid reconnaissance and high quality in all aspects of the work. It is a field with a long tradition and constant development of new knowledge based both on systematising experiences and various sciences. The ability of the police to solve investigation tasks is important for people's perception of safety and safeguarding the rule of law. It is therefore of great importance that the police have high investigator competence and that this is rooted in evidence-based knowledge. There is a demand for better competencies among leaders of criminal investigations to avoid such mistakes. The Norwegian Police University College now offers a master's in criminal investigation (90 ECTS).

Since the mid-1970s police officers in Germany—more or less—have enjoyed HE, aiming to become a Kommissar, a rank which is comparable to the Inspector in the UK system. So the German police have about 40 years of experience with HE. The importance of HE has grown over the years, for example, because of factual necessities in the context of social changes (knowledge society, democratisation, etc.); challenging developments in the fields of crime, terrorism, and so on; or the police unions' demands to improve the social situation of officers. The paper of Bernhard Frevel (University of Applied Science for Public Administration North Rhine-Westphalia) discusses the development of HE for the police against the background of the German framework for public services and the political decisions following a consulting report from the early 1990s. The system of HE will be presented and explained with the example of North Rhine-Westphalia. A critical view on the acceptance and effects of the system leads to a final discussion about the perspectives of a university-educated police.

Jan Heinen and Harry Peeters describe the training and study programme of the Politieacademie in the Netherlands. The Police Academy is the centre for training, knowledge and research for the Dutch National Police, offering training and knowledge programmes at the highest level, anticipating developments in society and translating these into customised education programmes. Consequently the Police Academy educates police officers at a vocational level but also offers fully accredited bachelor and master degree programmes in Policing and Criminal Investigation techniques. The Police Academy cooperates with the National Police and other (international) partners in the field of security, education, knowledge and research. This chapter considers the role of the Police Academy in light of the recent changes to the police organisation, which saw a reversal of previously fragmented and devolved police agencies to a more central and nationally controlled force. These problems include the 'lining up' of education and training for new positions and job profiles within a drive to professionalise the police organisation, with specific reference to the idea of labour market relevance (supply and demand).

Again, the other side of the world gets into focus when Tracey Green introduces Police Education at the Charles Sturt University, Australia.

Policing and HE in Australia have a long-standing and complex history. Whilst progress towards a full professional model has been made, levels of resistance are still evident in some quarters. This chapter focuses on the progress, which has been made towards policing achieving a professional status and discusses some of the changes and enduring partnership, which have evolved 'down under'. In particular the authors describe the collaborative recruit programme between the New South Wales Police Service and Charles Sturt University, which has endured for over 15 years with a new 10-year contract recently signed. This programme has stood the test of time whilst other such initiatives have failed to thrive. This paper explores the features of the collaboration in an effort to identify the factors, which may have led to the on-going resilience and success of this model for police recruitment within a HE programme. In addition the authors explore the patterns and trends of serving officers engaging in continual professional development within HE throughout Australia.

This introductory chapter highlights the perceived needs of police agencies in utilising HE to assist in dealing with potential strengths, weaknesses, threats and opportunities of the future on a global front, as well as dealing with internal organisational changes that affect the delivery of local policing.

Clearly there is a strong trend towards university-based qualification of police officers. Even though this book highlights and discusses some problems with this approach, the overriding belief is that the police need to have better qualifications through the HE route. The challenges for police and policing are growing, expectations of citizens are getting more diverse and demanding, the next generation of police officers expect to be part of a knowledge society and therefor desire a worthwhile qualification, which is up-to-date and opens job and career opportunities. The important question for the police is not whether the police should engage with HE, but rather 'how' this process is achieved. A modern police, faced with local, national and international challenges, should be underpinned by HE courses in order for them to be best equipped to deal with the challenges that will arise in the now and in the future.

References

Batts, A. W., Smoot, S. M., & Scrivner, E. (2012). *Police Leadership Challenges in a Changing World*. Available at https://ncjrs.gov/pdffiles1/nij/238338.pdf. Accessed 13 Mar 2014.

Castells, M. (2010). *The Rise of the Network Society* (2nd ed.). Chichester: Wiley-Blackwell.

Clarke, J., Newman, J., Smith, N., Vidler, E., & Westmarland, L. (2009). *Creating Citizen-Consumers: Changing Publics and Changing Public Services*. London: Sage.

Garland, D. (2001). *The Culture of Control: Crime and Social Order in Contemporary Society*. Oxford: Oxford University Press.

Goldstein, H. (1990). *Problem Oriented Policing*. New York: McGraw-Hill.

Greene, J. R., & Mastrofski, S. D. (1988). *Community policing: Rhetoric or Reality*. New York: Praeger Publishers.

Harfield, C., MacVean, A., Grieve, J. G. D., & Phillips, D. (2008). *The Handbook of Intelligent Policing*. Oxford: Oxford University Press.

Hebdon, R., & Kirkpatrick, I. (2006). Changes in the Organisation of Public Services and their Effects on Employment Relations. In S. Ackroyd et al. (Eds.), *The Oxford Handbook of Work and Organisation*. Oxford: Oxford University Press.

National Intelligence Council. (2008). *Global Trends 2030*. Available at http://www.dni.gov/files/documents/GlobalTrends_2030.pdf. Accessed 12 Mar 2014.

Rogers, C. (2012). *Crime Reduction Partnerships*. Oxford: Oxford University Press.

Schafer, J. A. (Ed.). *Policing 2020, Exploring the Future of Crime, Communities and Policing*. Available at http://fwg.cos.ucf.edu/publications/Policing2020.pdf. Accessed 12 Mar 2014.

Schafer, J. A., Buerger, M. E., Myers, R. W., Jensen, C. J., & Levin, B. H. (2012). *The Future of Policing, A Practical Guide for Police Managers and Leaders*. Boca Raton: CRC Press.

Spybey, T. (1996). *Globalisation and World Society*. Cambridge: Polity Press.

Wedlock, E. (2006). *Crime and Community Cohesion, Home Office Report 19/06*. Available at http://webarchive.nationalarchives.gov.uk/20120919132719/http://www.communities.gov.uk/documents/communities/pdf/452513.pdf. Accessed 13 Mar 2014.

Part I

Professionalisation

2

Education and the Police Professionalisation Agenda: A Perspective from England and Wales

Stephen Tong and Katja M. Hallenberg

Introduction

Police training/education in England and Wales has been, quite rightly, described as fragmented, problematic and unnecessarily complicated (Bolton 2005). It has remained an insular practice until relatively recently, hidden from the education world and in the periphery of the police world, taking place at many different levels and often lacking a clear responsibility or interest group. Furthermore, due to the changes wrought by reviews and reforms—most recently the organisational restructuring prompted by the Neyroud Report (2011) and the subsequent establishment of the College of Policing—the training arrangements have been in an almost constant state of flux. Police education/training is not a homogeneous practice but covers various types of approaches and levels of skills/knowledge, each with their own concerns and needs (Southgate 1988a).

Training and education of police officers depends on how the police role is perceived. The purpose of policing (the 'police mandate') is more

S. Tong (✉) • K.M. Hallenberg
Canterbury Christ Church University, Canterbury, UK

© The Author(s) 2018
C. Rogers, B. Frevel (eds.), *Higher Education and Police*,
DOI 10.1007/978-3-319-58386-0_2

complex and ambiguous the closer to the point of practice it is discussed (Thacher 2008), its orientation changing over time (Kelling and Moore 1988). What most approaches to defining police and policing ignore, Reiner (2010) argues, is the way in which policing reflects the broader social, cultural and economic conflicts and inequalities—something academic education has the potential to address by contextualising policing for those who practise it.

This chapter will provide an outline of the development of police education and training within the police in England and Wales, before moving onto the role of universities. The chapter will focus on the developments of police-university partnerships before describing the 'professionalisation agenda' and outlining potential challenges for policing in professionalising their workforce.

Historical Context

> At police schools, policemen learn from policemen what policemen have learned from policemen. (Reitz 1988: 33; translated and cited in Jaschke and Neidhardt 2007: 314)

During the establishment of the public police in 1829, and for a long time after, the training provided was minimal and largely drill-based. After all, there was little need for it: the work consisted mainly of foot patrol and occasional riot control, and the turnover was great (Martin and Wilson 1969). However, as the complexity of the work increased, so did the time and effort spent on training. Establishment of specialised departments, including the Criminal Investigation Department in 1878, led to corresponding training courses particularly in the large urban forces (ibid). After the First World War, the Desborough Committee started to standardise conditions of service and elevated police's economic and social status—something Martin and Wilson (ibid: 37–8) speculate to have been 'a conscious attempt to put police work on a more professional footing'. Notably, one of the Committee's recommendations was that the 'system of training and education be improved and assimilated throughout the Police Service' (Home Office 1919–1920). While such changes were slow in coming, police training during the period nevertheless saw an increased co-operation between forces and investment particularly in specialist training courses, for example, detective training centres opening in Hendon and Wakefield in 1936 and a couple of years later in Birmingham (Martin and Wilson 1969). Interest in the command-level training also began in the inter-war years with the establishment of the Hendon Police College in 1934 (ibid). Despite the initial attempt being short-lived (the College was shut prior to the Second World War), it inspired the founding of the Police College in 1948: the first national-level training project providing command rank courses (ibid; Lamford 1978).

The recruitment of large number of ex-servicemen after the Second World War and the growing investment in training resulted in the establishment of dedicated District Training Centres (DTCs) in 1946 (Martin and Wilson 1969; HMIC 2002). It standardised the recruitment training and moved it away from local forces to a few regional training centres (Martin and Wilson 1969), mirroring the wider trend towards centralisation brought by the beginnings of the welfare state. The curriculum was laid down by a committee of Chief Constables and teaching methods modelled after those used in the military (HMIC 2002). For example, Mathias (1988: 101) describes the probationer training at the Metropolitan Police Service as 'training for the masses, mass produced', teacher-centred, knowledge-based, done in a traditional classroom setting and completely from the point of view of the police officer.

The post-war period saw increasing specialisation and labour division among the police. By the mid-1960s, policing reoriented itself towards 'technology, specialisation, and managerial professionalism' (Reiner 2010: 79), and the practice of visible patrol, the 'bobby on the beat', began to decline as walking the streets was not seen to represent value for money (Bolton 2005). Instead, the officers 'retreated into vehicles, disappeared behind screens and disengaged with the public' (ibid: 89), resulting in a decrease in public confidence. Many officers no longer viewed policing as a lifelong career, and while they received more training compared to the industry standards at the time, it was of little value outside the service and became a strain on the manpower capacity (Martin and Wilson 1969). Already the 1960 Royal Commission had lamented the poor educational standards and lack of graduates within the police, and overall the recruitment and training were deemed inadequate for the complex and changing social context of police work (Reiner 2010).

The late 1960s and early 1970s were characterised more by 'the demand for change, the response to change and the understanding and handling of change' rather than any one event in particular (Mathias 1988: 102). Rise of counterculture, anti-war and anti-apartheid demonstrations contributed to a renewed politicisation of policing (Reiner 2010). The developments inside the organisation saw an increased number of female officers, growth in public and private transportation, and advancement in information, surveillance and investigative technologies and techniques. As a result of expansion of state schooling and mass media, the public became more educated and demanding. To survive, it was no longer enough just to get better at the old things; it was necessary to ask difficult and fundamental questions about the very purpose of the organisation (Argyris and Schon 1974; cited in Plumridge 1988).

This was reflected in training at all levels. For probationer training the 1973 Home Office Working Party recommended a shift away from legislation and drill towards 'public relations', whilst prompting the creation of Central Planning Unit, first of many such agencies aimed at centralising training design and delivery. The decade also saw the full integration of female officers into police ranks and active recruitment of ethnic minority officers (Mathias 1988). Introduction of 'Social Skills Training' heralded an official recognition that police work went beyond law and procedure (ibid), and aspects of social psychology, sociology, public administration and communication studies started to be incorporated into the recruit training (Bull and Horncastle 1988) and the senior management courses at Bramshill Police Staff College. There, the training fell into two distinctive categories of 'academic' and 'professional', the former concerned with a wider understanding of society and taught mostly by civilian instructors, with the latter consisting of courses on policing skills, tactics and strategies by police trainers (Lamford 1978). Interest in incorporating 'best practice' from the management world outside the police grew gradually (Plumridge 1988), at the same time as the officers on Bramshill scholarships to universities were returning to service and starting to ask some fundamental and uncomfortable questions about the way things were done (e.g. Young 1991).

In the 1980s, the police service experienced something of an identity crisis. Neither the organisation itself nor the society at large seemed to agree on what the role of the police should be (Brown 1983). The 'Brixton Riots', the subsequent report by Lord Scarman (1981) and the continuing inner city disturbances throughout the country brought home the shortcomings in training and preparation both at recruit and command level (Butler 1988). For the former, the second inspection of probationer training (MacDonald et al. 1987) brought a comprehensive revision of content and introduction of race relations training, workplace learning and tutor constable scheme. At the same time, the procedural changes from the Police and Criminal Evidence Act 1984 and the greater emphasis on the need to take the views of local communities into account when making policing decisions had to be incorporated. The philosophy of police training in the 1980s was characterised by active student-centred approach, introduction of computer-aided learning, equal emphasis on practical skills and theoretical knowledge, external consultation and multi-agency approach (Lightfoot 1988; Mathias 1988). For senior management training, the pressure from the Home Office meant the Bramshill College was unable to meet the demands directly and some on the training was devolved to local forces (Plumridge 1988). The increasing financial restraints of the public sector put emphasis on operational effectiveness, value for money, identification of policing priorities and political accountability (Butler 1988). It also resulted in what Butler (ibid) calls a 'siege mentality' among the police senior management, who was often more focused on making excuses than creating opportunities for improved service; part of which should have been investing a strategic plan for training and raising it higher on the agenda.

In the 1990s initial police training was still delivered at DTCs (Wood and Tong 2009). DTCs were police-only establishments where several forces would share training arrangements with police trainers delivering training usually over a 15-week period. Some DTCs were former military training establishments and thus still characterised by discipline, military-type drills, focus on fitness as well as learning law and procedure. These training centres did not share training with other public services and were organised on a regional basis across the country. In 1999, Janet Foster supported the idea of graduate entry in her evidence for the Home Affairs Committee on Police Training and Recruitment. In her submission,

Foster (ibid) argued that training should not be a 'self-contained activity' (Southgate 1988b: 233), that there should be more use of external expertise and that independent and reflective learning should be encouraged. Little changed and Her Majesty's Inspectorate of Constabulary (2002) argued in their 'Training Matters' Report that police probationer training was no longer fit for purpose and recommended the introduction of accreditation and qualification frameworks, links with further and higher education, alternative training delivery options and continuous professional development. This report was closely followed in 2003 by a BBC documentary entitled the 'Secret Policeman', a covert investigation conducted by undercover reporter Mark Daly on police training (BBC 2008). Daly joined the Greater Manchester Police and attended Bruche National Training Centre in Cheshire, revealing extreme racist views and behaviour among some recruits. The programme resulted in ten of the police officers involved resigning while twelve more were disciplined and three police trainers were removed. The documentary came only four years after the MacPherson Inquiry (1999), when the Metropolitan Police Commissioner, Sir Paul Condon, accepted his police service contained 'institutional racism'. This Inquiry was one of the most critical reviews into British policing and it appeared on the evidence of the documentary that a lot more still needed to be done to reform the police. These events and reviews continually raised questions around the way in which the police were recruited, selected and how and where officers were trained.

Indeed, the last decade and a half has seen an increasing focus on professionalising the police, particularly through education. The next section charts the changing relationship between the police and higher education, from which the more recent developments have stemmed.

Engagement Between Universities, Graduates and the Police Service

The co-operation between police and academia in England has a long history, though it has been relatively slow to develop (Wood and Tong 2009). It began with the establishment of forensic science services in the inter-war years, and the opening of the Metropolitan Police College in

1934, thanks to the efforts of the then Commissioner Lord Trenchard, who aimed to develop senior leaders within the service (Martin and Wilson 1969; Browne 1956). The College advocated a scientific approach to training and was aimed to attract (primarily middle-class) applicants with higher educational background, such as a university degree or a civil service qualification (ibid; Critchley 1967). The institution received constant criticism and was abandoned in 1939 without much opposition as the Second World War broke out (ibid, Martin and Wilson 1969).

The educational landscape of England changed in 1963 with the publication of the Robbins Report on Higher Education, as a consequence of which some professional training (e.g. in engineering, accountancy, architecture) moved into universities and colleges. However, the police remained unaffected with their separate training establishments. Nevertheless, the concerns over police legitimacy during the 1960s increased focus on training and education as a potential answer (Lee and Punch 2004) and with some forces turning to universities as a potential solution. For example, Essex Constabulary sent officers to university to do full-time degrees from 1967 onward (ibid) while the Bramshill Scholarship Scheme had started a year earlier in 1966, providing university education opportunities for management level officers. The year 1968 saw the beginning of the police Graduate Entry Scheme (ibid), which has continued under different names and formats ever since.

However, organisational attitudes to higher education were slow to change. Officers who attended university in the 1960s and 1970s often recount a response that was puzzlement at best, and open derision at worst (Lee and Punch 2004; Punch 2007). Young (1991) describes officers' experiences of being deliberately cut off, socially and professionally, and when returning to work being assigned to less demanding roles than they had held prior to their stint in the university. Young himself, who worked as a plainclothes detective in a drug squad before his anthropology degree, was assigned to Bridewell (a central prisoner lock-up) as a uniform inspector upon his return. This he saw not just as a reintegration to 'working in the real world' but also as a clear reassertion of control.

Nonetheless, links with higher education grew steadily. The Edmund-Davies 1978 pay awards encouraged more graduate applications to the police in the 1980s (Reiner 2010). By the following decade, the poor reputation of the police service and tensions with communities resulted in calls for 'reflective practitioner' officers, able to diffuse situations peacefully and build positive relationships with members of the public (Beckley 2004). Academia seemed to offer solutions, and Reiner (1994) describes the period as one of 'happy rapprochement'. Arrangements started to be formalised. For example, in 1996 the Institute of Criminology at Cambridge credited the Strategic Command Course offered at Bramshill.

Although there were a small number of university providers delivering policing degrees to police officers from the 1990s onwards, this increased from 2001 as more universities began delivering policing undergraduate degrees aimed at people aspiring to join the police. Before this, individuals wishing to obtain a degree before joining the police typically selected criminology, criminal justice or law degrees or programmes with not necessarily any overt connection to policing. There were no formal qualification requirements to become a police officer. The full-time 'pre-service' degrees were soon followed with five pilot schemes sanction by the Home Office in 2004 with police services sending their probationer police constables to universities for their initial training while gaining higher education accreditation (Wood & Tong, 2009). Partnerships were established between a number of universities with their local police services, but there was a lack of national coordination. Universities engaged with police education joined together founding 'The Higher Education Forum for Learning and Development in Policing' in 2009. The members consisted of universities across the country, hosting annual conferences focusing on various issues relating to police education and training. The forum is used to exchange ideas and practices between universities and police services, promoting university-based police education and supporting the College of Policing professionalisation agenda (discussed below).

The partnerships between universities and police services developed in different ways. Hallenberg (2012) described the academia-police relationship as one that increased in terms of frequency, moving from engagement with individual officers through to organisational engagement and emphasising the importance of hierarchy in relationship building:

1. **From rare to routine** – The interaction between academia and police developed from a rare occurrence to something far more routine, as a consequence of the increasing number of graduate entrants and links with higher education institutions.

2. **From individual to organisational** – In the past, academic education was encouraged and supported for *some* officers in *some* forces. However, the current approach is far more organisational; police service *as a whole* is linking up with higher education in a systematic manner and starting to build the supporting infrastructure for academic police education.

3. **From top end only to all levels of the organisation** – The relationship between police and the academia tended to exist mostly at the higher level of the organisation, for example, consulting relationships with senior academics, or command-level courses. Now, the changes are bringing academia closer to the experiences of police officers at all levels of the organisation.

At the same time the 'terms of engagement' between police and higher education institutions can reflect different arrangements and responsibilities between organisations including the police, universities, further education colleges and the private sector. Savage et al. (2007) presented the following models as reflecting the developing arrangements.

1. Scholarship model (Higher Education ownership): This model reflects programmes that are designed, quality assured and delivered by universities. Consultation usually occurs with police services in terms of curriculum development and student volunteering opportunities but this will not affect the 'ownership' or lead role in delivering the degree being firmly placed with the university. A typical example of this model would be full-time undergraduate programmes aimed at students pursuing a police career after graduation but can also involve programmes aimed at serving police officers and staff where the university maintains control on curriculum and delivery.

2. Partnership model (Joint ownership): The partnership model reflects a relationship between universities and police services where there is a shared ownership of curriculum design and delivery and where students are subject to both police (code of ethics) and university (student code of conduct) regulations.

3. Contract model—client/contractor (Police ownership): Police services construct a tender inviting education providers to submit a bid for training or education contracts. These tenders can invite applications

from universities, further education and private sector education providers. The contract determines the conditions of services provided and can be as narrow or as flexible as police service requires.

These models can overlap. For example, a contractual model can facilitate a partnership model of practice where a police service works closely with a university and both institutions mutually recognise different combinations of these models. The Neyroud (2011) and Winsor (2011, 2012) reports were significant in their influence in energising the police professionalisation agenda. The reports not only raised issues around current training but also argued for a professional body to be created. The new police professional body, the College of Policing, was introduced in 2013 and brought a new dynamic to the models above by leading on issues relating to standards and consistency among providers and improving engagement with universities. Holdaway (2017) describes these developments not only as 'The re-professionalisation of the police' but also part of the development of 'A new dynamic landscape of police regulation affording a central place to professionalism'.

The increasing number of universities offering policing degrees acted as drivers for a serious attempt at professionalisation while the government-widening participation policy encouraged higher numbers of graduates in society more generally. The Neyroud and Winsor reports and the establishment of the College of Policing also contributed to the development of direct entry scheme at the level of Inspector and Superintendent. The direct entry scheme is a national scheme providing 18 months of training aimed at recruiting candidates from other sectors to bring 'organisational and operational skills sets' from different contexts (College of Policing 2016a). Although educational qualifications are listed as desirable they are not required, subject to local variation in requirements. Currently, the numbers are low with further cohorts planned. Another initiative, 'Police Now', is a national programme that started in the Metropolitan Police (but has now spread to many other forces) aimed at 'exceptional' graduates. The programme reflects similar principles used in the 'Teach first' (teaching graduate programme) and 'Frontline' (social work graduate programme) in understanding social inequality, commitment to social change in communities and providing innovative leadership with communities (Spencer et al. 2014). The two-year programme is still in its early stages with first cohort accepted in 2015, but recruitment has seen increases in the appointment of female, black, minority and ethnic candidates (Police Now 2014). These reviews and initiatives have been paving the way for change in the police service in both the way police are recruited and how they learn.

The developments in relation to partnerships with universities and entry schemes for graduates are aimed at not only leadership but also the role of police constable. Although innovative, these developments have been lagging behind those in other public sector organisations (ambulance service, nursing, probation and social work) where higher education-level accredited training and education are established routes to qualification in various roles. The College of Policing recently introduced a consultation exercise in relation to developing a Police Qualification Education Framework (PQEF). The three options the consultation document considered are (College of Policing 2016b: 5):

1. The establishment of a qualifications framework for policing, working in partnership with the higher education sector to set minimum education levels by level of practice or rank.
2. The development of opportunities for existing officers and staff to gain accredited and publicly recognised qualifications equivalent to their level of practice or rank.
3. The development of initial entry routes which involve self-funded undergraduate programmes, police-force-funded graduate conversion programmes for graduates in other disciplines and higher level apprenticeships (HLAs).

The proposed entry routes reflect similar entry routes to established professions seeking accreditation for a professional role. Option 1: accepted named degrees for particular professions (law, education, social work and paramedics) are established with quality assurance involving professional bodies. Option 2: programmes recognising previous experience or Recognition of Prior Experiential Learning (RPL) allowing experienced professionals to receive academic credits for professional learning that can be demonstrated, usually allowing a programme of study to be shortened. These programmes are established in policing but also in other areas where universities apply RPL to their programmes. Option 3: the conversion programme follows similar examples mentioned earlier in relation to 'Teach First' and 'Frontline'. Graduates who have a degree that does not reflect the content of the profession they wish to join, can elect to do a short course that recognises their generic graduate skills and abilities and provides content to reflect the skills and knowledge required for their professional roles. Following the consultation a number of changes have been announced to how the police are recruited, how qualifications are recognised and the educational requirements for promotion (College of Policing 2017). The use of apprenticeships will allow aspiring police officers to join the organisation without a degree but accredit learning to degree level during the training and operational practice will be introduced in 2018. Postgraduate qualifications will be introduced for police leaders (from Sergeant and higher ranks) in 2020. Also by 2020 new recruits will need to join the police constable apprenticeship, join with a recognised policing degree or other graduates can join a police graduate programme. Senior leaders will require master's before applying for the rank of assistant chief constable.

The consultation marks a bold attempt from the College of Policing to collect views on proposed reforms before implementation. The consultation attracted over 3000 responses, with those responses in favour (46%), opposed (32%) and undecided (21%) in response to the proposal. The concerns that were raised about the PEQF proposal included future access to the police and appropriate representation, time and financial concerns in obtaining qualifications for current officers and the importance of experience and practical skills as an appropriate indicator for suitability rather than a degree (College of Policing 2016d). Among the responses from the College of Policing, a greater emphasis on the apprenticeship route into the policing with an emphasis on work place learning has been put forward and recognition for learning for serving police officers (College of Policing 2016d).

Challenges for Professionalisation and Change

The challenges to introducing professionalisation in the UK are multi-layered. Providing consistency, accrediting a range of learning, changes in police leadership, funding cutbacks, reduction in police training capacity and technological changes in policing and society are some of the issues confronting the push towards professionalisation (Tong 2017). The challenge of delivering consistent training across 43 police services has long been an obstacle to various national police training bodies. The College of Policing also acknowledges this:

> Policing does not currently have consistent, national education levels for all policing roles or ranks which reflect its current and future challenges, or an entry level qualification that would be considered commensurate with that of a profession. There is wide ranging, variable and inconsistent practice in terms of the implementation, assessment and accreditation of initial police education across the 43 forces. While some forces have already developed foundation or bachelor degree entry programmes, others deliver training to the appropriate level but do not require or enable officers to achieve the externally accredited Diploma qualification. Consequently, some officers have no recognised accredited qualification. (College of Policing 2016c)

Consistency can be particularly problematic with 43 police services, each with different Police Crime Commissioners (PCC) and chief officers and services that may have different approaches to police work and different local problems requiring a variety of solutions and skills. Similarly, the English higher education landscape is diverse and stratified, including research-intensive universities as well as more teaching-focused institutions, some recruiting internationally, others acting more as local education providers. Furthermore, cuts in policing have had an impact on the reduction of training resources within police services, with real estate sold off and experienced trainers/educators reduced in number. Providing consistent levels of training and curriculum nationally also presents challenges to localisation and accountability in responding to local needs. Changes in police leadership have resulted in a change of priorities in some forces from learning and development to operational demands. Building expertise in particular areas of training, and the development learning infrastructure that are sustainable takes a long time to establish but can be removed very quickly. In times of austerity, when operational demands are increasing in the context of less available resources, training resources are often the first to go.

Police training and education are inextricably linked to practice. As Southgate (1988b) argued, training should not be isolated but linked to organisational change and development. Changes in policing are not necessarily proactively reflected in training curriculums and can take time to be recognised. Similarly, it is difficult to predict the future role of the police and the areas of responsibility that the institution will continue to command (Tong 2017). In what is now termed 'the fourth industrial revolution' (Floridi 2014) the police will have to contend (and are contending) with rapidly changing technology (Tong 2017). This includes, for example, drones, driverless cars, retina scans for identification in police stops, body-worn cameras, artificial intelligence, big data, various forms of automation and police robots. Technological solutions and devices relevant to policing are predominantly researched and developed in the private sector. Technical knowledge and skills in using and manipulating technology are not traditionally developed in police training centres. As police work becomes more specialised and the manner in which crime is committed changes, new technologies will present new questions in terms of community safety and criminal opportunities. The police will need to ensure that they are able to identify the skills and knowledge base of future police officers and specialists required to address these challenges.

Conclusion

The landscape for police education in England, and its relationship with the higher education sector, has been one of continuous reorganisation. Effective education and research is dynamic and proactive, evidence-based (Wood et al. 2017) and providing a leading voice in innovation, reform and challenges in the society. The anticipated changes wrought by the College of Policing and the proposed PEQF will shape the trajectory for the police and higher education collaboration for years to come.

They reflect the continued professionalisation agenda, which has gathered momentum since the creation of the College of Policing in 2012. Influential reports (Neyroud 2011; HMIC 2002) have paved the way for opportunities for universities and other providers to play a key role in the delivery of education and accreditation of police learning. At the same time, police research in the College of Policing plays an important role in developing police practice.

As the police education curriculum is developed for various entry routes and qualifications for advancement there will be changes in negotiating the most appropriate approach. On the one hand, it will be useful for the police service to have content that develops practical policing skills. On the other, the content that helps officers understand local community and social issues, the ability to analyse problems, and develop criticality are crucial to the challenges officers are facing now. These are established graduate skills that are required for degree qualification awards. The balance of professional and academic knowledge/skills is important in developing effective curriculum. Debates around appropriate curriculum will be important for effective practice and credibility in the professional and academic world which future police officers will inhabit. Such debates also need to involve officers currently in the service with a recognition of the learning and training they have already attained.

References

ACPO. (1992). *Towards a Future Training Strategy*. London: HMSO.

Argyris, C., & Schon, D. (1974). Theory in Practice: Increasing Professional Effectiveness. London: Temple-Smith. Cited in Plumridge, M. (1988) Management and Organisation Development in the Police Service: The Role of Bramshill. In P. Southgate (Ed.), *New Directions in Police Training* (pp. 112–132). London: Home Office Research and Planning Unit.

BBC. (2008). *The Secret Policeman*. Available from: http://news.bbc.co.uk/1/hi/programmes/panorama/7650207.stm

Beckley, A. (2004). Police Training—Can it Cope? *Police Research & Management*, 6(2), 1–17.

Bolton, A. H. (2005). The Report. In Politeia Police Commission/Lawlor, S. (Series Ed.), *Policing Matters: Recruitment, Training and Motivation* (Social Science Research Series 8, pp. 7–91). London: Politeia.

Brown, L. (1983). The Future Face of Police Training. *Police Journal*, 56(2), 121–127.

Browne, D. G. (1956). *The Rise of Scotland Yard*. London: Harrap.

Bull, R., & Horncastle, P. (1988). Evaluating Training: The London Metropolitan Police's Recruit Training in Human Awareness/Policing Skills. In P. Southgate (Ed.), *New Directions in Police Training* (pp. 219–229). London: Home Office Research and Planning Unit.

Butler, A. (1988). Police Training for the 1990s: The Divisional Commander's Perspective. In P. Southgate (Ed.), *New Directions in Police Training* (pp. 83–99). London: Home Office Research and Planning Unit.

College of Policing. (2016a). *National Policing Vision 2016*. Available from: http://www.college.police.uk/About/Pages/National-policing-vision-2016.aspx

College of Policing. (2016b). *Policing Education Qualifications Framework Consultation*. Ryton: College of Policing.

College of Policing (2016c). *Policing Education Qualifications Framework*. Available from: http://www.college.police.uk/What-we-do/Learning/Policing-Education-Qualifications-Framework/Pages/Policing-Education-Qualifications-Framework.aspx

College of Policing. (2016d). *Developing and Delivering an Education Qualification Framework for Policing: The College of Policing Response to the Consultation*. December 2016. Available from: http://www.college.police.uk/What-we-do/Learning/Policing-Education-Qualifications-Framework/Documents/PEQF_2016.pdf

College of Policing. (2017). *An Education Qualification Framework for Policing*. Available from: http://www.college.police.uk/What-wedo/Learning/Policing-Education-Qualifications-Framework/Pages/Policing-Education-Qualifications-Framework.aspx

Critchley, T. A. (1967). *A History of Police in England and Wales*. London: Constable.

Floridi, L. (2014). *The Fourth Revolution: How the Infosphere is Reshaping Human Reality*. Oxford: Oxford University Press.

Foster, J. (1999). Appendix 22: Memorandum by Dr Janet Foster, Institute of Criminology, University of Cambridge. In *Home Affairs Committee, Police Training and Recruitment: Volume Two* (pp. 382–391). London: The Stationery Office.

Hallenberg, K. M. (2012). *Scholarly Detectives: Police Professionalisation via Academic Education*. PhD Thesis, University of Manchester.

HMIC. (2002). *Training Matters*. London: HMSO.

Holdaway, S. (2017). The Re-Professionalisation of the Police in England and Wales. *Criminology and Criminal Justice. Published online first January 21st 2017*.

Home Office. (1993). *The Future of Police Training*. London: HMSO.

Jaschke, H.-G., & Neidhardt, K. (2007). A Modern Police Science as an Integrated Academic Discipline: A Contribution to the Debate on its Fundamentals. *Policing & Society, 17*(4), 303–320.

Kelling, G. L., & Moore, M. H. (1988). *The Evolving Strategy of Policing* (Perspectives on Policing, 4). Washington, DC: National Institute of Justice.

Lamford, T. G. (1978). The Police College, Bramshill—Towards a Coherent and Comprehensive Command Training Structure. *Police Studies: International Review, 1*, 5–12.

Lee, M., & Punch, M. (2004). Policing by Degrees: Police Officers' Experience of University Education. *Policing & Society, 14*(3), 233–249.

Lightfoot, M. (1988). Community and Race Relations Training. In P. Southgate (Ed.), *New Directions in Police Training* (pp. 8–24). London: Home Office Research and Planning Unit.

MacDonald, B., et al. (1987). *Police Probationer Training: The Final Report of the Stage II Review*. London: HMSO.

Macpherson, W. (1999). *The Stephen Lawrence Inquiry: Report of an Inquiry*. London: HMSO.

Martin, J., & Wilson, G. (1969). *The Police: A Study in Police Manpower*. London: Heinemann.

Mathias, P. (1988). Paving the Way to Philosophy and Practices at Peel Centre, Hendon. In P. Southgate (Ed.), *New Directions in Police Training* (pp. 100–111). London: Home Office Research and Planning Unit.

Neyroud, P. (2011). *Review of Police Leadership and Training*. London: Home Office.

Plumridge, M. (1988). Management and Organisation Development in the Police Service: The Role of Bramshill. In P. Southgate (Ed.), *New Directions in Police Training* (pp. 112–132). London: Home Office Research and Planning Unit.

Police Now. (2014). *Police Now, 'On the Beat' Police Now Influence for Generations*. Available from: https://policenow.wordpress.com/page/5/

Punch, M. (2007). Cops with Honours: University Education and Police Culture. In M. O'Neill, M. Marks, & A.-M. Singh (Eds.), *Police Occupational Culture: New Debates and Direction*. (pp. 105–128). Bingley: Emerald Group Publishing.

Reiner, R. (1994). A Truce in the War Between Police and Academia. *Policing Today, 1*(1), 30–32.

Reiner, R. (2010). *The Politics of the Police* (4th ed.). Oxford: Oxford University Press.

Reitz, E. (1988). Die fachhochschulen für die öffentliche verwaltung—polizei—in den bundesländern und im bund. Eine vergleichende situationsbeschreibung. In Polizei-Führungsakademie (ed) Fachhochschulausbildung der Polizei. Polizei-Führungsakademie: Münster. Cited in Jaschke, H-G. & Neidhardt, K. (2007). A Modern Police Science as an Integrated Academic Discipline: A Contribution to the Debate on its Fundamentals. *Policing & Society, 17*(4), 303–320.

Savage, S., Clements, P. & Jones, J. (2007). Terms of Engagement: Police Involvement with Higher Education, British Society of Criminology, London School of Economics, September 18–20

Scarman, L. G. (1981). *The Brixton Disorders 10–12 April 1981, Report of an Inquiry by the Rt Hon The Lord Scarman OBE*. London: Home Office.

Southgate, P. (1988a). Introduction. In P. Southgate (Ed.), *New Directions in Police Training* (pp. 1–7). London: Home Office Research and Planning Unit.

Southgate, P. (1988b). Conclusions. In P. Southgate (Ed.), *New Directions on Police Training* (pp. 230–240). London: HM Stationery Office.

Spencer, D., Lloyd, M., & Stephens, L. (2014). *Police Now: The Case for Change*. London: Metropolitan Police.

Thacher, D. (2008). Research for the Front Lines. *Policing & Society, 18*(1), 44–59.

Tong, S. (2017). Professionalising Policing: Seeking viable and Sustainable Approaches to Police Education and Learning. *European Police Science and Research Bulletin*. Forthcoming Summer edition.

Winsor, T. (2011). *The Independent Review of Police Officer and Staff Remunerations and Conditions. Part 1* (Cmmd Paper 8024). London: HMSO.

Winsor, T. (2012). *The Independent Review of Police Officer and Staff Remunerations and Conditions. Final Report* (Cmmd Paper 8325). London: HMSO.

Wood, D. A., & Tong, S. (2009). The Future of Initial Police Training: A University Perspective. *International Journal of Police Science & Management, 11*(3), 294–305.

Wood, D., Cockcroft, T., Tong, S., & Bryant R. (2017). The Importance of Context and Cognitive Agency in Developing Police Knowledge: Going Beyond the Police Science Discourse. *The Police Journal: Theory, Practice and Principles* First Published February 28, 2017.

Young, M. (1991). *An Inside Job: Policing and Police Culture in Britain*. Oxford: Clarendon Press.

3

Police Basic Training in Sweden: Vocational or Academic? An Educational Muddle

Anders Green

A Prologue of Endings and Beginnings

For 15 years, between 2000 and 2015, I've been working on and off as a senior lecturer in criminology at the Swedish National Police Academy (SNPA) in the northern outskirts of Stockholm. The ups and downs have been significant, including admission closures and immense increases in the numbers of students. Not least have there been ample rumours about the future of the picturesque campus per se as well as the future of police basic training. In this chapter I'll try to elaborate the long-lasting, and a bit muddy, developments of Swedish police basic training and what its future might hold. To paraphrase the title of David H Bayley's (1994) classic book *Police for the Future*, in the case of Sweden the discussions regarding police basic training for the future has been going on for so long that the future has become the present. Noteworthy is that the perspectives for the future in Bayley (ibid) just contains the organization and new strategic ways of policing. Basic training is, on the whole, disregarded.

A. Green (✉)
The Swedish National Council for Crime Prevention, Stockholm, Sweden

© The Author(s) 2018
C. Rogers, B. Frevel (eds.), *Higher Education and Police*,
DOI 10.1007/978-3-319-58386-0_3

In the late fall of 2016 police students will for the last time graduate from the SNPA and that will be the final stage of five decades of vocational police basic training. From now on the police basic training will be located at three different universities: Umeå, Linnæus and Södertörn. The latter is the location, still in the greater Stockholm area, that replaces the SNPA. This could imply that steps will be taken towards higher education, but at present that is still not the case. A special feature in this development is that a political dimension has emerged between the Social Democrats, who clearly are in favour of a reform, and the Conservatives, who have been protracting the question of a merger with higher education.

Another lucid voice in this debate is the Police Union, which has been explicit in their critique and for years has expressed a distinct need to reform police basic training (Nitz 2012, 2014; Nitz et al. 2012). In the spring of 2005 the chair of the Police Union was very upset. The focal point in the agitation was that Sweden, from an international point of view, was losing so much by still pursuing vocational training with no natural platform for police research. Furthermore, it was scandalous that police officers couldn't continue as researchers within the police education. Conclusively, Swedish police needs a higher education and there must be preconditions for research.[1]

Since then three governmental investigations have looked into the future of police basic training. The overriding question is, if police basic training is ready to take the step into higher education, and following that, how can it be done? The governmental investigations and political debate have one thing in common, and that is that they all underline how the police must develop and prepare for a more complex and demanding future. A recurrent and crucial aspect for a prosperous development is a more diversified recruitment. It is necessary that more women and people with foreign background find the police basic training attractive.

Parallel to this protracted debate in January 2015 Swedish police was reorganized from 21 independent county police authorities into one national authority—The Police Authority.[2] This has been the biggest organizational reform ever in Swedish history, and the adaptation is still ongoing. Holgersson (2005) concludes in his earlier findings that reorganizations distinctly have negative implications for the police organization and that especially the police officers lose their feeling of work security.

Alas, at present not many days pass without articles in Swedish newspapers that underline that the state of the police in Sweden is plagued with muddiness, turbulence and an increasing employee turnover. An often emphasized remedy to these problems is a need for more police officers. For the semesters to come there will again be an increased number of students admitted to the police basic training. But, there is a determinant question yet to be answered—what are the features of the future of Swedish police basic training?

Police Basic Training History

The major part of the twentieth century Swedish police was run and administered within municipalities. Training was optional, and in the back countries training was sparse or absent, but in the bigger cities there were some police training (Lauritz and Hansson 2013). In 1965 Swedish police was nationalized and that also meant the beginning of mandatory police basic training, of which the new Swedish National Police Board was in charge. This initial vocational training took place in Stockholm with 35 weeks of theoretical training and eight weeks of internship. In 1967 the police basic training moved into a former regiment at Sörentorp and that was the genesis for the SNPA (Justitiedepartementet Ds 1996:11). Two significant features were that the students were paid during training and the recruitment was regional, meaning that the students knew exactly where to work afterwards. In short, as they were admitted to police basic training they were already police officers and the time at SNPA was just an "educative transportation", for which the police organization and the SNPA accordingly were responsible. These circumstances led to a minimal turnover.

Since then some police basic training reforms have taken place and, as early as 1979, suggestions have been made that the police training ought to become a higher education (SOU 2008:39; Polishögskolan 2012). It should develop towards more of a higher education alignment where subjects like psychology and social sciences needed to be amplified (ibid, SOU 2016:39). In this year the police basic training became a division under the Swedish National Police Board, and even though the setup and structure had undergone some changes the basic training continued to be vocational. It is noteworthy that the Swedish term for SNPA is "Polishögskolan",[3] which signals that the training is academic as the word per se refers to higher education. Another aspect to consider is that in earlier investigations and other writings students were referred to as "pupils" (SOU 1994:103).

In the 1980s police basic training was extend to three years: one year at the SNPA, 18 months of internship and finally another semester at the SNPA (Justitiedepartementet Ds 1996:11; SOU 2016:39). With this reform it was also decided that training should contain internships at other authorities, whereof the social service was particularly being stressed. The reform moreover led to an establishment of a unit for police research located at the SNPA (Knutsson 2010).

In the mid-1990s Swedish police experienced a vast organizational reform in order to develop community policing nationally. The national organization went from 118 police districts to 21 police county police authorities, which started functioning in 1998. At the same time one of the most significant police basic training reforms occurred that included a three-year admission closure (1994–1997). When the admission reopened in January 1998 the recruitment was national with the effect that the students had to apply for a position after graduating from the SNPA. Another important change was that training was no longer paid for, meaning that most students had to apply for study allowance. That particular question was too separately investigated (SOU 1994:103). In another investigation it was also suggested that the police basic training could start advancing towards a higher education, which in practice meant that the first year should be spent at a university (Justitiedepartementet Ds 1996:11). Simultaneously, a parallel focus was on how to enhance a diversified recruitment that mirrors society, for example, in terms of gender and foreign background. A noticeable change was that the percentage of applicants with academic backgrounds had started to increase.

In a memorandum presented by the Swedish National Police Board (Rikspolisstyrelsen 1997) these ideas were developed and consequently it was clearly suggested that the police basic training ought to be a higher education. At the same time, a step was taken in the opposite direction when the research unit at the SNPA was moved to the National Council for Crime Prevention. Knutsson (2010) discusses that after this move there came to be a pronounced "research ban" at the SNPA, of which he is quite critical.

Back to the reopening of the SNPA in 1998. The curriculum had also been altered and the reformed training setup comprised of four semesters at the SNPA and one semester of paid internship. The pedagogy was now problem-based with an aim to distinctly integrate different fields of knowledge. A vivid example of this is found in practical exercises where there is also input from law, behavioural science and crime prevention (Polishögskolan 2012; Bergman and Heder 2013).

The circumstance that the police basic training was just being pursued in Stockholm began to be questioned and a discussion of decentralizing was being discerned (Justitiedepartementet Ds 1996:11). The main reason was that a decentralization could cater for applicants from all over Sweden, with an emphasis on the back countries in northern parts. In 2000 police basic training commenced as contract teaching at Umeå University, situated 650 kilometers north of Stockholm. Besides the study period per se, a decentralization northwards was also seen as enhancing the possibilities for recruitment of newly graduated police officers to the northern parts of Sweden where the sparsely populated areas are significant. The following year, 2001, Växjö University,[4] 400 km south of Stockholm, was as well given the opportunity to pursue police basic training as contract teaching. Not just had the police basic training been geographically spread, but it had also entered the universities.

Police students at a university leads to specific questions, whereof one concerns the uniform and Jakobsson Öhrn and Stark (2014) noticed different solutions. At the SNPA the students got the uniform during the first semester and used it all over campus. The routine at Linnæus is a bit different as the students get the uniform during the second semester and wear it on campus to some extent. Finally, at Umeå the students get the uniform in the second semester and never wear it amongst other students on campus, which signals a higher degree of integration with the ambient university environment.[5]

Another feature from the early 2000s is the implementation of police basic training as distance learning (SOU 2008:39). The SNPA was in charge of this that commenced in 2002 and it simultaneously demanded a great deal of cooperation with the county police authorities who agreed upon supplying for the assets needed for the students to pursue their training regionally. The purpose was to stimulate the recruitment of students from back countries who were already locally established and also a bit older, and Jakobsson Öhrn and Stark (2014) also noticed that the age median was some years higher amongst these students.

Police Basic Training Anno 2016

To put an end to this historical odyssey it is adequate to describe how the basic police training is organized at present, which thus emanates from 1998. After doing an overview of the Swedish police basic training Jakobsson Öhrn and Stark (2014) conclude that the examination objectives are the same at all the locations, and hence the instruction for contract teaching is being followed. Even though the semesters are structured differently, in the end they contain the same, and graduating students should have a similar basis of knowledge and skills. After 2016, when the last students graduate from the SNPA, there will be three universities—Umeå, Linnæus and Södertörn—that pursue police basic training as contract teaching. The distance learning was closed in 2015, but will resume and be administered by Umeå and Linnæus. The Police Authority is still deciding the curriculum, the recruitment and the number of students admitted, which is based on an analysis of the forthcoming national needs.

Perhaps the most interesting concern is the disjunctive development of credits (ects). At the SNPA the students do not get any credits, at Linnæus the students get 22,5 (ects) and at Umeå 72,5 (ects). This was found in the overview done by Jakobsson and Stark (2014). Since then especially Umeå University has developed their mind-set for an academic future of the police basic training (Brulin et al. 2010). In 2015 an application was formulated to the Swedish Higher Education Authority in order to get full credits (120 ects) for the two years at the police basic training. And following this a new degree was suggested—university degree of police work. There are already substantial proposals for how police students can continue studying in order to fulfil a bachelor's degree (Polisutbildningen

Umeå universitet 2015). This new academic police basic training commenced in the fall of 2015, and Linnæus University is planning for an equivalent degree to start in 2017 (SOU 2016:39). At Södertörn University, where admission opened in January 2015, the police basic training is vocational and the students are not rewarded with credits.

Regarding the latter location the decision to commence police basic training was made as late as in November 2013 (Polisen 2013). Due to the short time-span all the facilities needed at the new campus could not be provided and there are still ongoing developments. The students are in the meantime obliged to use the facilities at the SNPA and will continue doing so for some time.[6] In the summer of 2017 the first police students will graduate from Södertörn University.

Throughout the years police basic training has been very popular and, for example, there were approximately 7000 applicants per semester in the mid-2000s (SOU 2008:39). The last couple of years this number has declined, and the most noteworthy experience lately is that there were not enough qualified applicants for the January 2016 admission (SOU 2016:39). Of stipulated 300 study places just about 260 students were admitted. This pattern continued until 2016s second admission in August, when roughly 35 study places of a total of 550 were empty (Schoultz 2016). The Police Union reacts strongly to this and claims that this lack of competition is utterly worrying. Not least is it perilous as it coincides with the ongoing reorganization and the Police Union foresees a major police crisis if nothing is done strategically (Nitz 2016). In January 2017 the number of study places will again be increased to approximately 800 and there seems to be an increase in the number of applicants. The question yet to be answered is whether there are any changes in the applicant's qualifications?

On the Political Agenda

> You get academic credits at the circus academy, but not at the police basic training. (Social Democrat former Minister of Justice, Interpellation 2009/10:221)

For several decades criminal politics was not of a major importance in Swedish politics (Green 1991). But in the 1991 election criminal politics made an impact. It was clearly put on the agenda by the Conservatives and that without doubt contributed to their success in the election.[7] The debate was mostly focusing on the prison system, including its ongoing failure and fear of crime. If the police were mentioned it was again by the Conservatives, with the message that there definitely is a need for more police officers to recreate law and order in society. Historically the Conservatives have been the advocates for policing matters in Swedish criminal politics (ibid).

Since then criminal politics have changed the focal point from punishment to crime prevention, and accordingly the police have become more important in the debate. Except the more extended debate, the Social Democrats have been more active in highlighting police matters, and amongst these especially police basic training. It can moreover be noted that during their governance police basic training as contract teaching at two universities commenced. In the 2014 election the Social Democrats put reforming police basic training on the top spot in their criminal politics agenda. This follows their criminal political programme, in which the creation of a safer Sweden is being thoroughly elaborated (Socialdemokraterna 2013). In their rhetoric a reformation of the police basic training is being stressed, as the ineluctable change for a modern and adequate police organization that is aiming to become the best in Europe in the year 2020. And the Social Democrats won the election in 2014,[8] but police basic training was most likely not the most crucial question for the average voter. Anyway, the promise was not neglected and in the Statement of Government Policy in October 2014, the Swedish Prime Minister Stefan Löfven put forth this promise: "Work will begin to make police training into a higher education programme" (Löfven 2014). After this postulate the reaction from the Police Union especially was tinged with greatest delight, as their perennial agitation finally was obeyed (Nitz 2012, 2014; Nitz et al. 2012). On the agenda for change, the Police Union furthermore referred to an opinion poll in which it is accentuated that 80 per cent amongst the public was in favour of police basic training as a higher education.[9]

Reforming the police basic training was overall sidelined during the eight years of Conservative-Liberal governance (2006–2014). Soon after winning in 2006 the Conservatives formulated another political goal to achieve: 20,000 police officers in the year 2010 (Motion 2005/06: Ju358). The focus was entirely on the numbers, and this increase with approximately 3 000 police officers was seen as the response to an ongoing decrease in the public's feelings of insecurity. An increased number of police officers as the remedy doubtlessly recalls some classic Conservative criminal politics with an amplification of law and order (Green 1991). This political goal put another form of pressure on the police basic training that had to practice "assembly line training" in the current form of vocational training. Consequently the numbers of students nearly doubled for some semesters, with the side-effect that the requirements for admission were lowered. In the year 2010 the goal was reached, but the effects were not that unambiguous as quite a number of the new police officers often just filled vacant positions. The promised effect with a higher police visibility in order to safeguard a safer society was overall fairly vague (Brottsförebyggande rådet 2013).[10]

As the debate on police basic training has grown, a political dividing line has emerged between the Social Democrats and the Conservatives, the two biggest parties. Örebro universitet (2011) committed a study on how the members of the educational, and judicial committees viewed the future of police basic training from the perspective of reforming it into a higher education. The Social Democrats were clearly in favour and the Conservatives expressed serious doubt. Amongst the other parties there were some varieties in the views, but the majority of the respondents agreed upon that in the longer run police basic training needs to become a higher education. A little interesting was that the two representatives from the Swedish Democrats, a right-wing populist party, gave contradicting answers: clearly positive and clearly negative. This can be seen as a token of their present balance of power in the Swedish parliament.

When it comes to the political debate the two most active parties are again the Social Democrats and the Conservatives, and it is quite clear that the former now have made the matter of police basic training theirs. Looking into the political debate in parliament the last decade it is noticeable how the interpellations nearly always are formulated by the Social Democrats (Interpellation 2006/07:208, 2008/09:616, 2009/10:221). A pattern is easily discerned, as the Social Democrats are pushing and demanding answers and the Conservatives are procrastinating and diverting. In the debate the Conservatives emphasize that they raise the police funding, as they are dodging the specific question of reforming the police basic training (Interpellation 2006/07:208).[11] On the other hand, the Conservatives repeat that they see the present police basic training as good and fulfilling, and that is not so often found in the Social Democrat rhetoric (ibid). The Conservatives see and emphasize that the Social Democrats are too eager to take the step that they will miss out questions like what kind of knowledge a police officer must have. "Content and quality are most important, not the form for training" (Conservative Minister of Justice, Interpellation 2007/08:616). But form is important to the Social Democrats, and preconditions for police research is repeatedly amplified as a prerequisite for the developments of policing in Sweden.

The Investigation Frenzy: A Three Strike System?

The most intense period began when the Social Democrat government formulated the directives for a governmental investigation in the beginning of 2006 (Kommittédirektiv 2006:10). The directive's focus was if and how police basic training, entirely or partly, could merge with higher education. This investigation met an abrupt ending. After winning the election in September 2006 the Conservatives plainly cancelled the process just a few weeks before the final report in January 2007. The main reason for the cancellation was that the directive was a bit "too narrow" (Interpellation 2006/07:208). But it was no secret that the investigation was about to confirm and suggest an academic future for the police basic training. On the other hand, directly after the lost election the Social Democrats continued emphasizing the importance of reforming the police basic training and at the same time suggesting police basic training at ten universities (Motion 2006/07: Ju377). The answer from the Conservatives was that when it comes to the number of locations for police basic training a limitation is needed, as the quality needs to be kept at a high level (Interpellation 2006/07:26)

The major concern for the Conservatives was the political goal with an increased number of police officers that put a massive pressure on the police basic training. At the same time they did not ignore the reform matter and thus initiated another governmental investigation about the future for police basic training (Kommittédirektiv 2006:139). The directive was, to refer to their criticism, wider and concerned suggestions for some kind of reform, without detailed elaborations. The academic imprint was still indecisive and to quote the Conservative Minister of Justice: "I'm both for and against police basic training as a higher education" (Interpellation 2008/09:616). By the end of March 2008 this new governmental investigation was presented, and the conclusions were significant (SOU 2008:39). The way forward was without doubt a merger with higher education. A reform was estimated to take approximately two years, whereby a new three-year police basic training would commence in 2010. An interesting feature was the suggestion that a higher number of students than needed, based on the Police Authority's perennial analysis, should be admitted in order to create a "healthy competition" and prepare for an increased student turnover. This way of thinking was quite unlike the police educational tradition.

At last, in 2008 there was now a governmental investigation that had settled the future developments for police basic training that ought to be agreed upon. The Social Democrats could not be displeased with a governmental investigation that basically confirmed their will. But a higher education was still something the Conservatives actually opposed (Interpellation 2007/08:616). During this period the Conservative's focus was on an increased number of police officers, and at the same time the existing police basic training was considered good and adequate. A decisive step was yet hanging around a long time and nothing consolidated a will to reform. Their passivity regarding the future of police basic training was of course not ignored and was repeatedly criticized (Interpellation 2006/07:208, 2009/10:221).

In December 2012, four years after that the governmental investigation (SOU 2008:39) was presented, there was a long-awaited governmental decision regarding the development of police basic training (Justitiedepartementet Ju 2012/8213/PO). In contradiction to their own investigation there was no reform as it was considered too substantial.

And there is already useful and ongoing research at the universities. But a closure of the SNPA was decided in order to find another university in the greater Stockholm area where vocational contract teaching could begin. But the police basic training would now be entirely located at university campuses. To put it mildly, the Police Union was very displeased (Nitz et al. 2012; Nitz 2014).

Strike Three; Police in the Future: Police Basic Training as Higher Education

As the years went by, the future became the present and then more or less the past. The change of government in 2014 revitalized the matter of reforming police basic training as it was imprinted amongst the Social Democratic election promises. Following the tradition, another directive was assigned for yet another governmental investigation, and this time there was no hesitation. A police basic training for the future demands scientific basis and evidence-based practice. Focus in the directive was entirely on *how* to reform it into a purposive higher education, including new legislation and a specific university degree in police work (Kommittédirektiv 2015:29).

And in June 2016 the third investigation was presented (SOU 2016:39). Referring to the investigation's title (which is the name of this heading, without the baseball reference) the content might be seen as the "manual" for how to finally reform the police basic training and merge it with the higher education. In the following section I will try to summarize the cornerstones of the investigation's 300 pages, though it can be noted that a substantial share of the argumentation and ideas are also found in the preceding investigation (SOU 2008:39).

The universities are independent authorities and it is suggested that the Swedish Higher Education Authority will be in charge of the governance and the dimensioning of the police basic training, which will include the degree system.[12] The importance of a well-functioning cooperation between the universities and Police Authority is repeatedly being stressed. The latter will still be taking part in some of the crucial decisions, that is, the numbers of students per semester. This also goes for the curriculum, as the training must adapt to the Police Authority's views on knowledge and needs and demands for employability. Regarding the location it is suggested that the training is pursued at an existing university, instead of initiating a university campus of its own.[13]

A significant change is that the basic training will be extended from two and a half years to three years. Of great importance is moreover that the students will not be employed during the internship, and hence no longer paid. To simplify it, the students will get paid in credits instead as the internship must be qualified as a higher education. This modification sums up to that the students, in practice, will need study allowance for six instead of, at present, four semesters.

There are several statutes within the university system that must be considered if a merger is implemented, and especially goes for the Higher Education Act and the Higher Education Ordinance. Police basic training is at present regulated in a specific ordinance (SFS 2014:1105) that will be revoked following a reform. In the investigation it is also suggested that the recruitment process must adapt to the higher education, and amongst the ideas is to cancel the personality assessment and IQ test. Unlike higher education in general the applicants have to be Swedish citizens and law-abiding and have an overall physical ability to be admitted to the police basic training. Of certain interest is that the reform hopefully can contribute to a higher percentage of female applicants, as higher education traditionally attracts more women. An already implemented and besides widening change is that the age limit for admission has been lowered from 20 to 18 years.

Of huge concern in the argumentation for a higher education is that knowledge needs to be resting on a scientific basis and evidence-based practice (see also SOU 2008:39). Contemporary societies are getting more multifaceted and globalized and that inevitably makes police work more complex. There is a growing need for students, as police officers to be, to be able to scrutinize, reflect upon and analyse information in order to solve problems adequately. Furthermore, in their everyday work, police officers meet academically trained social workers, lawyers and prosecutors with whom cooperation would improve. The advantages of a higher education will not just be beneficial for the students, but in a longer run the organization will too benefit from it.

In the era of internationalization the reform would enhance the possibilities for further cooperation with countries where the police basic training is a higher education. Amongst the vigorous arguments for a higher education is that in Norway, in several ways Sweden's closest neighbour, police basic training became a higher education in 1992. Since 2006 there is also a master's programme in police science in Norway and their police research is renowned. The other Scandinavian neighbours have also recently reformed their police basic training into a higher education: Denmark in 2010 and Finland in 2014. Regarding Denmark there was a recent change back to a two-year vocational degree, but with mandatory possibilities to continue for a bachelor. It can be noted that the Swedish neighbours still pursue police basic training at separate police academy campuses.[14]

New demands and roles for the teachers are other important and challenging aspects, and at present approximately 15 per cent of the police teachers have an academic degree whereof some at PhD level (SOU 2016:39). Brulin et al. (2010) are underlining an overall need for more academically trained teachers at police basic training. A significant question is whether the police teachers continue their teaching role as police officers or if they will be transformed into university lecturers. An employment as a lecturer at the university will lead to that their police role, including the authority, ceases to be valid. The bottom line in this context is that you are either a police officer or a lecturer.[15]

A merger with higher education would definitely enhance the preconditions for police research. This was one of the strongest arguments behind the reform, where it is emphasized that police researchers to some extent must be recruited amongst police students in order to develop evidence-based policing methods. Police research in Sweden is scattered and there is no clear responsible body for it, and that could be remediated by a designated graduate school for police work (see also Brulin et al. 2010).[16] At the same time the investigation suggests that the Swedish National Council for Crime Prevention ought to be responsible for building up a Swedish police research database. This can be seen in a historical perspective, as the research unit at the SNPA was moved to the Swedish

National Council for Crime Prevention in 1998, and that there ought to be a closer cooperation within the judicial system.

The reformed police basic training is suggested to commence in September 2018, located at the three universities with ongoing police basic training: Linnæus, Umeå and Södertörn. Following this, the first academically trained students will begin working in the summer of 2021, and a couple of them might also begin their careers as police researchers after being rewarded with a university degree of police work at a bachelor level.

After three consecutive governmental investigations, that all have been in favour of a merger with higher education, there soon ought to be a decision. Another noteworthy feature throughout the years is that most of the consultation bodies have sustained the proposals for a higher education. And right now—mid-October 2016—the views from the consultation bodies on the investigation will again soon be compiled.

From a Student's Point of View

When police students are asked why they applied for the police basic training the answers most often contain aspects of wanting to make a difference and looking forward to a profession that is practical (Olsson 2013). The academic aspects are rarely the most compelling. This dividing line between practical and academic training can easily be amplified during training by the staff. Or do the students carry these standpoints when admitted? Rohdin and Mikkonen (2008) found in their study that almost all the police students agreed upon that the recruitment demands were too low. Noteworthy is also that this critique was not just concerning the physical tests—the traditional "doings"—but even more so the skills in written Swedish.[17]

Newly admitted students are often eager and demanding as they early on identify with the profession, but some are surprised by that there is so much course literature to be read and not many practical exercises. Studies of the police basic training often confirm this contradictoriness that easily can make the students hesitant (Lauritz and Hansson 2013; Jakobsson Öhrn and Stark 2014). Bergman and Heder (2013) concur with this discourse as they noticed how students already during the internship are requested by their colleagues to be to just forget the basic training where nothing valid or of importance is being taught.

A common feature of studies on student's opinions is that quite often the students wanted more practical exercises during their training: more doing. Rohdin and Mikkonen's (2008) discuss that the theoretical parts of the training were nonetheless considered satisfying and there was a non-negligible concern that the training might be far too theoretical if it becomes a higher education. Conclusively, the respondents expressed doubt and resilience regarding a police basic training reform (ibid). Brulin et al. (2010) assume that this result stands for an apprehension that the present vocational training in a longer perspective might be downgraded.

In comparison to higher education police basic training has a special feature of a high degree of teacher-led learning activities (ibid). Police students who already were experienced from higher education put forth that too many students were "being served" to a higher degree (Jakobsson Öhrn and Stark 2014). An example of diversified traditions comes from the SNPA and regards the clear-cut resilience when course literature in English was suggested, but hence never implemented. This helpfulness was also noticed in Rohdin and Mikkonen's (2008) study, where they furthermore found that their respondents saw that students not suitable for the profession still could graduate as the routines for scrutiny were too vague. That opinion was also valid for faulty performances. This tradition of low turnover can most likely be explained by how the old system worked when students were paid employees and training just a formality. If admitted; you were a colleague to be and the organization needed you, and if the level of graduating students decreases it would severely inflict upon the expected employability.

Cultures and Traditions at Stake?

An ineluctable feature of the history of policing and the police organization is the military connotations. Not least are war analogies common within the world of policing, whereof the war on drugs or just against criminals has been significant (Brulin et al. 2010; Granér 2004). In general policing carries masculine insignias that build culture and over the years traditions have been fortified. These traditions include hierarchical organizations with ranks visible on the uniform, use of force and recruitment and training that more often attracts, and is suited for, men. The gender perspective will all the same need some attention, even though the number of female police officers in Sweden has increased throughout the decades.

Regardless of these traditions modern police work has developed and become ever so complex and contains several variables beyond the "all boys warzone". A question that repeatedly comes to mind is, what does a police officer need to know to be professional? Amongst others Granér (2004) and Olsson (2013) discuss knowledge, or rather know-how, from the traditional point of view of being able to perform. Police skills are to a high extent equivalent of doing, performing as problem solvers. And how to solve urgent problems often emanates from experiences gathered with colleagues; so there is a high degree of collective memories when it comes to making good use of skills and knowledge (Holgersson 2005). There is seldom any need for or interest in deeper understanding within this perspective, where police basic training and "real police work" are at odds (Olsson 2013).

The abovementioned authors see that policing often comes down to acting, or rather reacting to crime, and they continue to agree upon that knowledge is inherited within in the police force and learnings can hardly emanate from "outsiders" like academics. They are being too theoretical and completely lack contact with the "real world" in which there is no room for the artefacts taught during training (Granér 2004). Valuable and useful knowledge rarely comes from reading books.[18] Just those who have achieved police knowledge, or rather police skills, the hard way can know the trade. And conclusively, in this discourse they are the only ones who are legitimate to talk about policing. Academically achieved knowledge is therefore negligible in this discourse of negative connotations of police culture. Not surprisingly, Granér (2004) and Lauritz and Hansson (2013) remind us that the relations between the police and the academia every now and then have been strenuous, and that has had implications on the possibilities to do police research as there has been a lack of willingness to let academia take part. A quite important reminder in this elegy is that it takes two to tango. This point is clearly made by Olsson (2013) who sees how academics as well as police officers carry traditions of "self-sufficiency". This can be exemplified by doing research, as there are noteworthy differences between doing research for, on or with the police that implies different relations, interdependencies and trust between the academia and the police. Giving this mutual antagonism a historical, or rather a developmental, perspective the understanding and interdependence between police and academia has all the same improved over the years (SOU 2016:39).

Anyhow, with the above considered, still a huge, and maybe to some provocative, challenge is to reform police basic training into a higher education. And that will take some adaptations. The history of cultural incompatibility cannot, or rather must not, be completely neglected, and Olsson (2013) notices the importance of being wary of not ignoring several years of police experiences that the individuals as well as the organization carry. Beyond police basic training a professional life awaits where newly achieved knowledge meets experience, skills and traditions. Along the way forward there is a need for a paradigm shift, or perhaps several shifts, when it comes to how knowledge is valued and what will constitute police professionalism in the future. This calls for open minds amongst everyone concerned.

An Epilogue for the Future

Summing up this chapter is a bit precarious as there are some inconsistencies, procrastinations and muddy points in the pages above that I also quite easily can see. The history has been plagued with ups and downs, miscellaneous anticipations and different developments in what basically is a national and uniform education. Another historical feature is that vast police reorganizations happen to coincide with the efforts to reform police basic training.

However, Swedish police basic training is on the whole on the verge of taking some further steps into academia. After several governmental investigations, three just in the last decade, there finally seems to be a foundation for a reform to be implemented. The directives for the investigations have gone from *can* police basic training, fully or partly, be reformed and merge with higher education via *can and should* it be reformed to, at the final stage, *how will it be reformed*. Even though the major part of the consulting bodies repeatedly was in favour of a reform a change of government seems to have put new power into the matter. The Social Democrats had promised a police basic training reform in the 2014 election that was, and still is, vigorously supported by the Police Union. Or must a "probably" still be added? At present the comments from the consultation bodies have not yet been compiled and with the Swedish Democrats in a balance of power a vote in parliament is likely to be unpredictable.

Anyway, the closure of the SNPA cannot be seen in another way than that a higher education is forthcoming as police basic training is conclusively being located at universities from 2017. But there are differences to be aware of, and one regards credits that lead to some inequalities and variations. A concern in this context is if the new police officers will achieve different status due to where they graduate. On the path forward Umeå University has taken the lead in the ongoing development of police basic training as higher education. In the other end, police basic training at Södertörn University is at present still "under construction", regarding the training facilities, lack of credits and the fact that the first students have not yet graduated.

Maybe the most adequate point of entry is to look beyond the strategic and organizational levels and ask who the police officer for the future is. The focal point is whose applications for police basic training are the most needful. For years there have been incitements to stimulate a pluralistic and non-traditional recruitment. Foremost this aims at female applicants, but the male dominance is still evident. This also goes for Sweden-born. Of certain interest is the gap between the academic future and the applicant's preconditions to qualify for an admission and, in the longer run, being able to complete the basic training. It must be further discussed if the police basic training is to adapt to the students' conditions and preferences. Or perhaps is the other way around to prefer, so that students who are admitted must adapt to higher education. This matching aspect is crucial if the police basic training after a reform will sustain as a higher education. Moreover, this is important as police research, researchers included, for the future will emanate from the police basic training.

To resurrect the question from the Police Union it is worth noting that there were empty study places in the last two admissions, even though the qualification requirements overall have been lowered. The question is still unanswered what an increase in the number of applicants will lead to if they don't pass the different qualifying tests. It cannot be ignored that police basic training to a high degree still attracts "doers" before "academics", to put it bluntly, and this often makes an imprint on the anticipations during training. But at the same time the academic imprint has increased after each reform.

The last governmental investigation (SOU 2016:39) was given the directive to look into how reform should be implemented and the preconditions for a reform are at hand. So, now there is a "manual" to be followed, but there are still circumstances to consider before any conclusive decisions are made that will change the paradigm of police basic training. The first step in this progress must be attracting and recruiting the right applicants. And thereafter see to how to maintain them, because they are needed in the newly reformed Police Authority.

Notes

1. Speech given at the SNPA by the former chair of the Police Union Jan Karlsén, May 2005.
2. The Swedish Agency for Public Management published the first investigation regarding the reform (Statskontoret 2016). In the report there are more headings under "challenges" than under "implemented changes".
3. Högskola (high school) is like a parallel to "university college". See also the German term "hochschule".
4. Växjö University is nowadays called Linnæus University.
5. Rohdin and Mikkonen (2008) also found differences between the three locations in their survey of student opinions. (See also Brulin et al. 2010).

6. The distance between Södertörn University and the SNPA is 30 km. It can be noted that in the future there will just be further education at the SNPA, and the name "SNPA" will also cease to exist.

7. A Conservative win always leads to that they form a coalition government with two-three other parties that can be described as Conservative-Liberal, with the Conservatives as the biggest and most significant party.

8. After the 2014 election the Social Democrats formed a coalition government with the Swedish Green Party.

9. Nearly half of the respondents thought that police basic training already was a higher education, which of course the Police Union reacted strongly to (Polisförbundet 2012).

10. When this political numeric goal was reached the admission to the SNPA was closed for a year and employees were made redundant. In 2011 the SNPA reopened the admission and some formerly redundant staff was re-employed.

11. At the Conservatives homepage (www.moderat.se) there is nothing found about police basic training. Last accessed 27 September 2016.

12. The preceding investigation (SOU 2008: 39) suggested an administrative move from the Ministry of Justice to the Ministry for Education and Research.

13. There are continuous comparisons with the Swedish Defence University which became a higher education in 2008, but continued to be located outside existing universities when security issues were assessed.

14. In Norway there are two other locations (Kongsvinger and Bodö) where police basic training is being pursued in cooperation with the main in Oslo.

15. Police teachers to a high extent see a conflict in this matter and often conclude that it will discourage them from continuing teaching. The discussion also includes questions of where and when to wear the uniform.

16. A noteworthy novelty is that in 2016 two employees at the Police Authority (Stockholm Region) were admitted (with payment) as designated police researchers to the research programme in criminology at Malmö University, where no police basic training will be pursued.

17. Written Swedish was cancelled from the qualifying tests some years ago.

18. During my years at the SNPA the Teacher of the Year Award—Students' Choice was always won by a police teacher.

References

Bayley, D. H. (1994). *Police for the Future*. New York: Oxford University Press.

Bergman, B., & Heder, M. (2013). *Polisstudenters och polisers uppfattning om polisutbildningen*. Solna: Polishögskolan.

Brottsförebyggande rådet. (2013). *Satsningen på fler poliser. Vad har den lett till?* Rapport 2013:12 Stockholm: Fritzes.

Brulin, C., Eriksson, N., Ridderstad, A., & Sarre, R. (2010). *Extern utvärdering av polisutbildningen vid Umeå universitet.* Umeå: Umeå universitet.

Granér, R. (2004). *Patrullerande polisers yrkeskultur.* Lund Dissertations in Social Work, Lunds Universitet.

Green, A. (1991). *Brott och straff i partipolitiken. Kriminalpolitik på svenska.* Lunds universitet, Statsvetenskapliga institutionen.

Holgersson, S. (2005). *Yrke: Polis. Yrkeskunskap, motivation, IT-system och andra förutsättningar för polisarbete.* Linköping Studies in Information Science, Dissertation No 13: Linköpings Universitet.

Interpellation. 2006/07:26.

Interpellation. 2006/07:208.

Interpellation. 2008/09:616.

Interpellation. 2009/10:221.

Jakobsson Öhrn, H., & Stark, A. (2014). Polisiär grundutbildning. En kartläggning av höstterminen 2013 vid Polishögskolan i Solna, Linnéuniversitetet i Växjö och Umeå universitet, Solna: Polishögskolan.

Justitiedepartementet Ds 1996:11 Rekrytering och grundutbildning av poliser, Stockholm: Fritzes.

Justitiedepartementet Ju 2012/8213/PO Regeringsbeslut.

Kommittédirektiv. 2006:10 En ny polisutbildning.

Kommittédirektiv. 2006:139 En polisutbildning för framtiden.

Kommittédirektiv. 2015:29 En förändrad polisutbildning.

Knutsson, J. (2010). Den myndighetsanknutna polisforskningen—en kommenterad biografi, Växjö: Linnéuniversitetet.

Lauritz, L. E., & Hansson, J. (2013). Lära för livet—att vara polis i en föränderlig värld. In N. Eklund & L. Landström (Eds.), *Polisen—verksamhet och arbete* (pp. 66–82). Malmö: Liber.

Löfven, S. (2014). *Statement of Government Policy.* Available at: http://www.socialdemokraterna.se/upload/Samarbetsregeringen/Statement%20of%20Government%20Policy.pdf. Accessed 14 Aug 2016.

Motion. 2005/06:Ju358 Polisen i medborgarnas tjänst.

Motion. 2006/07:Ju377 En förbättrad polisutbildning.

Nitz, L. (2012, March 17). Lyssna på allmänhetens krav om en bättre polisutbildning, Beatrice Ask, *Aftonbladet*.

Nitz, L. (2014, September 23). Visa handlingskraft för en professionell polis, *Svenska Dagbladet*.

Nitz, L. (2016, April 17). Ingen konkurrens om man vill bli polis längre. *Expressen*.

Nitz, L., Johansson, M., Sarnecki, J., & Granér, R. (2012, December 20). Vi behöver en kompetent polis, *Expressen*.

Olsson, J. (2013). Från självskydd till akademisk teori—att förena den polisiära och akademiska världen. In N. Eklund & L. Landström (Eds.), *Polisen— verksamhet och arbete* (pp. 83–100). Malmö: Liber.

Polisen. (2013). *Södertörns högskola får utbilda poliser.* Available at: https://polisen.se/Arkiv/Pressmeddelandearkiv/Rikspolisstyrelsen/Sodertornshogskola-far-utbilda-poliser/. Accessed 10 Aug 2016.

Polisförbundet. (2012). *Åtta av tio svenskar vill reformera polisutbildningen.* Available at: http://www.polisforbundet.se/blog/2012/03/19/atta-av-tio-svenskar-vill-reformera-polisutbildningen/. Accessed 8 Aug 2016.

Polishögskolan. (2012). *Översyn av Polisprogrammet vid Sörentorp.* Slutrapport. Solna: Dnr: PHS-750-1750/11.

Polisutbildningen Umeå universitet. (2015). Ansökan om inrättande av huvudområde polisiärt arbete för högskole- och kandidatexamen. http://www.umu.se/om-universitetet/pressinformation/pressmeddelanden/nyhetsvisning//polisutbildningen-i-umea-ger-hogskoleexamen.cid253980 Accessed 8 Aug 2016.

Rikspolisstyrelsen. (1997). Ny grundutbildning för poliser.

Rohdin, B., & Mikkonen, M. (2008). *Uppföljning av Polisutbildningen för de studenter som tog examen vårterminen 2003 och 2005.* Växjö universitet.

Schoultz, E. (2016). 36 platser gapar tomma på polisutbildningen. *Polistidningen,* 17 October

SFS. (2014:1105) Förordning om utbildning till polisman.

Socialdemokraterna. (2013). *Ett tryggare Sverige. Bekämpa brotten och brottens orsaker.* https://www.socialdemokraterna.se/Documents/Ett%20tryggare%20Sverige.pdf. Accessed 8 Aug 2016.

SOU. 1994:103 Studiemedelsfinansierad polisutbildning. Delbetänkande av 1994 års polisutredning. Stockholm: Fritzes.

SOU. 2008:39 Framtidens polisutbildning. Slutbetänkande. http://www.regeringen.se/contentassets/7ff601e38a2842d495a8183c60e01ee1/framtidens-polisutbildning-sou-200839 Accessed 21 Feb 2016.

SOU. 2016:39 Polis i framtiden—polisutbildningen som högskoleutbildning. Betänkande av polisutbildningsutredningen. Stockholm: Wolters Kluwer.

Statskontoret. (2016) Ombildningen till en sammanhållen polismyndighet. Delrapport 1 om genomförandearbetet (2016:22).

Örebro universitet. (2011). Två frågor om polisutbildningen, http://www.blaljus.nu/sites/default/files/filarkiv/pdf/2012_arkiv/enkat_om_polisutbildn.pdf. Accessed 16 Aug 2016.

4

The New Zealand Context: Finding Common Ground in the Land of the Long White Cloud

Stephen Darroch

Introduction

Nullius in verba is the maxim of the Royal Society. It means "on the word of no one," and speaks to the determination of the Society to vigorously pursue the scientific method and avoid fallacious arguments from authority. *Nullius in verba* has been foundational to the development of the Royal Society and the advancement of science. Policing on the other hand, at least until the recent decades, might have adopted the motto *primo auctoritate* or "authority first," to characterise how wisdom was acquired and passed on. Whether from politicians, senior officers or community leaders how policing should be accomplished was apparently easily knowable and uncomplicated. Policing was a moral crusade and the task was straightforward: find the criminals responsible for breaking the law and put them before the courts. The degrees of freedom available when collecting evidence

S. Darroch (✉)
Royal New Zealand Police College, Porirua,
New Zealand

© The Author(s) 2018
C. Rogers, B. Frevel (eds.), *Higher Education and Police*,
DOI 10.1007/978-3-319-58386-0_4

allowed confessions to be extracted, with eyewitness identifications and generally cooperative witnesses and juries closing the loop. What could be simpler?

However, as the world became more complex, societies more diverse and glaring injustices more numerous, police organisations were forced to reflect on what they were doing and how to respond in more complex and nuanced ways to mounting pressures and community dissatisfaction. In effect, police were forced to figure out how to avoid being left behind.

One aspect of the police response was to consider how officers and managers might be better equipped to deal with growing social complexity and rapid change through better education. It seemed entirely straightforward that policing should move away from its vocational and blue-collar roots and instead mimic the professions with qualifications, professional bodies and portable careers. At least that seemed pretty clear in the 1980s and 1990s but as we will consider the picture is a lot more complicated now.

This chapter will do four things. First we will explore the recent history of police and higher education in Aotearoa, New Zealand. This will draw out some themes, which will be examined in the context of the much wider discussion around police and higher education. Here we will consider the critical issue of police higher education and research and the challenge of police professionalisation. All these issues coalesce around some key issues, which seem critical to the discussion but are not always clearly elucidated. In particular the importance of science literacy will be argued as critical to the advancement of police higher learning and education. Finally we will then draw these threads together and land on some conclusions.

Aotearoa/New Zealand

And so to New Zealand. While literally on the other side of the world from policing hot spots New Zealand Police pride themselves on keeping track of international developments in policing and following or leading where they can (Darroch and Mazerolle 2013; Darroch and Mazerolle 2015; Ratcliffe 2005). This section will plot the development of higher learning and engagement with academic institutions by New Zealand Police since the 1980s. My account will not look through a strict historical lens but explore a struggle of ideas endeavouring to emerge as New Zealand Police have gone through periods of reform and improvement.

For the record, New Zealand in 2016 is a country of 4.7 million people spread across a country about the size of the UK (Statistics New Zealand 2016a). It occupies two main islands, named perhaps a little uncreatively North and South. There are 9048 sworn officers and 2932 civilian staff forming a national police agency, which provides policing for the entire country (New Zealand Police 2015). The history and traditions of New Zealand are English, with the first national police service formed in 1886. New Zealand Police are very much in the Peelian tradition of a civilian police agency policing by consent with the goals of achieving an absence of crime and maintaining community support and standing (Hill 1995).

New Zealand and its Police have a mixed history with its indigenous people. The *tangata whenua* (people of the land) Māori people suffered many injustices during colonisation, which have echoed down the generations. Today, Māori make up 15.4% of the population but well over 50% of the prison population (Statistics New Zealand 2016b). Recent decades have seen significant national efforts to reconcile and address these injustices (Consedine and Consedine 2012). New Zealand is fast becoming an Asia Pacific country, with demographic trends well on track for New Zealand to be 21% Asian by 2038 (Local Government New Zealand 2016).

Looking back, the 1980s and 1990s seem like a much simpler time. I recall as a young 18-year-old cadet in 1981 being very impressed with Gary Burns an American and former officer running the Diploma in Police Studies at Massey University. Like many young police at the time no one in my immediate family had ever been to university and although qualified to attend university I was clueless but intrigued. How shiny and interesting this academic world seemed to be, what treasures did it hold? How smart they must be. David Burns is quoted in the *Bulletin* (New Zealand Police 1988) the internal police newsletter of the time encouraging staff to undertake the Diploma in Police Studies because "it indicates commitment to the career and concern about improving yourself to climb the ladder of success." He goes on to highlight the knowledge gained and personal benefits "such as improved communication, thinking and decision making skills" (New Zealand Police 1988, p. 10).

Whatever other benefits the Diploma might have brought, completing the undergraduate diploma allowed significant cross-crediting of academic papers for internal New Zealand Police examinations and healthy reimbursement of fees was also available. A well-designed undergraduate diploma or degree could see young officers quickly fully qualified to the rank of Inspector and applying for promotion, perhaps ahead of their peers. The same Bulletin (New Zealand Police 1988) reports a Wellington Detective qualifying for three of her four Senior Sergeant examinations and all of her Inspectors examinations on the basis of completing her Diploma in Police Studies.

This was the time in New Zealand Police when qualifications mattered. Higher education was in vogue and qualifications could lead to "blue flame" careers with an arms race in qualifications eventually seeing law degrees and Masters of Business Adminstration (MBA) and Masters of Public Policy becoming especially prized. In line with prevailing (or even at the time slightly dated) attitudes towards university qualifications, those with degrees and qualifications were seen as part of the elite. To be fair this view reflected thinking when fewer people went to university and those with qualifications were smaller in number.

Cross-crediting for police qualifications and valuing of higher educational qualifications for their own sake can also be linked to the birth of managerialism in policing. In the 1990s neoliberalism and managerialism drove concerns about performance, efficiency, effectiveness, structure and reform, even in the face of questions about the appropriateness and effectiveness of the reforms themselves (Cockcroft and Beattie 2009; Fleming and Rhodes 2004; Vickers and Kouzmin 2001). As a consequence interest in managerial qualifications accelerated. If management tools present the way forward then naturally managerial qualifications might form part of the tool kit to get the job done, hence the need for higher education and qualifications.

Unfortunately in New Zealand the credibility of managerialism was shattered by the very public failing of a new national Police computer system INCIS (Integrated National Crime Information System) in the late 1990s (Small 2000). INCIS was an effort to modernise police computer systems commencing in 1994. In 1999 it was very publicly abandoned after huge cost overruns and much public and private rancour. The final ministerial report into INCIS concluded the project was overly ambitious and lacked proper oversight and governance (Small 2000). INCIS undermined political, public and internal police confidence in managerialism and consequently higher education in policing. INCIS seriously undermined confidence damaging the link between higher education and the ability to get the job done.

Despite this challenge cross-crediting and an interest in university papers continued so, by the mid-2000s the New Zealand Police qualifications framework was in a blend of internal police examinations coupled with university papers. This was coupled with a requirement for newly graduated constables to complete university papers to qualify for their permanent appointment to New Zealand Police. This was known as the Certificate in Contemporary Policing and was administered through the Victoria (University) Police Education Programme VPEP (New Zealand Police 2007b).

This coupling didn't last as concerns were raised questioning cross-crediting and the prescription of university papers. Effectively Police began asserting ownership over their own business. As we will discuss in more depth in the next section, questions were sensibly raised about what the body of knowledge was that police should be expected to know, understand and apply? What knowledge should officers be expected to have? Setting knowledge of the criminal law, policy, processes and procedures contained in Police, set examinations alongside fairly dry and esoteric university papers like "organisational behaviour," "organisational process in police administration" or indeed at Inspector level any approved 200- or 300-level university papers (New Zealand Police 2007b) simply left many confused.

This melding of internal police examinations and academic papers led to a rethinking of the New Zealand Police internal qualifications framework. The rather public failings of qualifications with the INCIS scandal and a growing confidence in New Zealand Police about their ability to manage their own business also underpinned the rethinking.

By this time the link between higher education and career advancement was much more tenuous and higher education much less in vogue.

A review of the New Zealand Police Promotions Framework sets out the concerns clearly. Senior Non-Commissioned Officers and some Commissioned Officers "expressed a lack of appreciation of the tertiary components or the value of tertiary study to individuals or the organisation" (New Zealand Police 2007b, p. 3). Many expressed "bewilderment at the changes from the promotional requirements of circa 1996 (which introduced university qualifications into the framework) … there appears to be a perceived need amongst these members for a knowledge base in the areas of Practical Duties, Statutes, Evidence and Administration at all three levels" (New Zealand Police 2007b, p. 3). The paper goes on to explain that the rationale for the changes were not clear and were not fully communicated and in particular "the introduction of tertiary papers … was largely responsible for this perceived shift in focus" (New Zealand Police 2007a).

What emerged was a mature Police-owned promotions and leadership development model. Officers are expected to demonstrate core-policing knowledge through internal police examinations and demonstrate through interviews and internally managed police assignments that they had the right qualities to lead within New Zealand Police. All this is internally managed and unconnected to higher learning institutions. The model is stable, seemingly uncontroversial and evolving to meet the changing needs of the organisation.

Higher Education Bearing Fruit in Aotearoa, New Zealand

While higher education was struggling to find a stable home within New Zealand Police contemporary frontline managers and officers were enthusiastically consuming the fruits of higher learning, police research. While the introduction of community policing and problem solving helped, the rise of applied police research can be seen most clearly in the growth of Intelligence-led policing in New Zealand (Ratcliffe 2005, Darroch and

Mazerolle 2013, 2015) in the 2000s. From the early 2000s Intelligence-led policing was developing across New Zealand. The development was encouraged from the centre but was not command-driven change. While Jerry Ratcliffe (2005) noted the challenges within intelligence systems and process in the early 2000s, he was also a key influence on the development of intelligence systems and practice in New Zealand. Ratcliffe visited New Zealand on numerous occasions first in 2003 and consistently over the following decade. His 3I model (Ratcliffe 2003) was enthusiastically embraced over the 2000s in New Zealand, to the extent that New Zealand's own brand of Intelligence-led policing emerged under the banner of Crime and Crash reduction.

While the development of Intelligence-led policing in New Zealand was more ground up than top-down change, it nevertheless became normalised and accepted by senior management. In 2006 newly appointed Police Commissioner Howard Broad adopted the brand. The Police internal magazine of the time noted that "application of the proven crime and crash reduction model, enhanced by intelligence-led policing is where Howard will focus police direction. The track we've been on in recent years around crime and crash reduction and the evidence-based crime science model is the way to go," says Howard (New Zealand Police 2006).

The rise of Intelligence-led policing and thinking about evidence and crime science also shepherded key ideas and theoretical constructs into New Zealand Police. Crime science theories like Routine Activity Theory, Rational Choice Theory, Crime Pattern Theory and ideas like Crime Prevention through Environmental Design (Wortley et al. 2008) became accepted and utilised, not just within the Intelligence community but also across management and many frontline officers. Important related methodologies like Problem Solving and SARA (Scanning, Analysis, Response and Assessment) were also firmly adopted and embedded. All this built on a mature foundation of community policing practice within New Zealand.

In 2004 New Zealand Police hosted the Environmental Criminology and Crime Analysis conference (New Zealand Police 2004) at the Royal New Zealand Police College with leading international criminologists like Gloria Laycock, Ron Clarke, Johannes Knutsson, David Weisburd and Jerry Ratcliffe speaking. New Zealand Police took full advantage of having so much talent in the country conducting seminars and seeking advice. All of this helped propel the Crime and Crash reduction model and an appetite for effective evidence-based interventions. In 2006, 2008 and 2010 (New Zealand Police 2010) New Zealand Police organised research symposiums with, by 2010, more than 90 papers being submitted to the conference for consideration.

Over this time Intelligence systems steadily improved, becoming more professionalised and standardised with analyst training in particular being developed and delivered to a high standard. There was also some integration with higher education. A national diploma in intelligence analysis became offered as part of training for intelligence analysts sitting on the New Zealand qualifications framework (New Zealand Qualifications Authority 2016). The development of intelligence training and practice led to a closer relationship with Massey University with a memorandum of understanding between New Zealand Police and the university being signed in 2011 (Massey University 2011). It is insightful to look at the detail of the memorandum, in particular what it considered the relationship should be about. The focus of the memorandum was on:

- Delivery of a master's degree in international security
- Secondment of New Zealand Police staff to the Centre for Defence and Security Studies
- Joint teaching and research activities
- Participation in seminars and academic meetings
- Exchange of publications, academic material and other information
- Joint quality assurance benchmarking of programmes
- Teaching, learning and professional development

So, the focus of the relationship was in effect a start, an opportunity to concentrate on a few modest goals and see how the relationship might develop. The Master of International Security was offered within Massey University Centre for Defence and Security Studies based in Wellington and includes papers on security strategy, crime intelligence, international law, leadership and management (Massey University 2011). It provides development for 10–20 officers per year focused on strategic intelligence and international security. Intelligence training within New Zealand Police also offers internally a strategic intelligence course for a small number of staff at post-graduate level in partnership with Charles Sturt University in Australia (Charles Sturt University 2016).

The confluence of Intelligence-led policing and crime sciences approaches in the 2000s, and the perceived success achieved through adopting these approaches, demonstrated through the Crime and Crash reduction approach, gave New Zealand Police confidence that the fruits of higher education had value. Tools such as quality analysis, useful theories and models and the application of strong evidence-based practice proved themselves to be effective, if not exactly restoring confidence in higher education itself. Whether it was the particular offerings of universities themselves or a disconnect between police and academics, attitudes towards higher education remained lukewarm.

Core Foundational Initial Training (CFIT)

In early 2012 New Zealand Police began thinking about how to modernise its initial training offerings to new recruits. This involved a tendering process to identify a tertiary academic partner with the capacity, interest and vision to work with New Zealand Police to further develop its recruit-training programme. The successful tenderer was an Auckland-based polytechnic Unitec Institute of Technology (UNITEC) (New Zealand Police 2011b; Unitec to deliver foundation education for Police recruits n.d.). Interestingly a university was not selected but a polytechnic institute of technology with many existing practice-based vocational education and training courses. It is easy to see that courses offered by UNITEC like three- and four-year degree programmes training nurses, social workers and teachers might have a lot of crossover in content and approach with police work. This raised the question—is it possible the more practical nature of the polytechnic environment, where skills similar to policing, like nursing and social practice are taught, may help bridge the gaps between academe, research and front line practice when this did not seem entirely achievable up to this point.

In 2016 as part of relationship building with UNITEC I had the chance to meet and talk with Heads of School at UNITEC. I found the discussion with the Head of Nursing particularly insightful. For me it contrasted the differences between the attitudes of police to higher education and research and those of the medical (in this case the nursing) profession. We talked about the training our new recruits would receive. She explained that a principal goal of year one was to understand research. A key goal of year two was how to apply research and year three was to do research. Nurse graduates were expected to constantly ask "why?"—why are we doing this, this way and not another way—what is the evidence base for doing this procedure or practice this way rather than any other way? I was hugely impressed. However, I could not help reflecting on how such questioning might be received within a police organisation. I wondered about the kind of reflective police culture needed for everyone to be comfortable with these kinds of questions. Surely, I thought, this kind of detailed questioning and analysis of what police actually do and what they should be doing, with a profound focus on outcomes is what is needed to build an evidence base of effective policing practice.

To date the relationship is developing and the training offered is proceeding as hoped. However, as the discussion with the Head of Nursing illustrated there is still work to do to determine how higher education might evolve into something impacting on the whole of policing and not just discrete components like intelligence practice and recruit training.

What looks promising for even more engagement with universities and higher education is the strategic direction of the New Zealand Police. The current operating model is the "Prevention First" strategy launched in 2011 (New Zealand Police 2011a). The model builds on its predecessor, the Crime and Crash reduction model, but with a much sharper focus on repeat victimisation, family violence prevention and wider issues of deploying to demand and focus on the drivers underpinning crime. As the model develops a focus on the addressing the drivers of offender behaviour to enhance prevention is emerging. The next stage of developing the model is being developed through a transformation programme entitled Policing Excellence the Future (New Zealand Police 2015). Two elements of this programme are key to a more enhanced engagement with higher education, Safer Whanau (Māori for families) and Evidence-Based Policing. These challenging aspects of policing, working with families to address the causes of crime and endeavouring to build an evidence base for policing, suggest an obvious need for a productive engagement with higher education. Working to minimise harm in families is hugely challenging, requiring both effective day-to-day policing and strong and effective partnerships to address complex and persistent areas of family discord. These challenges provide an obvious focus for the testing of police interventions and experimentation to build effective partnerships.

There is a lot going on across strategic thinking and forward-looking approaches within New Zealand Police. The progenitors of current initiatives draw from the best in analytical thinking and policing tools from the late 1990s and 2000s which all have their roots in academic institutions and higher learning across the globe. But whilst higher learning academics and institutions have made a real contribution to the evolution of policing in New Zealand, meaningful engagement with higher education itself remains ambiguous. There still seems to be a missing piece of the puzzle preventing development beyond a certain point. As crime evolves policing will need to develop or risk falling behind. A big part of keeping pace with evolving challenges will be developing the critical thinking of emerging leaders to meet these new challenges and, for this, higher education needs to be a big part of the mix.

The Wider Context: The Barriers and Opportunities to Meaningful Engagement with Higher Education

The New Zealand context sits within a much broader discussion about policing and higher education. In this section I want to explore how the New Zealand fits into that broader discussion and land on some conclusions. Thinking about the issue of police and higher education immediately draws us into a conversation about the relationship between policing and the normal rewards of higher education, research and evidence. As we have seen, research evidence and theoretical constructs have been enthusiastically adopted in New Zealand but this has been accompanied by reticence about higher learning itself. As well as this tension the persistence of critical criminology (Carrington and Hogg 2002) asking uncomfortable questions about issues like the goals of policing, what police actually do and what evidence exists to support policing approaches, underpins police suspicions about the intentions of academics and the possible outcomes of research.

Ben Honey's (2014) study of the tensions between policing and higher learning identified the continuing challenges all police organisations face as they wrestle with the place of research in policing. Honey (2014) concludes that police organisations are non-learning with continuing elements of anti-intellectualism. Qualifications may be used to identify talent, but police-led research is not to be encouraged. Honey (2014) confirmed that police management culture remained politically dense and the crucible of "observed failure" (Honey 2014, p. 137) is ever present. Moreover, police culture remains isolated and inward looking. In the hot politics of policing, the modest measured progress offered by research struggles to compete with command and control, media friendly crackdowns. Finally, Honey (2014) confirms the continuing importance of tacit knowledge to policing. Police know what needs to be done and just need to be given the space to get on with it. Not a very promising start.

Another way to think about engagement between policing and higher education is the idea of higher education being a necessary step in the professionalisation of policing. Green and Gates (2014) do a nice job in setting out the challenges police face in professionalising their discipline. While professionalisation in policing is often discussed, precisely what professionalisation means is often left opaque. For me, becoming a profession organises the world (as far as possible) around a discrete topic or discipline to allow a defined group to overcome systematic errors and biases in thinking to advance or assist the cause of humankind. Or put more concisely, to bring the disciplines of science to a collective endeavour. In this way engineers can build bridges, pilots fly planes and dentists straighten teeth.

Green and Gates (2014) set out the key characteristics of a "profession": identifying autonomy; an accepted body of knowledge; and a commitment to lifelong learning and higher education as the key elements. These characteristics strike me as actually pretty serious barriers. While it would be nice to think police officers can and do act autonomously this is a moot point. Discussion could start with the command and control aspects of policing, the lack of compelling research and evidence to make clear professional self-directed decisions as opposed to gut feeling decisions (should I prosecute or divert this 16-year-old offender with complex problems, exhibiting poor self-control—who is currently drunk and stoned and spitting at me?). Other barriers would include the pressures of exigent police culture and the ever-present influence exerted by oversight bodies (internal and external) likely to pressure officers to make safe decisions close to existing norms rather than evidence-based or innovative decisions.

As Green and Gates (2014, p. 79) note "practitioner led research is necessary to drive the establishment of the 'complex body of knowledge' that is distinct from existing disciplinary knowledge and constitutes the knowledge base of the profession." Green and Gates (2014) describe the vacuum of shared knowledge in policing and the lack of practitioner interest in researching best practice and developing the "science of policing" (p. 79). Linking all this back to higher education they go on to conclude "yet still there is no agreed position on where higher education fits within the recruitment, advancement and lateral development of police officers ... there appears to be no common agreement that a university education is either necessary for policing or that such qualifications would be representative of the community" (Green and Gates 2014, p. 80).

Or, put another way as Michael Buerger (2010, p. 140) notes "researchers should ask police (at all levels from street cop to agency head) what sort of information they need to make better operational decisions." Answering this question would be the start of building a distinct police discipline and scholarship. This discipline would build on the limited evidence and theories that exist, which are situational, place and opportunity based (Wortley et al. 2008) to include much more detail about how police should conduct themselves day to day to address the complex behaviours they are presented with and to some extent the complex social problems that underpin those behaviours.

A big barrier to making a meaningful start is police understanding of science, or overall levels of science literacy in policing. Cops need to first agree on the place of science in policing and then on a level of science literacy for the emerging profession to begin to build the discrete body of knowledge necessary to build the discipline. Effective science literacy will mean police will be able to overcome their own cognitive biases and systematic errors in thinking to effectively change their own professional practice. This is a very challenging thing to do. Wenning (2006) both defines science literacy and simultaneously identifies challenges for any emerging science-based profession. "The truly scientifically literate person will know not only content knowledge, but also understand the scientific process whereby that knowledge has been developed. The person will understand the importance of observation and experimentation in science, and will be capable of questioning, using logic for induction and deduction, relying upon evidence, and having a proper understanding of the nature of science. This would include a basic understanding of the history, values, and assumptions of science. Perhaps only 4% or 5% of the US population ever achieves this level of scientific literacy, and almost all of them will be scientists or professionals" (Wenning 2006 p. 9). The only thing missing in this quote is to emphasise the importance of a scientifically literate person understanding their own cognitive biases and systematic errors in thinking likely to lead them to false conclusions and unscientific thinking.

Buster Benson (2016) provided an excellent overview of known cognitive biases, neatly summarising why and how our brain presents such a distorted view of the world to us. In short, our brains have evolved to aggressively manage our perception and thinking to deal with:

- Too much information—we aggressively filter (leading to biases such as the availability heuristic and confirmation bias)
- Not enough meaning—lack of meaning is confusing, so we fill in the gaps (leading to biases such as the halo effect and hindsight bias)
- The need to act fast—lest we lose our chance, so we jump to conclusions (leading to biases such as the sunk cost fallacy and illusion of control)
- What should we remember? This isn't getting easier, so we try to remember the important bits (leading to biases such as recency effect, next-in-line effect)

Coming back to higher education for a moment the role of tertiary academic scientific training now becomes much clearer in the development and maintenance of a profession. Higher education provides the cognitive, scientific, statistical, mathematical and modelling tools to assist professionals to advance their profession. The scientific method provides a systematic way to accurately represent reality to allow for real development and advancement. In this way doctors can actually cure people and not make things worse. Engineers can actually build bridges and buildings that stand up. Psychologists might apply talk therapy to relieve anxiety. Nurses administer evidence-based treatments. Social workers use interventions that address and reduce the behaviours driving child abuse. And police might manage individual criminals, communities and environments promoting crime prevention in a manner that is evidence based and effective. The point is none of this matters if the agents of the proposed profession are unable to see past their own cognitive biases to apply science. None of this matters if there is little empirical evidence to inform practice. And none of this matters if command and control and politics overwhelm the emerging profession.

I propose that police need science literacy and a willingness to overcome their own cognitive biases. As Benson (2016) notes so clearly these biases and errors keep the world simple and straightforward. We can see the impact of these biases and errors across the population in the ease with which the tobacco industry was able to manipulate public views about smoking for 50 or more years (Cummings and Proctor 2014) and currently in the challenges of climate change denial (McCright and Dunlap 2011). It is discomforting to suffer cognitive dissonance and disrupt the more comfortable status quo of believing what you have always believed. It is entirely reasonable that police will suffer from the same biases as the communities they are drawn from, given that police are representative of the population and have not been through the extensive winnowing and high-level education processes which typically shape the membership of professional elites. As Honey (2014) observes police organisations are typically non-learning and this is entirely consistent with the bulk of the population being non-learning and comfortable having existing modes of thinking unchallenged.

Worryingly, David Kennedy (2010) suggests that these issues are not just a police problem but endemic across the whole criminal justice system. Kennedy hammers the point home, "we spend enormous amounts of time, resources and authority doing things we know from the outset will be unsuccessful" (Kennedy 2010, p. 167). Kennedy (2010) claims that it is simply routine in the criminal justice system for loyalty to be to an individual's occupation and occupational norms rather than any particular set of outcomes. Kennedy (2010) further argues that individuals in the system are well aware that a vast amount of what is done will not actually reduce the overall burden of crime on the community or prevent future offending. Regrettably evidence pales in the face of business as usual.

Kennedy (2010, p. 167) goes on, "other disciplines devoted to practical reasoning do not behave like this." He argues that the key missing element is the relentless focus on outcomes seen in other disciplines and professions. What is encouraging here is evidence from both New Zealand and beyond, that where a focus on outcomes is applied, progress can be made. Kennedy (2010, p. 168) notes that tools, which are proven to be effective, focus on outcomes and rely on "information, analysis and impact assessment." Outcomes can be and have been achieved (as we saw in New Zealand) through tools like "community and problem-oriented policing, situational crime prevention, routine activity theory, attention to hot spots, repeat offenders, and repeat victimisation, innovative deterrence frameworks and the like" (Kennedy 2010, p. 168).

Critically these approaches are the tools of science and these tools represent the extent to which science has penetrated policing. Perhaps the opportunity, which now presents itself, is the prospect of doing wider science and analysis with a focus on outcomes across the whole policing and criminal justice endeavour, from the behaviour of frontline officers and the outcomes of arrests and prosecutions, to the high-level strategies and interventions undertaken by police. Police and the wider criminal justice endeavour needs to break the constraints of existing role functions and loyalties and instead adopt a commitment to outcomes supported by evidence. As Kennedy (2010, p. 169) notes "fundamentally, criminal justice actors feel role responsibility; they do what they are called upon to do as police officers, prosecutors, judges, defence lawyers, etc. Their obligation is to the role, not to effective strategies and good outcomes." He concludes that "criminal justice is fundamentally agnostic about outcomes but uncompromising about methods," and "until we change this, there will be no possibility of a real and meaningful integration of research and practice" (Kennedy 2010, p. 168).

As I have argued already in this chapter until this tension is resolved the place of higher education in policing will be murky. This tension helps us understand why there is often confusion about what the police should actually study at academic institutions. Questions like "should officers study law, psychology, management or political science?" Possibly they should study all of that at some point, but first they should acquire the foundational skills needed for more advanced study and research within their own discipline—the scientific method, statistics, qualitative and quantitative research methodologies and the history and critics of their own discipline.

In these circumstances it is much clearer what a real engagement with higher education might look like. It would entail supporting a redesign of the profession from the ground up, which would start with developing the unique body of knowledge describing policing and how to do it effectively. Immediately this brings us back to questions I asked reflecting on the engagement of New Zealand Police and UNITEC; is policing ready for the "why" questions? Why are we doing this and what is the evidence that this is the best way to do it? While engineering, medicine and nursing embrace these conversations—is policing ready?

As a thought experiment it is worth asking where science and evidence is going to lead policing and what will we be asking police to do in 100 years? What will be the skills we expect police to have and how will we then be training them? If policing does become a genuine profession what will we be expecting police to actually do and have a deep well of professional competence in? It is not hard to imagine a profession of policing looking radically different to the way it does today. Perhaps the way medicine looks back a little sheepishly on the era of butcher surgeons and bloodletting. One presumes there will always be a need for police to deal with emergencies but beyond that one can see police applying expert knowledge with other community and health professionals to limit the opportunities for crime and "treat" individuals, families and communities experiencing criminal behaviour. Along the way police will need to develop its own body of professional knowledge and engage with developing knowledge about the transmission of crime and the behaviour of people in time and space to exploit criminal opportunity. Inevitably this process of development, of training generations of police to build their profession will require a significant engagement with higher education. Weisburd and Neyroud (2011) signalled an important step on this journey when they called for police ownership of their own science. They argued for Clinical Professors of Policing to lead the research required to make policing a genuine profession (Weisburd and Neyroud 2011).

A significant remaining challenge is the law itself. If, as Kennedy (2010) suggests, much of what is done within wider criminal justice has little impact or does not work, then the role of police in enforcing the law needs to be drawn into thinking about the role of science, higher education and the professionalisation of policing. An obvious question is how do police resolve conflicts between the law and the evidence presented by a new police science? While it is generally accepted that police have reasonable discretion to pick and choose when and where to enforce some laws (cannabis, disorder, minor traffic) this discretion extends only so far. It may be that police science, education and professionalisation can only develop to a point while constrained by a fairly strict requirement to "enforce the law" whatever the downstream consequences. Perhaps until a whole of criminal justice evidence-based inquisitorial system emerges with a focus on community safety and outcomes, police development is constrained.

Such a wider criminal justice science might allow deeper thinking about the causes and treatment of crime. Remarkably while clear scientific evidence continues to emerge about the precursors of crime and the drivers of crime within individuals and families, there has been remarkably little response to applying this knowledge. This is pertinent for New Zealand where two landmark longitudinal studies, the Dunedin Longitudinal Study (Dunedin Multidisciplinary Health and Development Research Unit 2016) and the Christchurch Longitudinal Study (Christchurch Health and Development Study 2016), have provided tremendous insights into the familial and individual factors underpinning criminal offending and anti-social behaviour, pathways in and out of offending, and the opportunities to address criminal behaviour (e.g. see Fergusson et al. 2015). If policing and wider criminal justice does build a police science, with clear goals and a focus on outcomes, this will allow challenging questions to be raised which beg deeper inquiry into what crime actually is and the best response to it. This is important because there is evidence that we might account for nearly all crime in five ways:

1. as an outcome of opportunity, so reduce the opportunity and reduce or eliminate the crime (Wortley et al. 2008)
2. as a consequence of damage in the first 1000 days of life (adverse childhood experiences) that sets individuals up for predictable poor health and social outcomes across the board (Danese et al. 2009; Felitti et al. 1998; Fergusson et al. 2015; Reavis et al. 2013)
3. as a consequence of drug and alcohol addiction (very often led by point 2) (National Council on Alcohol and Drug Dependence 2016; Payne and Gaffney 2012)
4. as a consequence of the transmission of violence within communities (Patel et al. 2012)
5. as a result of predictable adolescent behaviour and socialisation processes (Moffitt et al. 1996)

Given this more science-based account of crime what should police and the criminal justice system be doing? What are the outcomes they could or should be focusing on? What is the body of professional knowledge that might support the best possible outcomes in the short, medium and long term? To what extent should police be professional gatekeepers and guides into well-researched treatment programmes once they have diagnosed the conditions underlying criminal behaviour? Again, it is worth asking, if police and the criminal justice system pursue science for 100 years then given this more scientific account of crime what could be achieved? And of course what higher education do police need to support this development across generations of police?

Drawing the Threads Together to Reach a Conclusion

New Zealand Police has been on a journey with higher learning. Various attempts have been made to build meaningful long-term relationships without really getting to grips with what a clear and evolving substantive relationship should look like. Different configurations have emerged and then faded without settling on exactly how to fully engage with universities and higher education. What has been most successful is the integration of police research into intelligence practice and the current operating model of the New Zealand Police which focuses strongly on prevention. New Zealand Police has adopted the best of research and thinking from higher education into the organisation and there is real interest in doing more of what has been successful to date.

In New Zealand the appetite for helpful applied research theory and practice remains very strong. The new strategic direction of New Zealand Police looks promising for a more long-term relationship to emerge. Both the Prevention First operating model (New Zealand Police 2011a) and the new strategic approach Policing Excellence the Future (New Zealand Police 2015), are asking the right questions about the causes of crime. Under the banners of Safer Whanau (Families) and evidence-based policing (New Zealand Police 2015) both the right solutions and a much stronger relationship with higher education and universities is likely to emerge, if the new strategic direction is able to deliver on its promise. Building practice-based training and learning also looks promising. Learning from closely related but more advanced professions like social work and nursing through a close relationship with UNITEC should support police development and enable further development and integration of higher learning.

Seen from a wider international frame, the challenges New Zealand Police faces in engaging with higher education are common to police and criminal justice agencies across the globe. It is likely that cultural challenges remain and learning barriers focused around persistent anti-intellectualism still exist (Honey 2014). Overcoming population wide cognitive biases and building science literacy is extremely challenging. Learning to focus on outcomes through the application of science and research will be far from easy. Like the rest of the criminal justice system police will need to break entrenched occupational loyalty and learn, like other professions, a new kind of loyalty. Fidelity to science, lifelong learning and delivering long-term quantifiable outcomes must become the new standard.

Pursuing science over generations could ultimately professionalise policing with a clear and growing role for higher education and learning. A significant necessary precursor to this is the emergence of professional autonomy. Occupational loyalty and slavish adherence to the "law" needs to be replaced by clearly defined and widely accepted desired outcomes operating within an agreed legal framework if police and wider criminal justice professions are to emerge. Scientific tools can then be employed to achieve those goals providing both professional autonomy and assurance to the community.

It is not hard to see what kind of policing profession might emerge over time with clear implications for the kind of higher learning needed to support that development. The profession of policing is likely to be about excellence in emergency response and critical incident management. Police will need to be expert in reducing the opportunity for crime in the physical environment and at the individual, family, community and national levels. They will understand how to reduce victimisation within highly and predictably at-risk populations. They will deal expertly with the day-to-day behaviour of offenders. They will understand, treat and refer offenders for behaviour arising from drug and alcohol addiction or a myriad of health-related problems like mental health challenges that spill over into behavioural and social problems. Police will be proficient in dampening the transmission of violence within communities as it begins to emerge. They will recognise and treat families as the crucible of predictably poor health, social and criminal justice outcomes and expertly prevent and treat all forms of violence within families. Police will understand and deal effectively across the life course with crime arising from predictable adolescent developmental and socialisation processes. What might emerge is a science of criminal justice and policing that addresses the real causes of crime and socially dysfunctional behaviour, which can be clearly traced back to the home and the communities around those homes.

What would be exciting is police adopting the maxim of the Royal Society *Nullius in verba*—on the word of no one. The Royal Society was founded in 1660. Through continually asking the "why" question, learning and applying the disciplines of science and adopting the accoutrements of other professions, it is worth considering what the profession of policing might evolve into over the next 350 years. On this journey an enduring relationship with higher education, mirroring that seen in other professions, will be a predictable and necessary outcome.

References

Benson, B. (2016). *You Are Almost Definitely Not Living in Reality Because Your Brain Doesn't Want You to Quartz Online.* Available at: http://qz.com/776168/a-comprehensive-guide-to-cognitive-biases/#. Accessed 8 Oct 2016.

Buerger, M. E. (2010). Policing and Research: Two Cultures Separated by an Almost Common Language. *Police Practice and Research, 11*(2), 135–143.

Carrington, K., & Hogg, R. (2002). *Critical Criminology: Issues, Debates, Challenges.* Portland: Willan Publishing.

Charles Sturt University. (2016). *The National Strategic Intelligence Course.* Available at: https://www.csu.edu.au/__data/assets/pdf_file/0003/543540/F3168-AGSPS-NSIC-flyer_WEB.pdf. Accessed 25 Oct 2016.

Christchurch Health and Development Study. (2016). Available at: http://www.otago.ac.nz/christchurch/research/healthdevelopment/. Accessed 22 Oct 2016.

Cockcroft, T., & Beattie, I. (2009). Shifting Cultures: Managerialism and the Rise of "Performance.". *Policing an International Journal of Police Strategies and Management, 32*(3), 526–540.

Consedine, R. C., & Consedine, J. (2012). *Healing our History: The Challenge of the Treaty of Waitangi.* Auckland: Penguin Books.

Cummings, K. M., & Proctor, R. N. (2014). The Changing Public Image of Smoking in the United States: 1964–2014. *Cancer Epidemiology, Biomarkers and Prevention, 23*(1), 32–36.

Danese, A., Moffitt, T. E., Harrington, H., Milne, B. J., Polanczyk, G., Pariante, C. M., Poulton, R., & Caspi, A. (2009). Adverse Childhood Experiences and Adult Risk Factors for Age-Related Disease: Depression, Inflammation, and Clustering of Metabolic Risk Markers. *Archives of Pediatrics and Adolescent Medicine, 163*(12), 1135–1143.

Darroch, S., & Mazerolle, L. (2013). Intelligence-Led Policing: A Comparative Analysis of Organizational Factors Influencing Innovation Uptake. *Police Quarterly, 16*(1), 3–37.

Darroch, S., & Mazerolle, L. (2015). Intelligence-Led Policing: A Comparative Analysis of Community Context Influencing Innovation Uptake. *Policing and Society, 25*(1), 1–24.

Dunedin Multidisciplinary Health and Development Research Unit. (2016). Available at: http://dunedinstudy.otago.ac.nz/. Accessed 22 Oct 2016.

Felitti, V. J., Anda, R. F., Nordenberg, D., Williamson, D. F., Spitz, A. M., Edwards, V., Koss, M. P., & Marks, J. S. (1998). Relationship of Childhood Abuse and Household Dysfunction to Many of the Leading Causes of Death in Adults the Adverse Childhood Experiences (ACE) Study. *American Journal of Preventive Medicine, 14*(4), 245.

Fergusson, D. M., Boden, J. M., & Horwood, L. J. (2015). From Evidence to Policy: Findings from the Christchurch Health and Development Study. *Australian and New Zealand Journal of Criminology, 48*(3), 386–408.

Fleming, J., & Rhodes, R. (2004, 29 September–1 October). *It's Situational: The Dilemmas of Police Governance in the 21st Century*. In Australasian Political Studies Association Conference University of Adelaide.

Green, T., & Gates, A. (2014). Understanding the Process of Professionalisation in the Police Organization. *The Police Journal, 87*, 75–91.

Hill, R. S. (1995). *The Iron Hand in the Velvet Glove: The Modernisation of Policing in New Zealand 1886–1917*. Wellington: Dunmore Press.

Honey, B. A. (2014). *Study in Blue: Exploring the Relationship Between the Police and Academia Professional Doctorate*. UK: University of Portsmouth.

Kennedy, D. (2010). Hope and Despair. *Police Practice and Research, 11*(2), 166–170.

Local Government New Zealand. (2016). *The 2050 Challenge: Future Proofing Our Communities A Discussion Paper*. Available at http://www.lgnz.co.nz/assets/42597-LGNZ-2050-Challenge-Final-WEB-small.pdf. Accessed 23 Oct 2016.

Massey University. (2011). *NZ Police and Massey University Forge Closer Ties*. Available at http://www.massey.ac.nz/massey/about-massey/news/article.cfm?mnarticle_uuid=AF1421EA-F9D3-C9FB-52C9-4C07C09F2948. Accessed 18 Sep 2016.

McCright, A. M., & Dunlap, R. E. (2011). The Politicization of Climate Change and the Polarization in the American Public's View of Global Warming of Climate Change and, 2001–2010. *The Sociological Quarterly, 52*, 155–194.

Moffitt, T. E., Caspi, A., Dickson, N., Silva, P. A., & Stanton, W. R. (1996). Childhood-Onset Versus Adolescence-Onset Antisocial Conduct in Males: Natural History from Age 3 to 18. *Development and Psychopathology, 8*(8), 399–424.

National Council on Alcohol and Drug Dependence Inc. (2016). *Alcohol Drugs and Crime*. Available at: https://www.ncadd.org/about-addiction/alcohol-drugs-and-crime. Accessed 18 Oct 2016.

New Zealand Police. (1988). *The Bulletin* (p. 10). Wellington: New Zealand Police.

New Zealand Police. (2004, June 29, Tuesday). *NZ Police to Host Environmental Criminology and Crime Analysis Symposium*. Available at http://www.police.govt.nz/news/release/1423. Accessed 6 Oct 2014.

New Zealand Police. (2006, May). *Ten One Community Edition*. Available at: https://www.police.govt.nz/tenone/20060428-284/feature_broadview.htm. Accessed 6 Oct 2014.

New Zealand Police. (2007a, February 27). Promotions Review Report, Stakeholder Consultation.

New Zealand Police (2007b, February 27). Promotions Review Report, Current Model – Summary.

New Zealand Police. (2010, August). *Ten One Community Edition*. Available at: http://www.tenone.police.govt.nz/tenone/Aug10Research.htm. Accessed 8 Oct 2016.

New Zealand Police. (2011a). Memorandum of Understanding Between Massey University New Zealand and the New Zealand Police.

New Zealand Police. (2011b). *Prevention First Strategy*. Available at: http://www.police.govt.nz/sites/default/files/publications/prevention-first-strategy-2011-2015.pdf. Accessed 23 Oct 2016.

New Zealand Police. (2015). *Annual Report*. Available at: http://www.police.govt.nz/sites/default/files/publications/annual-report-2015.pdf. Accessed 23 Oct 2016.

New Zealand Qualifications Authority. (2016). *National Diploma in Intelligence Analysis*. Available at: http://www.nzqa.govt.nz/nzqf/search/viewQualification.do?selectedItemKey=0899. Accessed 25 Oct 2016.

Patel, D. M., Simon, M. A., & Taylor, R. M. (2012). Rapporteurs Contagion of Violence: Workshop Summary Forum on Global Violence Prevention; Board on Global Health; Institute of Medicine The National Academies Press. Available at: http://www.nap.edu/catalog.php?record_id=13489. Accessed 18 Oct 2016.

Payne, J., & Gaffney, A. (2012). *How Much Crime Is Drug or Alcohol Related? Self-Reported Attributions of Police Detainees, Trends & Issues in Crime and Criminal Justice No. 439*. Canberra: Australian Institute of Criminology.

Ratcliffe, J. H. (2003). Intelligence-led Policing Trends & Issues in Crime and Criminal Justice No. 248. Australian Institute of Criminology. Available at:

http://aic.gov.au/publications/current%20series/tandi/241-260/tandi248. html. Accessed 23 Oct 2016.

Ratcliffe, J. H. (2005). The Effectiveness of Police Intelligence Management: A New Zealand Case Study. *Police Practice and Research, 6*(5), 435–451.

Reavis, J. A., Looman, J., Franco, K. A., & Rojas, B. (2013, Spring). How Long Must We Live Before We Possess Our Own Lives? *The Permanente Journal, 17*(2), 44–48.

Small, F. (2000). Ministerial Inquiry into INCIS New Zealand Government.

Statistics New Zealand. (2016a). *Population Clock*. Available at: http://www. stats.govt.nz/browse_for_stats/snapshots-of-nz/top-statistics.aspx. Accessed 23 Oct 2016.

Statistics New Zealand. (2016b). *New Zealand's Prison Population*. Available at: http://www.stats.govt.nz/browse_for_stats/snapshots-of-nz/yearbook/ society/crime/corrections.aspx. Accessed 23 Oct 2016.

Unitec to deliver foundation education for Police recruits. (n.d.) Available at: http://www.scoop.co.nz/stories/ED1504/S00046/unitec-to-deliver-foundation-education-for-police-recruits.htm. Accessed 18 Sep 2016.

Vickers, M. H., & Kouzmin. (2001). A New Managerialism and Australian Police Organizations A Cautionary Research Note. *The International Journal of Public Sector Management, 14*(1), 7–26.

Weisburd, D., & Neyroud, P. (2011). *Police Science: Toward a New Paradigm New Perspectives in Policing*. Available at National Institute of Justice Harvard Kennedy School Program in Criminal Justice Police and Management. https://www.ncjrs.gov/pdffiles1/nij/228922.pdf. Accessed 23 Oct 2016.

Wenning, C. J. (2006). Assessing Nature-of-Science Literacy as One Component of Scientific Literacy *Journal of Physics Teacher Education Online, 3*(4) 3–14. Available at: www.phy.ilstu.edu/jpteo. Accessed 24 Oct 2016.

Wortley, R., Mazerolle, L., & Rombouts, S. (Eds.). (2008). *Environmental Criminology and Crime Analysis*. Cullompton: Willan.

Part II

Innovation

5

The College of Policing: Police Education and Research in England and Wales

Colin Rogers and Bethan Smith

Introduction

Educating police officers has been a topical subject for many years. Since the days of August Vollmer at the start of the twentieth century, how police officers were educated was open to discussion and sometimes quite emotional debate. Vollmer was the first police chief to require that police officers attain college degrees, and persuaded the University of California to teach criminal justice. In 1916, UC Berkeley established a criminal justice programme, headed by Vollmer. At Berkeley, he taught O. W. Wilson, who went on to become a professor and continued his efforts to professionalise policing, by being the first to establish the first Police science degree at Municipal University of Wichita (now Wichita State University). This is often seen as the start of criminal justice as an academic field.

C. Rogers (✉) • B. Smith
University of South Wales, Pontypridd, UK

© The Author(s) 2018
C. Rogers, B. Frevel (eds.), *Higher Education and Police*,
DOI 10.1007/978-3-319-58386-0_5

87

Over the years, there have been many reports and inquiries into the way police officers in England and Wales have been educated, including the Trenchard report which led to the foundation of Hendon Police College in 1934.

The future of policing in England and Wales will require a different kind of police officer. Citizen expectations are rising, we live in a consumerist society where individuals know their rights and expect to be treated as a customer, whether they are in a supermarket, booking a holiday or reporting something to the police. Many people want to get involved in service delivery, and it is no longer right to say the public get the policing they deserve, which was a derogatory phrase often heard over the past few decades.

Global society has become more complex, with such topics as cyber-crime, financial crime and organised crime increasing. The use of social media means most events are instantaneously recorded and posted on websites within minutes of them having occurred. There is a realisation that we need smarter police and smarter policing, to deal with such issues and this is why the way we educate our police in the future is so important.

The College of Policing

When considering the College of Policing (CoP), it is necessary to outline the historical developments that have given rise to the establishment as we know it today. Following the Second World War, the British Home Office fronted by senior civil servant Sir Frank Newsam set about to establish a National Police Training College. This was hailed "a landmark in the history of the police force of England and Wales" by the then Home Secretary James Chuter Ede (Harris 1949, p. 217). As explained by Harris (1949), the Bramshill Police Training College was established in 1948 by the Home Office for the purpose of providing training to officers serving at, or seeking promotion to the rank of Inspector or above. With the rationale that

In order to raise the standards and efficiency of the Police Service college training should widen the interests, improve the professional knowledge, and stimulate the energies of men in the middle or higher ranks of the Service. (Harris 1949, p. 219)

Described as an "outstanding example of cooperation between the central Government, the local authorities, and the Police themselves" (Harris 1949, p. 218), the establishment of the Police Training College set the precedence for a national body that aimed to provide training and to improve standards of policing in the UK. Albeit targeted towards the upper echelons of policing, this establishment laid the foundations for the future of police training and development, and its successive replacements.

The National Police College was later named the Police Staff College in 1979 and continued its work through until 2001. Under the New Labour administration, Part 4 of the Criminal Justice and Police Act 2001 saw the Police Staff College replaced by the Central Police Training and Development Authority (CPTDA), commonly known as Centrex. Essentially, Centrex was responsible for overseeing police recruitment processes, training and promotions, whilst it also sought to "to provide advice and consultancy services, generally with respect to best police practice" (Criminal Justice and Police Act 2001).

Centrex was made up predominantly of seconded police officers and civil servants, on the belief that good police practitioners would automatically be good trainer. Whilst this would appear to be a logical presumption, Reiner (2000) explains this model is indicative of the insular nature of the police force and its resistance to external agencies (such as higher education and academics) in the provision of education and in advisory roles (Rogers 2011, p. 5).

Further reform under the 2006 Police and Justice Act saw the dissolution of Centrex and the establishment of the National Police Improvement Agency (NPIA), formed by the amalgamation of Centrex along with other relevant agencies including the Police Information Technology Organisation, the National Centre for Policing Excellence and a number of Home Office staff roles (Home Affairs Committee 2011). As explained by Rogers (2011, p. 5), the idea of the NPIA was to "work in partnership with forces and other policing agencies to improve the way they work across all areas of policing". This effectively saw the mainstreaming of the idea of collaboration in police work, training and policy development, acknowledging that policing was not solely the job of the police.

The Home Affairs Committee stated:

> The NPIA has done much to bring about welcome changes to policing. In particular, it has acted as a catalyst for identifying areas for efficiency gains within forces, encouraging greater collaboration and identifying where economies of scale can be realised through national procurement frameworks. It has succeeded in the first stage of rationalising a number of different agencies responsible for supporting police forces. But now is the right time to phase out the NPIA, reviewing its role and how this translates into a streamlined national landscape. (Home Affairs Committee 2011, p. 3)

The creation of the College of Policing was first announced by the Home Secretary in December 2011 and became effective in February 2013 (College of Policing 2015a). The CoP inherited much of its responsibility from its predecessors (the National Police Improvement agency and Centrex) as well as the Association of Chief Police Officer (ACPO). However, the College of Policing differs in the fact that it is:

> The first professional body of policing, [it is] a different entity from the NPIA, with a different mission and objectives. Its governance is different and inclusive, and its priorities are evidence-based and commissioned with partners within and outside policing. (College of Policing 2013, p. 1)

The College of Policing came into existence as a registered limited company. Notwithstanding this, it has been stated by the College of Policing that "although the Home Secretary is its only shareholder, the Home Secretary has been clear that she does not believe the Government should be responsible for the day-to-day running of the College" (College of Policing 2013, p. 4). It has further been added that "as soon as Parliamentary time allows, the College of Policing will be established as a statutory body, independent of government" (College of Policing 2015a). Notwithstanding this, the notion of independence is disputed as this piece will later go on to discuss.

The overall strategic aim of the CoP is "to ensure all officers and staff have the right knowledge and skills to do their job", ultimately aiming to create an efficient and professional police service within the UK (College of Policing 2013, p. 1). According to the college its main strategic aims include the following:

- set standards of professional practice
- accredit training providers and set learning and development outcomes
- identify, develop and promote good practice based on evidence
- support police forces and other organisations to work together to protect the public and prevent crime
- identify, develop and promote ethics, values and standards of integrity. (College of Policing, 2013:1)

One way in which the College of Policing set out to achieve such aims is through collaboration with academics and the Higher Education (HE) system. This research paper predominantly focuses on the collaboration aspect of the College of Policing work (particularly between the police and the academic sector), for the purpose of developing evidence-based policy and practice within operational policing.

At present, the College of Policing has increased the emphasis on action research, bringing together both police and academic researchers to work in collaboration, with the intention of generating evidence-based policies that can be mutually understood and translated into well-reasoned practices; whilst allowing ongoing evaluation and development of the "What Works" evidence base (College of Policing 2013). However, its aim is not

> just the creation and availability of rigorous evidence on what works best to reduce crime, but also an understanding of how this evidence is adopted throughout an organisation and the extent to which it is accepted and valued within the professional culture. (Ritter and Lancaster, 2013 cited in Hunter et al. 2015, p. 3)

As explained by Sharples (2013),

> The most effective mechanisms for bridging the inherent gaps between research knowledge and practice are frequently debated. Recommendations focus on the accessibility and format of information, the need to involve

practitioners as evidence producers so research is more firmly embedded in and relevant to frontline experience; increasing skills and capacity through training and development programmes and the 'championing' of research-based practice within the organisation. (Sharples 2013 [cited in Hunter et al. 2015, p. 3])

As claimed by the CoP, there is a positive correlation between police knowledge of research; and willingness to incorporate evidence-based practice into police work (Miller 2013). Therefore, through the use of academic collaboration the CoP aims to "increase receptivity and engagement of the Service to research & scientific practice; to encourage excellence in development and application of research into practice; to support continuous professional development of practitioners [and] strengthen the evidence base for policing" (Miller 2013, p. 4).

Educating Police Officers

With the demise of Centrex in 2007 and the workforce modernization programme starting in 2004, the question of addressing police education became more pressing. The Her Majestey's Inspectorate of Constabulary (HMIC) report Training Matters suggested there was more scope for partnerships between police and further and higher education and a plethora of police related course sprung up around the country.

The current situation is that we have 43 different police forces in England and Wales, each doing their own thing in terms of educating their police officers. Each one is in the situation, it appears, that they can pick and choose to some extent what is delivered in their curriculum. There are often good reasons for this based upon geography or social/demographics of the area to be policed. Some police forces are linked to higher education establishments which offer full-time/part-time, undergraduate or foundation degrees or certificates.

Whilst there may appear to be good reasons for such a diversity of approaches and contents, such a structure makes it difficult to develop a coherent national structure for police learning. In addition, some forces will not recognise internal or external courses delivered to an individual

Table 5.1 Work undertaken by the college to support professionalisation of police

Criteria	Position
Specialist knowledge base	Some way into being developed
An ethical code of conduct	Some way into being developed
Up-to-date professional development	Some way into being developed
Meeting a standard of education verified by nationally recognised qualifications	NO

officer from within a force, which seems quite ludicrous but another topic for debate. Against this backcloth in 2012 the College of Policing was introduced.

The college has a difficult task, as highlighted by the recent Home Affairs committee report (June 2016) which suggests that recognition of the college has been problematic, including the fact that topics such as standards and improvements are not currently binding upon individual chief constables. Indeed, the report concludes that with regard to the Code of Ethics introduced by the CoP, not all forces have adopted it in its entirety with some partial implementation in some. A major area of the colleges work is aimed at increasing the professionalisation of the police to meet future challenges. Table 5.1 illustrates the work undertaken by the college thus far and the current situation in the development of criteria to support the professionalisation of the police.

Table 5.1 clearly illustrates the four main areas which are believed to be the building blocks for the professionalisation process. It reflects what colleagues in police education and training across many other countries are undertaking, which is highlighted in other chapters within this book.

Degree Entry Proposals

From 2019, it is proposed by the College of Policing that there will be two main entry routes into the police service. Firstly by degree which would be either a specific police degree or other degree followed by a conversion course on policing. Secondly through an apprenticeship scheme for those individuals who join the police and do not have a degree already.

For those already in the service who would wish to obtain a degree, it appears opportunities for prior accredited learning opportunities will exist. This means an officer can submit a portfolio of experiences, courses and training to universities who will award credits for this activity, thus shortening the length of a traditional degree. However, it is the apprentice scheme that I wish to briefly concentrate upon.

This approach is designed for individuals who do not have a degree, but would otherwise become a police officer.

The programme envisages a three-year duration, which may necessitate a change in the Police Act, but the idea is the scheme will lead to a degree in policing.

Table 5.2 illustrates research findings from the USA regarding the effects of police educated degree/college programmes. Overall, it would appear to suggest that police officers are less authoritarian and cynical, are more ethical and professional with less complaints and a generally improved attitude towards minority groups. All of this seems to support the idea of professionalising the police. However, these findings are not without criticism, they being quantitatively focused and of course some of them are now older research.

There are of course some issues or concerns with the proposals that need to be highlighted. Firstly, there is the cultural resistance to change that any organisation would probably have in these circumstances. Police tend to be conservative and traditional, and a change such as this is bound to produce resistance. One commentator compared introducing change into the police as trying to walk through treacle. However, society has changed dramatically and there is a need to reconsider the

Table 5.2 Synthesis of early research into degree educated officers in the USA

Research findings	Research authors, etc.
Police less authoritarian	Parker et al. (1976); Roberg (1978)
Police less cynical	Regoli (1976)
Police have a more flexible value system	Guller (1972)
Police have improved attitude towards minorities	Parker et al. (1976)
Police more ethical and professional with less complaints	Roberg and Bonn (2004); Mons et al. (2008); Lersch and Kunzman (2001)

Source: The authors

education of police officers as being fit for purpose. Of course the degree entry is a pre-application course so it has to be paid for by the individual with no guarantee that they will become employed after they have completed their studies. On the subject of finance there is the question as to how the apprenticeship schemes will be funded and if this will be adequate to maintain numbers for this sort of entry. If the idea of the degree programme is to encourage a different way of thinking about police and policing, particularly for future challenges, then there is a need to ensure the degree programme, delivered by former police officers employed by universities, is not just a geographical relocation of police training centres possibly perpetuating the same cultural mentality, but actually produces thinkers and reflective practitioners capable of problem solving and working with others. In addition to the work of the college on educating police officers, a separate and important role it has is to produce a database of knowledge for the professionalisation process. This means that the CoP has a major role to play in the support of research into policing, particularly utilising expertise available in Higher Education establishments, which has not always been a comfortable relationship.

Police Research in Context

Reiner (2010, pp. 11–12) identifies four distinct stages in the development of police research and scholarships since the 1960s. These are "consensus", "controversy", "conflict" and "contradiction". The consensus period of research is often credited as the starting point at which policing begins to be considered a standalone academic discipline. This period of study was typified by studies based upon the identification of police successes and the development of policing based on previous work. This period was also associated with scholars such as Michael Banton and his work *The Policeman in the Community*, which sought to understand the work of the police and what made it successful, drawing upon contrasts and comparisons between the UK and USA. This is widely considered to be "the first study of policing by an academic social scientist in Britain, and virtually the first in the world" (Reiner 1995, p. 121). Whilst it was not expressly critical of police work, Banton's work acknowledged the need for reform and development in line with the rapid social change of the time (Banton 1964).

In stark contrast, this was followed by the controversy period of research in the late 1960s. The controversy period, as described by Thomas et al. (2014, p. 3) was more interested in "police practices (and malpractices), and academic researchers began to take a greater interest in policing, particularly in its limitations". The controversy period was later identified by Greenhill (1981) as the beginning of the professionalisation of the police service, as researchers began to question traditional policing methods, pushing the police to develop alternatives.

This was later followed by the conflict phase of police research. Throughout the late 1970s and early 1980s, the provision of policing became shrouded in political rhetoric. Often highly critical of police work and seeking increased police accountability, the conflict period promoted the objective oversight of independent research as a vehicle to stimulate change within policing policy and practice (MacDonald 1987). Academic works such as Simon Holdaway's (1979) *The British Police* brought the notions of police subculture and ethics to the forefront of policing research, increasing the critical study of the police institution.

Reiner (2010, pp. 11–12) describes the later contradiction agenda of police research as having developed since the late 1980s arguably though until the present day. It is characterised by "a clear (though not unchallenged) crime control agenda" (Reiner and Newburn 2007 cited in Reiner 2010, p. 11). Unlike its predecessors the contradiction phase of research focused on being "*policy-oriented*" and sought primarily to develop "concrete, immediately practicable tactics for crime control" in search of greater economy, effectiveness and efficiency (Reiner 2010, p. 12). This has been evident through the works of governmental police research in the Home Office and academic works alike, and the increased prominence of the "what works" framework.

As explained by scholars such as MacDonald (1987), early police research, particularly during the controversy and conflict periods (between the late 1960s and early 1980s) can be seen as a form of critical criminology, having taken place with little or no police engagement whatsoever (Reiner 2010). In early police research, data was commonly generated from sources such as public media outlets, freedom of information requests and observations, as was the case for much of the pioneering police research, such as Holdaway's (1983) "Within the sociology of policing, The British Police: a force at Work". Whilst Holdaway himself was a serving officer, his research was carried out in a covert manner with no formal police approval (Heslop 2012).

Such a relationship was seen to further strain trust between police and researchers, creating a sense of suspicion between the two. It is argued that as a result of the persistent fault-finding and perceived disparagement from academia, police attitudes in general were seen to become increasingly insular and defensive towards academia (Young 1991).

The critical research tradition is still evident today and maintains a vital role in contributing to debate and scrutiny in the field of policing. However, given its shortcomings and the rise of New Public Management since the 1980s, it has since been acknowledged that academic research can be used to improve policy, practices and cost-effectiveness of police work; hence giving rise to the pre-eminent Evidence-Based Policy research tradition (Sherman 2013). Sherman defines Evidence-Based Policing as

> A method of making decisions about "what works" in policing: which practices and strategies accomplish police missions most cost-effectively. In contrast to basing decisions on theory, assumptions, tradition, or convention, an evidence-based approach continuously tests hypotheses with empirical research findings. (Sherman 2013, p. 1)

The College of Policing appear to have adopted Evidence-Based Policy/Policing as their *sine qua non*. However, historically with researchers having little or no experience in practical law enforcement and with most police officers having little or no academic research training, the effectiveness of how this has translated into practice has been questioned.

With each party failing to understand the rationale of the other, this approach has been seen to fall short of its desired outcomes, creating a sense of "mutual misunderstanding that negatively impacts on the police–academics relationship" (Bradley and Nixon 2009, p. 423).

As explained by Wincup and King (2008), during the 1980s the Home Office began to take a more profound interest in policing and policing research, with the development of the Home Office Research and Planning Unit (later known as the Research Development and Statistics Directorate). This period of time became associated with the themes of Rational Choice Theory, Routine Activity Theory and Environmental Criminology (Walklate 2007).

However, as explained by Walklate (2007, p. 46)

> Work emanating from the Home Office during the 1980s was characterized as 'administrative' insofar as its central concern became administering, that is, managing the crime problem, rather than working to explore its underlying causes.

In 1992 the Home Office established the Police Research Group (which splintered from the Research and Development and Statistics Directorate) headed by Gloria Laycock. Unlike the Research Development and Statistics Directorate, who had "a strong policy orientation across all aspects of the criminal justice system" the Police Research Group was concerned only with policing; and specialised in producing research findings that were operationally relevant and usable (Laycock 2014, p. 47).

The use of Evidence-Based Policy research is clearly defensible, it has distinct methodological leverage, as explained by the WhatWorks Centre for Crime reduction (2015). The What Works model aims to systematically review and "label the evidence on interventions in terms of quality, cost, impact, mechanism (why it works), context (where it works) and implementation issues". As a result of the methodologies involved with Evidence-Based Policy, subsequent research tends to be based upon random control sampling, predominantly quantitative, somewhat results oriented and geared towards the cost-benefit payoff (with research falling outside the parameters of the tenets of the Campbell Collaboration, or lower on the Maryland scale, largely being overlooked in the realm of policy creation) (Pawson 2001).

Hence, the use of means Evidence Based Policing (EBP) as an underpinning principle for the College of Policing's collaboration model has the potential to influence the types of research funded and possibly the associated outcomes, which ultimately poses the question "to what extent is the CoP responsible for setting the agenda and influencing the direction of any subsequent research?" Furthermore, a number of the CoP funding streams have contributions from third parties such as the Economic and Social Research Fund (ESRC) (WhatWorks Network 2014). This may also play a part in determining the sort of bids and applications that are funded as funding streams are often prescriptive as to what research methods are used, as explained by Buerger (2010, p. 137) "funding, in turn, depends upon political winds of outrage, interest, and chance". Thus, by influencing what types of research are funded, the CoP can indirectly influence research methodologies, and in effect the subsequent findings. Hence it can be argued that a premium is placed on statistical analysis as opposed to practicality or the wider concomitants of the intervention. Particularly as much of the work relating to What Works measures only what matters to the individual study, as Beurger (2010, p. 137) highlights, "'Measuring What Matters'; contrarians retort that 'what can be measured matters,' to the exclusion of important variables not captured in standard data sets".

In addition, it is worth noting that policing and crime exists within a complex system, in that there are a multitude of variables with both direct and indirect impacts and causal relationships on crime control. Therefore, occurrences of crime and disorder are somewhat unpredictable phenomena. The uncertain nature of occurrences of crime means the use of private business models (as advocated by New Public Management) such as Key Performance Indicator measurements are rather unreliable (Johnson 2005). Given the complexity of crime, policing must be understood in a localised context, and the results of "What Works" interventions should not be treated as definitive or entirely generalisable, as what may work in one situation may not work in another, for a multitude of circumstantial reasons. As stated by Bassey (2013) "good research only provides an indication of what may work, rather than a definitive solution. Instead of expecting policy to be evidence-based, it should be seen as evidence-informed". It should also be highlighted that due to the democratic nature of the British system "policy is sometimes not based on the research findings but more on public opinion" (Punch 2010, p. 157).

From a strategic perspective, when operating within a complex system, problems are best solved at a localised level through multiple safe to fail experiments, as opposed to attempting to develop a larger fail-safe response. Due to the nature and complexity of the issues facing policing, a one-size-fits-all policy is easily overwhelmed by the diversity of problems affecting the institution (Snowden 2015a). Whilst the CoP is actively encouraging regional research networks and local research partnerships, by modelling research on the What Works methodology, the criticism can be made that research risks over focusing on "calculability, efficiency, control and predictability", concepts that run counter to the stimulation of professionalism (Ritzer 1993 in Heslop 2010, p. 3). As Ritzer argues, "predictability is tied to the imposition of discipline, order, systematisation, formalisation, routine, consistency and methodological operation" (Ritzer 1993: 83 cited in Heslop 2010).

Structures of Collaboration

The College of Policing Chair Professor Dame Shirley Pearce explained that the funding of the collaboration model would assist in

> Developing effective relationships between forces and universities is a key part in growing the knowledge base for policing [... it will] help cement these relationships and enable ideas from Frontline practitioners to be considered alongside knowledge from academics. It is a significant step in developing the policing profession. (College of Policing 2015b)

With the following strategic aims, this technique offers the prospect of improving the "relationships between the key parties—government policy-makers, police management, and university academics" (Bradley and Nixon 2009, p. 431):

- Generate the evidence base in policing;
- Encourage and stimulate new ideas for research by practitioners;
- Provide greater coherence to police-academic engagement;
- Develop skills and confidence of the Service in creating, seeking and using research evidence. (College of Policing 2015c)

However, Buerger (2010, p. 140) explains that it also takes into account

> The success of operational research of this type depends upon a joint ability to identify or create sources of information specific and relevant to the operation, tactic, or approach under study [...] though actively incorporating the police [both management and front line] in the crafting of the research.

In theory, this research technique potentially offers the ability to develop policies and practices that are practical to use, whilst also adhering to the tenets of economy, efficiency effectiveness. It is also worth noting a distinct differentiation can be made between police managers and front line officers being involved in policy and research generation. Reuss-Ianni (1983) highlights a distinct division between "street cops" and "management cops" and their different cultures, roles and priorities; therefore representing different ideals.

Introduced in order to create institutional capacity for collaboration in the hope that it will help police and academic partners to develop future bids for funding from other sources, the following initiatives support the development of partnerships by providing the necessary funding to develop the structures and networks required to successfully collaborate (College of Policing 2015c):

> Innovation capacity building grants- The College of Policing awarded one-off grants of up to £50,000 in 2013/14 to partnerships of educational establishments, police forces and Police and Crime Commissioners (PCCs), to test models and ideas that will support innovation and getting evidence into practice.
>
> Police Knowledge Fund- The College of Policing, the Higher Education Funding Council for England (HEFCE) and the Home Office launched the £10m Police Knowledge Fund earlier this year to encourage collaboration between academia and police forces in order to increase evidence-based knowledge, skills and problem solving approaches within policing. (College of Policing 2015d)

However, particularly with the Innovation Capacity Building Grants the emphasis is placed upon the financial aspect of collaboration and the ability to draw upon external resources, which begs the question "to what extent is austerity perceived as the driving force behind the College of Police's focus on collaboration?" The description of the Police Knowledge Fund in contrast focuses on the professionalisation aspects of introducing the collaboration model, which conversely puts forward the question "to what extent do practitioners view police professionalisation the *raison d'etre* for police and academic collaboration?"

The Evidence Base Camp initiative was introduced "with the aim of developing critical thinking, appraisal skills, giving experience of searching the evidence base and identifying what works" (College of Policing 2015e). Providing intensive training on the use and generation of research and evidence-based practice, the Evidence Base Camp has taken place involving officers from all ranks of the police along with academics and College staff.

> Evidence base camp-training session taken place over a few days that brought together police of all ranks, college staff and academics. (College of Policing 2015e)

Although it has only taken place on a small scale at present, on a larger scale it is believed that the Evidence Base Camp scheme has potential to assist in the professionalisation and development of the individual officers involved, as well as mainstreaming the use of evidence-based practice into police professional culture (College of Policing 2014). This highlights the professionalisation and cultural change aspects of the collaboration model, but does participation in such schemes affect police perceptions of research, academia and the CoP?

Conclusion

The College of Policing aims to assist and facilitate the building of partnerships between police forces and academic institutions, namely universities, in both education and research. Prior to the creation of the College of Policing, Laws and Rein (1997) identified three distinct stakeholders in the process of evidence-based policy development and application:

> Front line officers who deliver the service; policy makers and upper managers who define agency goals; and the perspective of researchers who attempt to develop knowledge that is both useful and generalizable. (Laws and Rein 1997, p. 53)

The idea of police and academic collaboration is not an entirely new concept, with research consortiums such as the University Police Science

Institute (UPSI) and the Applied Criminology Centre having forged successful police and academic partnerships predating the College of Policing (UPSI 2015; University of Huddersfield 2015). The creation of the College of Policing, however, discernibly introduces a new stakeholder in the process of facilitating police and academic partnerships.

References

Banton, M. (1964). *The Policeman in the Community*. London: Tavistock.

Bassey, M. (2013, April 6). *The Current Enthusiasm for Evidenced-Based Policy Needs to be Met with a Greater Degree of Methodological Caution*. British Politics and Policy. Available at: http://blogs.lse.ac.uk/politicsandpolicy/what-works-or-what-may-work-and-bets-on-whether-it-will/. Accessed 2 Feb 16.

Beurger, M. (2010). Policing and Research: Two Cultures Separated by an Almost-Common Language. *Police Practice and Research: An International Journal, 11*(2), 135–143.

Bradley, & Nixon. (2009). Ending the 'Dialogue of the Deaf' Evidence and Policing Policies and Practices. An Australian Case Study. *Police Practice and Research: An International Journal, 10*(6), 423–435.

College of Policing. (2013). *Frequently Asked Questions*. Available at: http://www.college.police.uk/About/Documents/FAQs_College.doc. Accessed 5 Oct 15.

College of Policing. (2014). *Putting the Evidence Base into Policing*. Available at: http://www.college.police.uk/News/archive/2014mar/Pages/news-evidence-base.aspx. Accessed 20 Dec 15.

College of Policing. (2015a). *About Us*. Available at: http://www.college.police.uk/About/Pages/default.aspx. Accessed 5 Oct 15.

College of Policing. (2015b). *College of Policing Supports Collaboration between Academics and Forces*. Available at: http://www.college.police.uk/News/College-news/Pages/COP-collab-academics-forces.aspx. Accessed 11 Dec 16.

College of Policing. (2015c). *Police and Academic Collaboration*. Available at: http://whatworks.college.police.uk/Involve/Pages/collaboration.aspx. Accessed 5 Oct 15.

College of Policing. (2015d). *Police Knowledge Fund*. Available at: http://whatworks.college.police.uk/Involve/Pages/Knowledge-Fund.aspx. Accessed 11 Dec 15.

College of Policing. (2015e). *Evidence Base Camp*. Available at: http://whatworks.college.police.uk/Involve/Pages/ebc.aspx. Accessed 24 Nov 15.

Great Britain: *Criminal Justice and Police Act 2001. Elizabeth II chapter 16*. (2001). London: The Stationary Office.

Greenhill, N. J. (1981). Professionalism in the Police Service. In M. D. Pope & N. Weiner (Eds.), *Modern Policing*. London: Croom Helm.

Guller, I. (1972). Higher Education and Policemen: Attitudinal Differences Between Freshmen and Senior Police College Students. *The Journal of Criminal Law, Criminology and Police Science, 63*(3), 396–401.

Harris, R. E. (1949). New Police College Opened in Britain. *Journal of Criminal Law and Criminology, 40*(2), 217–222.

Heslop, R. (2012). A Sociological Imagination: Simon Holdaway, Police Research Pioneer. *Police Practice and Research, 13*(6), 525–538.

Holdaway, S. (1979). *The British Police*. Oxford: Basil Blackwell.

Holdaway, S. (1983). *Inside the British Police: A Force at Work*. London: Edward Arnold.

Home affairs Committee. (2011). *New Landscape of Policing: Report*. London: Parliament House of Commons.

Hunter, G., May, T., Wigzell, A., & McSweeney, T. (2015). *An Evaluation of the 'What Works Centre for Crime Reduction' Year 1: Baseline*. Available at: http://whatworks.college.police.uk/About/Documents/WWCEvaluation_Year_1.pdf. Accessed 12 Nov 15.

Johnson, L. (2005). *The Rebirth of Private Policing*. Taylor & Francis e-library: Taylor & Francis [online]. Available at: https://books.google.co.uk/books?id=IeSIAgAAQBAJ&pg=PA55&lpg=PA55&dq=police+performance+indicators+private&source=bl&ots=RgYEq4xQhP&sig=iru9dW_8MZjXmnOwhjTboyqzCuk&hl=en&sa=X&ved=0ahUKEwj0n_rwhOTLAhVFxxQKHQ0cD2MQ6AEIUTAH#v=onepage&q=police%20performance%20indicators%20private&f=false. Accessed 28 Feb 16.

Laws, D., & Rein, M. (1997). Knowledge for Policy and Practice. In D. Tucker, C. Garvin, & R. Sarri (Eds.), *Integrating Knowledge and Practice*. Westport: Praeger.

Laycock, G. (2014). Trust Me I'm a Researcher. In E. Cockbain & J. Knutsson (Eds.), *Applied Police Research: Challenges and Opportunities*. Oxon: Routledge.

Lersch, K. M., & Kunzman, L. L. (2001). Misconduct Allegations and Higher Education in a Southern Sheriff's Department. *American Journal of Criminal Justice, 25*(2), 161–172.

MacDonald, B. (1987). *Research and Action in the Context of Policing: An Analysis of the Problem and a Programme Proposal*. London: The Police Foundation of England and Wales.

Miller, N. (2013). *Evidence Matters*. Available at: http://www.law.leeds.ac.uk/assets/files/events/2015/Miller-Evidence-Matters.pdf. Accessed 2 Feb 16.

Mons, J., et al. (2008). Exploring the Impact of Police Officer Education Level on Allegations of Police Misconduct. *International Journal of Police Sciences and Management, 10*(4), 509–523.

Parker, L., et al. (1976). Higher Education: Its Impact on Police Attitudes. *The Police Chief, 43*(7), 33–35.

Pawson, R. (2001). *Evidence Based Policy: I. In Search of a Method*. Available at: https://www.kcl.ac.uk/sspp/departments/politicaleconomy/research/cep/pubs/papers/assets/wp3.pdf. Accessed 21 Dec 15.

Punch, M. (2010). Policing and Police Research in the Age of the Smart Cop. *Police Practice and Research: An International Journal, 11*(2), 155–159.

Regoli, R. M. (1976). The Effects of College Education on the Maintenance of Police Cynicism. *Journal of Police Science and Administration, 4*, 340–345.

Reiner. (1995). From Sacred to Profane: The Thirty Years War of the British Police. *Policing and Society, 5*, 121–128.

Reiner, R. (2000). *The Politics of the Police*. Oxford: Oxford University Press.

Reiner, R. (2010). *The Politics of the Police* (4th ed.). Oxford: Oxford University Press.

Reuss-Ianni, E. (1983). *Two Cultures of Policing: Street Cops and Management Cops*. London: Transaction Publishers.

Roberg, R. (1978). An Analysis of the Relationships Among Higher Education Belief Systems and Job Performance of Patrol Officers. *Journal of Police Science and Administration, 6*, 336–344.

Roberg, R., & Bonn, S. (2004). Higher Education and Policing: Where Are We Now? *Policing: An International Journal of Police Strategies and Management, 27*(4), 469–486.

Rogers, C. (2011). Introduction. In C. Rocers, R. Lewis, T. John, & T. Read (Eds.), *Police Work: Principles and Practice*. Oxon: Routledge.

Sherman, L. (2013). The Rise of Evidence-Based Policing: Targeting, Testing, and Tracking. *Crime and Justice, 42*(1), 377–451.

Snowden, D. (2015). *Introduction to Sensemaker*. Available at: http://cognitive-edge.com/resources/videos/. Accessed 12 Feb 16.

Thomas, G., Gravelle, J., & Rogers, C. (2014). Research on Policing: Insights from the Literature. In C. Rogers & J. Gravelle (Eds.), *Policing in the 21st Century*. Basingstoke: Palgrave Macmillan.

University of Huddersfield. (2015). *Applied Criminology Centre*. Available at: http://www.hud.ac.uk/research/researchcentres/acc/. Accessed 20 Dec 15.

UPSI. (2015). *About Us*. Available at: http://upsi.org.uk/about-us/. Accessed 20 Dec 15.

Walklate, S. (2007). *Understanding Criminology*. Berkshire: Open University Press.

WhatWorks Network. (2014). *What Works Evidence For Decision Makers*. Available at: https://www.gov.uk/government/uploads/system/uploads/attachment_data/file/378038/What_works_evidence_for_decision_makers.pdf. Accessed 21 Dec 15.

Wincup, E., & King, R. (2008). *Doing Research on Crime and Justice*. Oxford: Oxford University Press.

Young, M. (1991). *An Inside Job: Policing and Police Culture in Britain*. Oxford: Clarendon Press.

6

Police Higher Education in China

Zheng Chen

Introduction

This chapter provides an overview of the development of police higher education in China since the founding of the People's Republic of China (PRC). Different from Western countries, police higher education in China bears its own characteristics. There are both national police universities and provincial police colleges or academies around the country, providing associate degree, undergraduate degree and postgraduate education. The education in these institutions includes both liberal studies that other universities provide and specialized courses aimed to train a police officer. Most graduates from these institutions will become police officers after attending competitive State Civil Service Examinations. These institutions also provide courses for in-service police training nationally or within a certain province. In addition, some comprehensive

Z. Chen (✉)
Criminal Investigation Police University of China, Shenyang, China

© The Author(s) 2018
C. Rogers, B. Frevel (eds.), *Higher Education and Police*,
DOI 10.1007/978-3-319-58386-0_6

universities in China have also set up colleges or schools that offer police studies programmes or forensic studies courses. In this chapter, the author first introduces the history of police higher education in China, with an emphasis on the development after the adoption of the reform and opening-up policy in 1978. The author also illustrates the police education and training system in China and introduces the main police universities, police colleges and police academies together with the main education and training programs they offer.

The History of Police Higher Education in China

The development of police education in the new China can be traced back from the period of Liberation War.

Before the Creation of Police Higher Education in China

The Beginning of Police Education in PRC (1949–1965)

In China, as the People's Liberation Army (PLA) won victory after victory against the KMT Army, more police force were needed to maintain social order and defend the new regime. As the first police academy founded in the history of Communist Party of China (CPC), Shandong Provincial Police Academy was established in May 1946 (Wang et al. 2008). Later, Lyuda Municipal Police Bureau Academy was founded in August 1946. Since then, many police academies were established to meet the requirement of fostering more police officers to keep public security during the transfer of power to CPC.

Since the founding of the PRC in 1949, Chinese government aimed to create an effective police force as soon as possible in order to consolidate its sovereignty over the country. The top police department—the Ministry of Public Security was established on November 5, 1949, while the

Central Public Security Cadre School was founded on the basis of the former North China Public Security Cadre School (extended as Central People's Public Security College in 1953). Gradually, all the provinces, autonomous regions and cities established their own police training schools. Up to 1956, there were altogether 52 police academies nationwide (MPS 1997). At that time, the main functions of the police academies were police recruits training and backbone officers training (Wang et al. 2008). For backbone police officers training, police academies of different levels had their own task division. Central People's Public Security College and its branches were responsible for county and above police chiefs training nationwide; provincial and municipal police academies were responsible for deputy county police chiefs and below.

With regard to the training contents, there were mainly three types of knowledge that were compiled into the teaching materials. The first type of training focused on political and ideological education due to the Marxist ideological definition of police organs as "an armed force which represents the interest of the ruling party and maintain national security and public order on the basis of violent, coercive, and special manners" (Yuan 2007, pp. 130–131). The police departments were considered to be one of the most important components of the state apparatus, a coercive department of People's Democratic Dictatorship (Yuan 2012). Therefore, the principal aim of police training was to build a Communist outlook toward life and the world. Ideological courses, such as principles of CPC, current affairs and policies, patriotism, ideology and working style, account for 60% of the curriculum (Ju and Gao 1996). The second type of training contents included policing-related and legal courses, such as political security, economic security, prison administration, public security administration, police station work, traffic management and fire control. In addition, police academies also provided police professional and ethical courses. There were four main requirements for a professional and ethical police officer: loyalty to the CPC, abiding by the law, service awareness and paramilitary organizational discipline (Yuan 2012). Most of Chinese police education and training principles, methods and structures were created in this period (Wong 2009).

The Devastating Period of Cultural Revolution (1966–1976)

During the Cultural Revolution period, many schools stopped normal operation for a long time, senior high schools stopped student recruitment for up to six years, and universities stopped recruitment for an even longer period (Andreas 2009). During this period, the Red Guards were called on to smash the police, the procuratorate and courts (Wong 2009). This virtually destroyed the whole criminal justice system and also disrupted all levels of police education and training system (Yang 2014). Police academy campuses were forcibly occupied; teachers were sent to the May Seventh Cadres Schools for prosecution; teaching facilities, books and reference materials were destroyed.

The Beginning Period of Police Higher Education in China (1977–1985)

After the Cultural Revolution, CPC set up a new requirement for state cadre: "the contingent of cadres should become more revolutionary, better-educated, professional, and younger in age" (Yuan 2012, p. 152). Until 1978, almost all the provincial and municipal police academies resumed their training programmes for in-service officers. The key event that represented the new development stage for Chinese police education is the first meeting of National Public Security Education Conference held in 1984. During this conference, many deficiencies of Chinese police force were pointed out, such as low education level due to less schooling, lack of specialists in various fields of police work, lack of capable police administrators and so on (Hu 1999). In order to meet the requirement of more high-level police practitioners and administrators, a new plan of police education development was established to enhance police officers training and specialists fostering. In China, three levels of police education providers were designed: police colleges (four year), police vocational colleges (three year) and police vocational secondary schools. These police education providers were set up under three levels of administration system: national, provincial and municipal. In early 1980s, four national police universities or colleges were established independently or transformed from other institutions, including China People's Police University (incorporated into China People's Public Security University in 1998), Chinese Armed Police Force Academy, China Criminal Police College (new name as Criminal Investigation Police University of China) and China People's Public Security University. Meanwhile, 12 provincial police vocational colleges were set up all over the country. Both the national and the provincial police universities and colleges recruited senior high school graduates and issued Bachelor's Degree or Associate Degree to graduates. In addition, police vocational secondary schools and local police academies were also built around the nation to provide training for local in-service officers and secondary education to junior high school graduates.

30 Years' Development of Police Higher Education in China (1986–2016)

With the further development of the reform and opening up of China to the outside world and the dramatic social transformation, crime rates soared unprecedentedly. Among all the crimes, three types of them posed great threat to social stability, namely, high-tech crimes, organized crimes and unexpected violent crimes. Meanwhile, as people's legal consciousness and right-protection awareness grow, they had higher requirements of police officers' professional, civil, fair and standardized manner of law enforcement. Therefore, in 1990, the Ministry of Public Security called on all police departments to enhance police qualities through education and increase police effectiveness. A year later, on the 18th meeting of National Public Security Conference, the main topic was to strengthen police education construction. Again on the 19th meeting of National Public Security Conference in 1995, the topic was to enhance police education in order to strengthen the police with science and technology. In order to upgrade the educational background of the police force, the National Public Security Conference held in 1999 proposed that all provincial and municipal police vocational secondary schools transfer to police vocational colleges or police academies, some provincial police vocational colleges (three year) transfer to police colleges (four year).

For postgraduate education, China People's Public Security University was the first police university to be authorized to provide postgraduate education in 1993 by the Academic Degrees Committee of the State Council. In 1995, China People's Public Security University (CPPSU) began postgraduate students' enrollment. In 1998, China People's Police University was incorporated into CPPSU, making the new CPPSU bigger in scale and more complete in discipline range. In 2004, CPPSU was permitted to start doctoral education in the major of criminal procedural law. This represented that for the first time in the history, a Chinese police university was able to foster police recruits with potential PhD qualifications. Meanwhile, China Criminal Police College also started the enrollment of postgraduate students from 1999.

Up to now, there are 37 police universities or colleges in China. Among them, five are under direct administration of Ministry of Public Security, namely, China People's Public Security University, Chinese Armed Police Force Academy, Criminal Investigation Police University of China (CIPUC), Railway Police College and China Maritime Police Academy; one is affiliated with State Forestry Bureau. Of these six universities, CPPSU, CAPFA and CIPUC offer both postgraduate and undergraduate education. The other three colleges only offer undergraduate education. Besides these six national police colleges, the rest of the police colleges are under the administration of the related provinces, autonomous regions or direct-controlled municipalities. Among them, 18 colleges offer four-year undergraduate education, while the others only provide three-year associate degree education.

An overview of police higher education through two national police universities (CPPSU and CIPUC) and a provincial police university (Hubei University of Police).

CPPSU

China People's Public Security University is affiliated with Ministry of Public Security. In 1984, CPPSU started undergraduate education, while China People's Police University and Beijing Traffic Police School were incorporated into CPPSU in 1998 and 2000 separately. CPPSU has 12 departments: law school, school of public order, school of criminal investigation, school of criminology, school of police administration, school of international police and law enforcement, school of forensic science and technology, school of policing information engineering, school of cyber defense, school of counterterrorism, department of police command tactics and department of traffic management engineering. CPPSU provides undergraduate education at 13 majors related with the aforementioned 12 departments. In addition, it offers master degree education at law, public security studies, psychology, security science and engineering, forensic technology and doctoral education at law, public security studies, and forensic technology. Meanwhile, the university also covers a wide range of training programmes, including senior police officers training, police professional training, army soldiers training and training for foreign police officers. There are around 14,000 students for degrees and nearly 10,000 trainees per year.

CPPSU aims to train qualified police officers through a model incorporating teaching, studying, practice and combat. This model connects class teaching and field practice with an emphasis on practical abilities. During the college period, students not only learn foundation courses and theoretical courses but also need to grasp practical skills such as policing tactics, information battle, enemy capturing and self-defense skills. There are two campuses in Beijing, covering an area of over 600,000 square meters. CPPSU has many laboratories, including DNA identification, fingerprint identification, trace evidence analysis, toxicological and drug analysis, document identification, bullet trace inspection, simulated crime scene investigation, security precautionary technology, traffic management and control. In addition, there are many facilities, such as comprehensive training gym, police tactic training center, multifunction shooting range, multimedia classrooms, language labs and so forth.

Besides police education and training, CPPSU also endeavors to become one of the best think tanks in the field of policing, providing theoretical support and technical support for police work. This is based upon the high-level research in the field of policing studies conducted by leading scholars in this university. In September 2015, Institute of Public Security Development Strategy, Ministry of Public Security was established in CPPSU. In addition, there are more than 20 research institutes and judicial expertise centers affiliated with CPPSU. In the recent five years, researchers in this university hosted more than 300 province-level research projects and won more than 20 research awards. The university also edits four academic journals, including *Public Security Education, CPPSU Journal, Modern World Police* and *Police Digest.*

CPPSU attaches great importance to international cooperation and academic exchange. It has connections with police academies in more than 60 countries and regions around the world. It has long-standing cooperation with the City University of New York, German Police University, College of Policing (UK), National University of Public Service (Hungary), the Danish National Police College, Turkish National Police Academy, the Academy of the Ministry of Interior of the Republic of Uzbekistan, Korean National Police University, the Law Enforcement University of Mongolia, the Vietnam People's Police Academy and the University of Moscow Ministry of Internal Affairs of Russia. CPPSU provides training courses for police officers in Asian and African developing countries, Hong Kong SAR and Macao SAR. Each year, the university holds an international police forum in Beijing. During the forum, policing experts and scholars around the world are invited to discuss over the focus issues in the field of policing and law enforcement and provide suggestions and countermeasures.

CIPUC

Formerly named as China Criminal Police University, CIPUC is also affiliated with Ministry of Public Security of China. While CPPSU is a relatively comprehensive police university that covers almost all aspects of police work, CIPUC is a university that emphasizes criminal investigation and forensic sciences. CIPUC is the first police university that provides undergraduate education. CIPUC has developed a school-running mode of integrating teaching with research and case-handling. Upholding the school spirit of "Loyalty, Honesty, Unity, Endeavour", CIPUC has cultivated more than 100,000 cadres, personnel and specialists for judicial and public security organs, and has been honored as "the Top Police University of China" and "the Cradle of Oriental Sherlock Holmes".

CIPUC offers undergraduate courses in the majors of criminal investigation, economic crime investigation, public order, anti-narcotics, police intelligence, foreign policing, information security, cyber security and law enforcement, forensic science and technology, audio-visual technology for the police, forensic medicine and police canine training technology. There are 15 departments in the university, including department of criminal investigation, department of police intelligence, department of anti-narcotics, department of economic crime investigation, department of cybercrime investigation, department of trace examination technology, department of document examination technology, department of audio-visual material examination technology, department of forensic chemistry, department of forensic medicine, department of public order, department of public security basics, department of law, department of police skills and tactics training, and department of police canine training technology. CIPUC also provides postgraduate courses in the majors of criminal law, procedural law, analytical chemistry, practical computer technology and forensic medicine.

Besides degree education, the university is one of the earliest police training providers in China. It has been nearly 70 years since CIPUC started police training courses. Currently, the university has organized different levels of police training programmes, including criminal investigation, economic crime investigation, cybercrime investigation, trace examination, document examination, audio-visual material investigation technology, forensic medicine and forensic chemistry. In addition, the university also provides training for the army, the procuratorates and the courts. CIPUC also conducts education through correspondence nationwide.

CIPUC attached great importance to research. There are two key labs of Ministry of Public Security: Document Examination Key Lab and Trace Examination Key Lab, one Liaoning Province key lab: Cyber Law Enforcement and Video Investigation Lab, one Liaoning Province University key lab: Forensic Science and Technology Lab, one Shenyang Municipal key lab: Forensic Medicine Lab. The university issues two academic journals: *Journal of CIPUC* and *China Criminal Police*. *Journal of CIPUC* is the journal issued by all police universities and colleges in China. It introduced the latest development of criminal investigation and forensic science and technology in China. China Criminal Police is jointly issued by Criminal Investigation Bureau of Ministry of Public Security and CIPUC. It has been considered as one of the best journals for criminal police in China.

CIPUC actively carries out international academic exchanges and cooperation and has already established cooperative relationships with higher education institutions and police organizations in more than ten countries including the United States, Canada, the United Kingdom, Germany, France, Netherlands, Russia, Serbia, Australia, the Republic of Korea and Singapore, as well as in Hong Kong SAR, Macao SAR and Taiwan Province. In addition, CIPUC holds a large-scale international academic conference every year. Through the student exchange programmes with foreign universities such as Ulster University in the UK and Charles Sturt University in Australia, CIPUC cultivates multiskilled policing talents with double bachelor's degrees. Being entrusted by the Ministry of Commerce and the Ministry of Public Security, the university commenced to undertake police trainings for foreign countries from 2007 and have trained almost a thousand criminal investigation specialists for about 70 countries.

Hubei University of Police

Hubei University of Police is one of the two earliest provincial police colleges. Established in 1948, HUP started undergraduate education from 2002 and has been permitted to begin the preparation for postgraduate education programmes. Although HUP is affiliated with Hubei Province, it is under joint support by both Hubei Province and the Ministry of Public Security of China. Different from national police universities like CPPSU and CIPUC, HUP is mainly responsible for the education and training for police cadets and in-service police officers within Hubei Province. This university has designed a discipline structure with legal studies as its foundation, public security studies and forensic technology as its main disciplines, computer science and technology as its supporting discipline. This structure aims to integrate legal studies, computer science and technology with police-related disciplines.

There are currently six police-related undergraduate majors, including criminal investigation, public order, police command and tactics, forensic science and technology, Internet security and law enforcement, fire protection engineering, and five non-policing majors, including information security, law, computer science and technology, public affairs administration and English. HUP actively promotes teaching quality enhancement and teaching reform. Procedural law and public security studies have been listed as key disciplines in Hubei Province; criminal investigation has been listed as key discipline by Ministry of Public Security. A number of high-quality courses have been established: criminal investigation and public order as state key courses, interrogation, Internet security, policing basics, criminal procedural law, the study of police facing battles, investigation measures and tactics, dangerous goods management as Hubei Province key courses.

HUP aims to integrate teaching, case-handling and research into an organic whole. This is based upon several important platforms, such as forensic lab, electronic evidence acquisition lab, social public order management research center and the *Journal of HUP*. With these platforms and the structure, HUP put a focus on the training of practical skills of students, incorporating practical course, experimental course, internship, social practice and research into teaching system. Many practical training bases were built in cooperation with local police departments, including Henry Chang-Yu Lee Studio, DNA lab, Teaching Base in Dongyue Police Sub-bureau and Teaching Base in Gedian Economic Technological Development Zone Police Bureau.

Besides degree education, HUP also provides in-service police training for both the country and Hubei Province. It has been selected as the national training bases for police chiefs, immigration and border control officers, law enforcement department chiefs, police intelligence officers, as the provincial training bases for political and legal cadres, police chiefs, police branch chiefs, police officers and forest police officers. In addition, this university also provides training programmes for police officers from other developing countries, such as Myanmar and Laos.

Key Issues of Police Higher Education in China

The Contradiction Between the Position as a University and the Position as a Police Academy

After more than 60 years' development of police education in China, most national and provincial police universities and colleges provide both undergraduate education and in-service police training. This is quite different from most police training providers in Western countries where police academies provide only policing training for police recruits and in-service police officers. Let's take the way how NSW Police Academy and Charles Sturt University cooperate in police recruits education and training. I studied in School of Policing Studies, Charles Sturt University as a PhD candidate of policing studies from 2012 to 2016. Those who plan to become a police officer in NSW need to pass the police entrance examination and apply to the NSW Police Academy. The NSW Police Academy and CSU jointly provide the Associate Degree in Policing Practice (formal entry level studies) to police recruits to gain entry to the NSW Police Force. The cooperation between a university and a police academy gives the students both police-related training and police force entry and university education and the degree.

In China, police universities and colleges need to meet both the two requirements and provide in-service police training as well. This seems to be a simple method that is able to solve many problems, but there is an unavoidable contradiction between the role of a higher education provider and a vocational training provider. This contradiction lies in the distinct difference between the two types of instruction that could be represented through the two names themselves to some extent: education and training.

> Higher education is about preparation for working life, not for a specific job in the first couple of years after graduation. Graduates who have studied the more academic subjects will require a longer transition period into employment than those who have studied more vocational degrees. The transition may well entail further training in a professional field, which either the employer or an educational institution may provide. (Brennan 2014)

Police universities in China aim to provide higher education to those who planned to become a police officer in the future and also to equip them with essential skills and professional knowledge to become a member of the police force. However, there are some intrinsic contradictions that are not difficult to deal with. First of all, policing is a practical career that needs a lengthy and serious training process to become qualified and firm and strong beliefs and determination to achieve. If these have been settled when students come to the university, liberal education that is essential for higher education but not related to policing is easily ignored or walked through by both the university and the students (Zhou and Zhu 2014). For most police universities in China, students are under a paramilitary-style management. Students' entry and exit of the campus are strictly limited except for the weekends; police uniforms are required to be worn at all times in the campus; most of the lectures that are arranged are practical rather than academic, policing-related rather than diverse. All of these arrangements are for the policing profession and against the liberal education spirit that aims to dig out students' unidentified potentials and creative thinking and reasoning abilities. It seems that students skipped the step of learning to be a good man and directly went to the step of learning to be a good policeman. This is really a pity for both the students and the education providers.

Besides the education issues, problems also arise when students graduate. Students need to attend the competitive State Civil Service Examination and a two-way selection process. Not all police university graduates are able to get entry to the police force and become a police officer. Those who are not able to gain the position need to find another relevant job or a completely irrelevant job in the society. This is awkward for both the students and the society in that these students were educated and equipped with knowledge and skills to fight crimes.

If police education is not only for policing bound students, there is a real question why para-military discipline and police curriculum is necessary. More practically, why teach police tactical skills – marital arts, shooting, driving – when students do not intent to and have no prospect of ever becoming police? (Wong 2009)

Conclusion

From this brief review of police higher education in China since the founding of new China, it is easily observed that the development of police education in China is far from smooth and quite different from Western countries. The specific way of combining higher education and police entrance training in police universities and colleges is also only in its beginning stage and needs further development and time to prove its effectiveness. No one can deny that police higher education in China is developing faster than ever before with its unique characteristics. It has made great contributions and will continue to contribute to the growing need of policing practitioners and administrators in China.

References

Andreas, J. (2009). *Rise of the Red Engineers: The Cultural Revolution and the Origins of China's New Class*. Stanford: Stanford University Press.

Brennan, J. (2014). *Higher Education is More Than Vocational Training*. Australia. Retrieved October 16, 2016, from http://theconversation.com/higher-education-is-more-than-vocational-training-23759

Hu, Z. (1999). Jianli gonmganjiaoyutixi nulikaichuang gonganjiaoyugong-zuode xinjumian [Try to Establish the Police Education System]. In MPS (Ed.), *Gonganjiaoyu wenjianhuibian* [Documents of Police Education]. Beijing: Police Education Press.

Ju, F., & Gao, Y. (1996). Gonganjiaoyude lishipianzhang [The History of Police Education]. *Liaoning Higher Education Research*, *3*, 120–123.

MPS. (1997). *Gonganjiaoyu gailun* [A Brief Introduction to Police Education]. Beijing: Mass Press.

Wang, Q., Zhang, Z., & Li, C. (2008). *Zhanlueshiyezhongde zhongguo jingcha gaodengjiaoyu* [Chinese Police Higher Education from Strategic Perspective]. Beijing: China People's Public Security University Press.

Wong, K. C. (2009). *Chinese Policing: History and Reform*. New York: Peter Lang.

Yang, T. (2014). A Review of Police Education and Training in China. In P. Stanislas (Ed.), *International Perspectives on Police Education and Training* (pp. 193–208). London: Routledge.

Yuan, G. (2007). Hexieshehuixia woguojingchade juesedingwei [The Status of Chinese Police in a Harmonious Social Approach]. *Journal of Chinese People's Public Security University (Social Sciences Edition)*, 2, 127–134.

Yuan, G. (2012). Goujian Gong'anxue Xuekeliluntixi de Fangfayucelue [Methods and Strategies to Establish the Discipline of Public Security Studies]. *Journal of Chinese People's Public Security University (Social Sciences Edition)*, 3, 31–36.

Zhou, Z., & Zhu, G. (2014). Gonganyuanxiao tongshike wentiyanjiu [On Liberal Education in Police Colleges]. *Public Security Education, 3*, 50–54.

7

Higher Education and Democratic Policing: Challenges from Latin America

José-Vicente Tavares dos Santos

Introduction: The Issue of Police Education

In the age of social conflict, the project to prevent violence and reduce violent crime has been multiplied in the perspective of new alternatives for public security policies that could guarantee the right to security of citizens.

These are the multiple effects of the globalisation of the human rights issue since the Second International Conference on Human Rights held in Vienna in 1993 and the World Conference on Women in Beijing in 1995.

At the beginning of the twenty-first century, one can perceive that the crisis of the nation-state, due to the process of formation of the global society, and the vicissitudes of the welfare state, in the face of neoliberal policies, both have brought increasing difficulties for the exercise of the office of police.

J.-V. Tavares dos Santos (✉)
Federal University of Rio Grande do Sul, Porto Alegre, Brazil

© The Author(s) 2018
C. Rogers, B. Frevel (eds.), *Higher Education and Police*,
DOI 10.1007/978-3-319-58386-0_7

There is a crisis in the office of a policing, either because of difficulties in securing public order, it is internationalised conflicts and crimes and the privatisation of some police, and even because of limitations in contributing to the construction of consensus. Community bases no longer exist in complex societies and with a large amount of unstructured work patterns. There would remain an option for the growth of the repressive social control functions of the police, through the systematic appeal to the use of illegal and illegitimate violence, configuring a "state of criminal social control".

The purpose of this text is to analyse the police education developed in contemporary society: we intend to analyse police education in a selected set of Latin American countries, highlighting the current aspects of innovative educational experiences but we can't forget the resistance to changes in many educational police institutions. To analyse the documentation, we have classified the curriculum of training and educational courses in the following categories: social sciences, law studies, policing technologies, professional skills, management, professional internships and other activities.

Experiments of Police Education in Latin America

From the 1990s, violence in cities and in the countryside began to appear on the public agenda in Brazilian society (Zaluar 1999, 2004; Barreira 2004) and also in Argentina, with a lot of fear of crime (Pegoraro 2015; Kessler 2009). Social control seems to have exhausted its functions within traditional models (Fabian Sain 2008).

The issue of security and public security professionals emerges very slowly in the transition from military rule to civilian rule, since 1983 in Argentina and 1985 in Brazil. If we look at the functions of the democratic rule of law, we have the feeling that scientific and technological advances, including social technologies, have been incorporated into education, health, housing and food. However, in what would be one of the fundamental rights of the human person, the security of life – as contractualists have written since the seventeenth century – it seems to be a huge backwardness in relation to police studies and education (Tavares dos Santos 2002, 2004, 2009, 2010, 2014; Tavares dos Santos et al. 2009).

The Case of Argentina

The Argentinian Federal Police has created a university, in which they offer several courses open to all people, civilians and policemen. In it, there is a School of Cadets, whose Course for Policing presents the distribution of disciplines in Fig. 7.1.

It's evident that the policing technologies and the professional skills are the most important matters learned to young police students. In contrast, at the Master Degree, the relevance of social sciences appears (Fig. 7.2).

The predominance of social science disciplines is verified, followed by legal studies and those of public management.

The Universidad Nacional de Villa Maria, in Córdoba Province, offers a course for the Province Police, presenting this profile (Fig. 7.3).

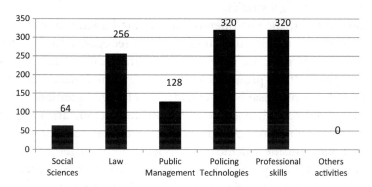

Fig. 7.1 Argentina – Policía Federal – Police Officer – Escuela de Cadetes – Bachelor's degree in public security – Class hours by subjects (2007)

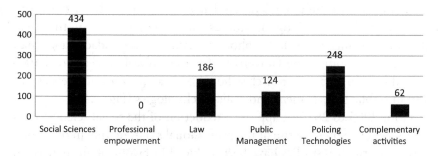

Fig. 7.2 Universidad de la Policia Federal Argentina – Master in public security – Class hours by subjects (2007)

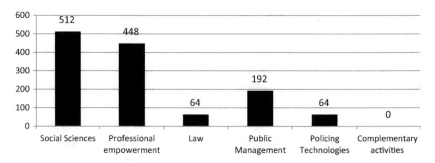

Fig. 7.3 Argentina – Universidad Nacional Villa Maria – Córdoba – Bachelor's degree in Public Security – Class hours by subjects (2008)

There are two main areas: social sciences and professional skills. It follows the area of public management, and with reduced presence, police technologies and legal studies.

Finally, the Province of Buenos Aires created a Community Police, requesting the University of Lannus to guarantee education. The definition of this undergraduate programme in Citizenship Security is based on an approach that promotes citizens' rights in general: The main objective of this proposal is the elucidation of many questions. Among them, for example, is it possible to formulate a democratic citizenship without responsible public security, or to propose a consistent public security policy outside a democratic conception of citizenship? So, the general objectives are proposed: "Promote the conditions of social existence, the preservation of rights and professional protection of citizenship. To professionalise existing issues and open new areas of intervention regarding their instructions, whose limitations and obsolescence have been proven harmful to citizens. And acquire the aptitude for the development and undertaking of studies and investigations in the area" (http://www.unla.edu.ar/index.php/licenciatura-en-seguridad-ciudadana).

The curriculum of the University of Lannus reveals a scenario characterised by a high number of class hours dedicated to social sciences but also in public management and police technologies (Fig. 7.4).

From 2005 to 2016, it appears a reduction of the social sciences class hours but an expressive rise of the professional skills, mainly in data analysis. Also, the law studies have been reduced in favour of an increase in

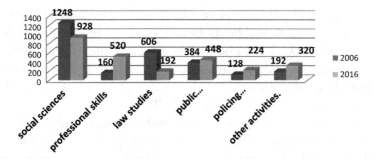

Fig. 7.4 Argentina – Universidad de Lannus – Provincia de Buenos Aires – Bachelor's degree in public security – Class hours by subjects (2005 and 2016)

public management, policing technologies and other activities that include a final research paper.

A very innovative process of police reform in the Provincia de Buenos Aires has been established in 1998, to be organised by a High Institute of Public Security. But the political process couldn't really accomplish this transformation (Fabian Sain 2008). Nevertheless, in the case of Police Education in Argentina, it is important to note that the presence of universities in police education leads to a greater presence of the social sciences in the police education curricula. There is a heavy presence of the social sciences, followed by the study of police technologies, legal studies and disciplines related to management. Perhaps, this side of the reform has been followed at least partially, leaving untouched the other main dimensions concerning the definition of a new model of policing.

A Comparative Research in Brazil

A new period of transformation in Brazilian society has been open since the 1988 democratic constitution. In the process of transition to democracy in Brazil, since 1985, there has been a wide mobilisation of different sectors of society and the state to propose changes during the process of debate and voting of the new constitution. As a result, the Constitutional Charter of 1988 introduced the incorporation of democratic proposals in relation to civil, political and social rights.

In the sphere of public security, paradoxically, problems arise both for civil society – because mobilisations and social struggles against violence are organised – as well as for political institutions, the state and the legislative and judiciary powers, in order to deepen the rules democratic – whether those of representative democracy or those of participatory democracy (Soares 2000; Pinheiro et al. 2000).

However, the issue of police reform and changes in police education has been little discussed: there is a deficit in the political and educational agenda in Brazil for all institutions – political parties, police organisations, civil society associations – which did not take into account the need to reflect on police training.

In Brazil, each state has two main law enforcement agencies – military and civil police forces – while cities are responsible for unarmed municipal guards, even if big cities could have armed municipal guards. The military police in the states are charged to the law enforcement against criminals and to maintain the public order, with patrol and ostensive functions; it has normally in all Brazilian states the following dual hierarchy: high officers – colonel, lieutenant-colonel, major PM and captain PM – and police officers – lieutenant, sergeant, cable and soldier. There are in each state two police academies, one for the high officers and another for the police officers.

The civil police has judiciary functions, with also a dual hierarchy: The police delegates are responsible for management of the civil police and are in charge of presiding over the police investigation, an instrument that formalises the criminal investigation by the Brazilian judicial police, called enquiry. On the other hand, the civil police have the police officers: (1) the investigators or inspectors are really responsible for the criminal investigation – taking proofs, interviewing people and analysing reports, intercepting, financial analysis, analysing links, breaches of secrecy, and so on; (2) the registrar takes care of all the bureaucratic work of the police station and follows the entire police enquiry, from collecting the first reports to closing the case and (3) the agent, a first police officer in the base of the hierarchy.

This dispersion is reflected in police training, since there is a doubling of police education institutions – almost all Brazilian states have two institutions, the Military Police Academies and the Police School of the

The Military Police Academies

The modalities of police training resent structural problems of Brazilian police organisations, especially the fragmentation of operational services, the overvaluation of legal culture, the orientation of positive law, a methodology based on the disproportionate enumeration of contents. A fragmentation of services expresses a dispute of competencies between the different police – federal police, civil police, military police, military fire brigade, municipal guards – as well as the problems related to the regulation of private security companies.

This dispersion is reflected in police training, because there is a doubling of police education institutions – almost all Brazilian states have two schools: the military police academies and the police schools of the civil police – there are no systematic training centres. In fact, still there is a legacy from the army model of training, a survival of the Military Dictatorship that ruled the country from 1964 to 1985 (Fernandes 1974; Castro 1990; Araujo Filho 2003).

There are at least 24 academies and 24 training, improvement and specialisation centres of the military police in 17 Federation Units, of which only 10 offered a graduate course in 2005. Among the 24 military police academies, in 2006, the collective equipment they have is 11 auditoriums, 5 gymnasiums, 15 dining rooms, 10 study rooms, 14 sports courts and 7 swimming pools; and 12 academies registered to have computer laboratories. However, there is no information on the existence of libraries.

Information on the professional corps existing in the military police academies and military fire brigade, according to the level of education, indicated in 2006, in a universe of 2266 professionals, 22% completed higher education and post-graduate courses. The promotion of integrated courses with other institutions of public security happened in 75% of the academies. The institutions with which this type of integration is most frequent are the civil police, the military fire brigade, the public universities (15 academies in 2006) and the National Secretariat of Public Security. Less registered are articulations with civil society organisations and national civil defence.

Civil Police – and there are no systematic patterns of education and tra
ing. And each is also divided into two: in the military police, one to hi
officers, who graduate as a captain PM, and another to police office
who finish their course with the grade of a soldier of the military poli
In the civil police, there is one programme to the police delegates an
second to the police officers.

The fragmentation of police academies and schools expresses the m
tiplicity of competences between the Brazilian police – federal pol
(from the Union), civil police, military police, municipal guards – as w
as the problems related to the regulation of private security compan
(Mingardi 1992; Kant de Lima 1995; Lima and Paula 2006). This is t
case of decentralisation through the "municipalisation" of some pol
functions, since most of the municipal guards (except for large cities)
not have systematic training centres.

Brazil has a federal police very specialised in federal crimes such
violent crimes, drug trafficking, corruption, immigrant's problems a
other hate crimes. But the curriculum for the managers and superinte
dents, the delegates, high police officers, shows a very restrict model
policing (Fig. 7.5).

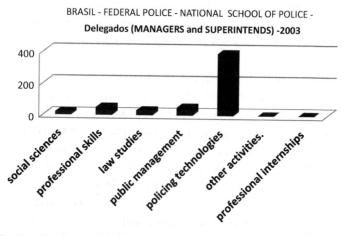

Fig. 7.5 Brazil – Federal Police – National School of Police – managers an
superintends – 2003

with other countries. In most cases, the evaluation of the subjects was done from a questionnaire completed by the students at the end of the period.

Most of the teachers are police officers selected through an invitation process of the directions; less than half of them being for expertise in the area or career of the teacher's origin. Only 30% of the units mentioned the existence of continuing education programmes, although almost all of them follow the SENASP Curriculum Matrix.

In most cases, there is no provision for retraining classes or for misconduct or improper operations; although in half of the cases, there is some kind of psychological counselling. It was observed that a significant percentage of Units of Education have not yet been certified by the Ministry of Education or by the State Board of Education. Meanwhile, for half of the units, there is no project to create undergraduate technologist degree.

In the case of Rio de Janeiro Military Police, the curricula reveal a similar situation (Fig. 7.7).

The data show a huge predominance of professional skills and of policing technologies, followed by law studies. The public management and the social sciences have a very low importance in the whole programme. A similar pattern is observed in the most important academy, the Barro

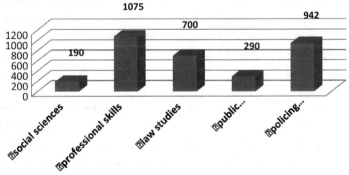

Fig. 7.7 Brazil – Military Police of Rio de Janeiro – undergraduate course for high officers – 2006

BRAZIL - STATE OF SAO PAULO -
BARRO BRANCO MILITARY POLICE ACADEMY - 2006

Fig. 7.8   Brazil – State of Sao Paulo – Barro Branco Military Police Academy – 2006

Branco Military Police Academy, of the State of Sao Paulo. Both reveals a great number of hours dedicated to law studies but few opportunities to learn how to interact with the public in the streets, a lack of efforts to improve a community policing (Caruso 2006), as some US police departments (Dias Neto 2000) (Fig. 7.8).

Here, we observe a large presence of policing technologies, followed by law studies after we have the professional skills. Also, in this case, the public management disciplines and the social sciences aren't so important. So, it has been written that "police training continues to be embedded in programmes and practices that mould the subjectivities of trainees in line with a paramilitary ethos that undermines formal commitment to human rights principles" (Wood and Cardia 2006).

It is possible now to summarise some trends in police education. All police organisations expressed the crisis of police professionalisation. The dimensions of this problem are the following.

In the first place, the dualities of careers in the selection and training of the police professional, both military and civil, the career will be double, a career for police officers and another for graduate officers; one career for policemen and detectives, one for superintendent. Secondly, in the process of police socialisation, in the case of several military police academies, alongside the official curriculum, there is a hidden curriculum. Thirdly, there is a lack of content concerning information systems – from the computerisation of news bulletins, online networks to the geo-reference of occurrences that is obviously very important for ostensive policing because it allows in planning for the placement of patrols and policemen on the street and also for enquiries.

The question of the education of ostensive police is based on a difficulty to reduce crime and violence. However, there has not yet been a break with the model of police training guided by the perspective of the army, based on the doctrine of national security, according to which, the police should function as the defence of the state.

Therefore, attempts to change the police education system in Brazil occurred in a fragmented institutional context in which archaic pedagogical practices coexist with democratic and critical curricular proposals.

In other words, police education institutions in Brazil present a framework of needs, remnants of a militarist and legal legacy of the past and a corporate segmentation. Military Police Academies maintain residues of a militarised organisational culture, with the exaltation of discipline, military hierarchy and training in military operations, allied to a pedagogical archaism, with few exceptions.

Rites of transition, by which one must break with the civil identity and assume a new existence, mark the professional training of the military police. Normalisation is sought through the relation of docility utilities, through the constant exercise of a disciplinary power.

It was evidenced that there are situations of psychological risk in which the policemen can be involved in the day to day routine. Hence, they need to develop a lifelong learning programme, but a police mental health is a service that is not offered yet in academies or throughout their life careers.

There have been changes in the training courses for military police officers, since they began the requirement of high school in the selection, and some police begin to predict the need for higher education to enter the initial levels of the career. The importance of the relationship with the universities and the need to overcome reciprocal stigmas were evidenced.

Therefore, attempts to change the police education system has shown a fragmented teaching in which curricular, democratic and critical proposals coexist with archaic pedagogical practices and the continuity of the traditional mode of police education.

There are experiments of curricular innovation, teaching-learning processes, didactic methodologies and institutional integration. In Rio Grande do Sul, in 1997, a new law was passed for the military brigade, whereby people enter only with law degree and remain there for two years (Rudnicki 2007, 2014); also, a brief experiment in discussing gender diversity has been observed in late years (Aquino da Silva 2010). In Minas Gerais, a law was passed in the same terms in 2010. In São Paulo, there is already a debate on the issue, still unfinished. It seems that the state military police are still in a dilemma between a more professional approach and a law model of education.

The Schools of the Civil Police

In the case of the Civil Police Schools, police training is guided by positive law, leaving little space for discipline related to the exercise of police duties, such as criminal investigation, conflict mediation, police performance management and information. The legal and criminological formalism present in the curricula of most Brazilian police education institutions confirms the critical analysis of the law formulated by Sousa Santos (Sousa Santos 2000; Zaverucha 2003; Sadek 2005).

The concept of criminality is understood as the question of public security through criminal law logic, where law enforcement repression is a solution to crime. The penal paradigm is observed, above all, by the great workload devoted to the study of legal disciplines in the training of police officers. A few hours are devoted to criminal investigation or the construction, monitoring and analysis of information systems. On the other hand, the incorporation of the human sciences is only beginning to occur in several training courses for police officers.

It is also part of this culture that guides the practical work of the police, inserted in a hidden curriculum of the police academies. And the effects of the mass media provoke the transformation of the acts of extraordinary violence into ordinary violence, with the exaltation of the repressive police or the figure of the police hero, which disregards all the social

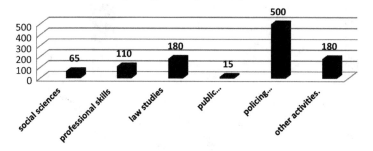

STATE OF RIO GRANDE DO SUL - CIVIL POLICE
PROGRAMME FOR DELEGATES
(Managers and Sperintend) - 2006

Fig. 7.9 State of Rio Grande do Sul – Civil Police – programme for managers and superintend – 2006

relevance of the office of police officer and, especially, the functions of crime prevention, police investigation of occurrences and social responsibility of the police. Some changes in the US police departments also show this concern with law and order (Costa 2004).

Two examples from the state of Rio Grande do Sul will be very demonstrative of this pattern. First is the programme for delegates, with 1050-hour class (Fig. 7.9).

The data shows that half of the period is dedicated to policing technologies and also a lot of disciplines to law studies (reminder that the students have already a law school degree) and other activities. The place for social sciences is very small and it is worst for public management. Secondly, the programme for registrar, with 830-hour class, appoints the same importance to policing technologies and law studies, minimising the period for social sciences (Fig. 7.10).

However, there are some experiments of curricular innovation, teaching-learning processes, didactic methodologies and even institutional integration. Since the 1990s, a prodigious series in innovative police teaching experiences, both inside police educational institutions and in the agreements made with universities, happened in several Brazilian states, indicating a movement of transformation of curricula, contents and conception of the office of policemen.

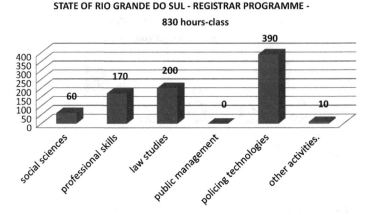

Fig. 7.10   State of Rio Grande do Sul – Registrar programme – 830 hours-class

Educational Integration Programmes Experiments

The experiments of integrated training that took place in Brazil were very important, as were the agreements with universities, which began with the late professor Paixão in Minas Gerais, in the 1980s, with an association between the military police and the UFMG – Federal University of Minas Gerais. At the same time, Professor Theotonio dos Santos, in the first Brizola government of Rio de Janeiro, also in the 1980s, organised courses on human rights at police schools in Rio.

We can now analyse the curricular framework of some experiments: the Fluminense Federal University, Rio de Janeiro; CRISP, Federal University of Minas Gerais; the IESP – Institute of Public Security Studies of Pará; and the Federal University of Rio Grande do Sul (Fig. 7.11).

This institutional relationship is perhaps the best legacy of the 1990s, so much so that there have been five forums on police education in partnership with universities. Such integration allowed, for example, that SENASP inaugurate agreements with universities for collaboration on forensic laboratories, forensic genetics, forensic biology and legal medicine, trying to incorporate science and technology into police work.

We emphasise that the objective of this item is to carry out an evaluation of the cases of institutional integration of the Military Police

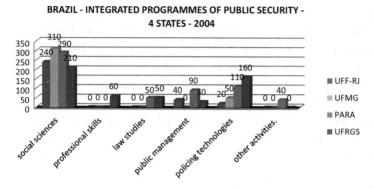

Fig. 7.11 Brazil – Integrated programmes of Public Security – 4 States – 2004

Academies and of the Civil Police Schools, particularly in the states of Rio Grande do Sul, Ceará and Pará. All the social actors involved in such activities – managers, administrators, teachers and students – as well as the pedagogical objectives formulated, the curricular maps, the disciplines (menus, contents, bibliography and evaluation system) and the teaching-learning methodology.

The period chosen for analysis begins in 1993, in Rio Grande do Sul, and with emphasis on the agreement between the Academy of the Military Brigade and the Federal University of Rio Grande do Sul, whereby university professors taught courses to officials. During the Olívio Dutra (1999–2002) administration, with the completion of the Unified Training Course for new civilian police, military and prison officers, about 90 teachers and post-graduate students were involved in teaching activities.

In the state of Ceará, in the mid-1990s, during the Jereissati administration, there were similar agreements with both the Federal University of Ceará and the State University of Ceará. The state secretary signed an agreement with the State University of Ceará (UECE), through the Institute of Studies and Research and Projects (IEPRO), with the objective of technical-professional and cultural improvement of public safety professionals in 2000 (Brasil 2000; Brasil et al. 2015; Granjeiro et al. 2001). There was also the involvement of teachers and post-graduate students of the Federal University of Ceará.

In Pará, an integrated police education system was formed, with the Pará Safety Education Institute (IESP) and the Centre for Training and Improvement of Squares (CFAP) as its main bodies. The policy of integration of the public security and social defence system, adopted in the state of Pará, has a great importance in the training of security officers at the level of official and superintendents.

Co-operation processes were unleashed between the academies of several states, such as Minas Gerais, Rio Grande do Sul, Ceará, Pará. Consequently, the constitution of a unified academy is debated, although the resistances are blatant.

The case of Rio Grande do Sul, between 1999 and 2001, is quite interesting. The fundamental axis of the Integrated Academy of Public Security was to transform police practices, containing the valorisation of human resources, with the aim to build up of new civil servants in public security. That is, newly enrolled in the career of soldiers of the military brigade, holders of a diploma of second degree; in the career of researchers and clerk of the civil police, holders of secondary degree diploma with many already attending higher education; and entering the penitentiary service, holders of a secondary degree diploma, some already having attended higher education or still attending. Another objective was the professional updating of the servers within the new pedagogical conception, as well as the structuring of an advanced training centre in public security.

The proposal was that the courses would develop a space for building social awareness of the different actors involved in the implementation of a pedagogical process. The relationship between students and teachers was generally quite satisfactory, with interactions derived, on the one hand, from the didactic methods of the professors coming from the universities and, on the other hand, from the novelty that the contents offered to the students, many of them newcomers of the second degree.

One of the main changes that occurred was practised in the classroom. Another way of teaching with new assumptions was encouraged; therefore, new disciplines were introduced and new readings were stimulated to debate a new police model.

Another element was a theoretical reflection on social and existential practices, leading to students an exercise in theoretical activity that was certainly a novelty in police education. However, the reading difficulties on the part of the students were marked, accentuated by the lack of libraries and access to books.

In the case of Pará, during the debates about the new professional programme, critics of the traditional training model stood out in asserting that the success of the integration would fundamentally result from the alignment of three dimensions: (1) to expand a democratically thought about public security; (2) to build up the principle of integration; and (3) to exercise effective actions to transform the reality. In short, they suggest that one should think, speak and act in an integrated way.

However, critics note that years after the creation of the institute, its academic units, that is, the training academies of the civil and military police and the state fire brigade continue to work autonomously as before, that is, they plan and coordinate their professional courses. The difference is that they are now installed in the same physical space. Based on this empirical observation, we assume that the model implemented in the IESP is not really integrating, but rather preserving the distance between institutions.

Since 2001, two important pedagogical initiatives have been carried out, which, in fact, integrate students from different institutions of the public security system of the state and the teaching staff of public universities, in the process of building a new professional knowledge. These are three graduate programme carried out in partnership with the Federal University of Pará and the State University of Pará: in Public Security and Social Defence; Strategic Management in Public Security and Social Defence; and Strategic Management in Social Defence and Citizenship.

In the case of Ceará, the partnerships directly related to training and consequently to the qualifications of the state police can be understood and described from three initiatives. The first one concerns the partnerships to carry out activities that involved projects aimed at meeting short-term needs such as the Special Intelligence Programme given to intelligence professionals. Another case was the graduate programme in Management of Public Safety, for high officers of the military police and for commissioners of the civil police, carried out in the period 2001–2002. Finally, the training course for policemen of the military police organised in 2001.

The third initiative is responsible for the development of a long-term continuity partnership between the State University of Ceara and the Secretary of Public Security. The design of the integration process involves the participation of instructors from military and civilian police academies in the teaching of disciplines considered more operational; and, also in the disciplines of theoretical foundation, of the domain of human and social sciences and those directly related to the issues of citizenship and human rights.

This movement of reform of police work has been marked by the collaboration between universities and academies and police schools in several Brazilian states in the last years, indicating a slow movement of curriculum transformation, content and conception of the office of policemen.

Somewhat outwardly, we have witnessed some training initiatives in penal techniques guided by respect for human life. With regard to matters of police techniques, the International Red Cross Course on the use of force and the use of firearms, guided by respect for human rights, police officers and citizens was a significant experience. Police officers from various states (Bahia, São Paulo, Minas Gerais, Rio Grande do Sul, etc.) participated in the period 1998–2002. This interesting case has developed the training in police techniques that reduce the risk of life, an even greater issue when dealing with the military police officers who are in service and need a permanent education.

The most recent experience was the ESPC – Public Safety School of Ceará, set up by Professor César Barreira who has been the first director, between May 2011 and August 2012. His period provided a humanistic approach to police education, with a dialogic approach, an enormous empowerment of the policemen students, a large invitation to scholars and policemen to give lectures and a huge innovation of the curricula. Unfortunately, the governor of the Ceara State fired him in one year and half of his duty, mainly due to corporate resistance to these interesting pedagogical innovations.

In the midst of such process, there was an improvement in the police training, another indication of the presence of several professionals, who came to teach in police academies, somehow bringing other visions of society.

There was then the incorporation of the human sciences, the relativisation of military training, the reduction of the positivist approach in the teaching of law and the absorption of human rights contents. In fact, a democratic public security system passes by human qualification and technical training of direct system operators, civilian and military police and military fire fighters. There is no training without academic education. Therefore, we could conclude that non-linear processes of transformations in police education are under development.

The most relevant phenomenon of this dialogue was the implementation of RENAESP – National Network of Public Safety Studies, by SENASP of the Ministry of Justice, in 2006 until 2014. The objective of RENAESP was the accreditation of higher education institutions to promote graduate certificate programmes in public security. The goal is to disseminate among public security professionals and, therefore, among the institutions in which they work, the knowledge and critical capacity required to construct a new way of doing public security committed to citizenship, human rights and the construction of social peace and articulated with scientific advances and accumulated knowledge.

The National Network of Higher Studies in Public Security – RENAESP of SENASP/MJ, organised in 2004, consists of graduate certificate programmes in public security, in order to disseminate among public security professionals "the knowledge and critical capacity needed to build a new way of doing public safety, committed to citizenship, human rights and the construction of social peace and articulated with the scientific knowledge and accumulated knowledge" (http://portal.mj.gov.br).

The objectives of RENAESP are to articulate the practical knowledge of the police officers, acquired in their professional life, with the knowledge produced in the academic environment; to disseminate and reinforce the construction of a culture of public security based on the paradigms of modernity, intelligence, information and the exercise of strategic, technical and scientific competences; and to encourage the elaboration of studies, diagnoses and research applied in public security that contribute to the process of institutionalisation of SUSP (http://portal.mj.gov.br).

In 2010, there were 85 graduate certificates programme in public security, human rights and citizenship, in 63 higher education institutions, having as professional students of public safety and the general public. These programmes comprehend 360 regular class hours plus a research dissertation. Notably, there are some mandatory contents: sociology of violence, human rights, violence against women and children, analysis of homophobic violence and public administration. The universities could organise the remaining contents, with great emphasis on social sciences and the mediation of conflicts.

These programmes approached the public security sectors of the states and universities in Brazil; on the one hand, traditional technical and operational training and the study of laws, on the other, it incorporates the academic education, with the scientific understanding of social, historical, economic and cultural phenomena. Thus, a process of dialogue was established between universities and public security agencies, setting up a debate on new directions for policing models towards the democratisation of social relations. We could observe an important orientation to the Security Sector Reform proposed by the United Nations (https://unssr.unlb.org).

The Crisis of Police Education

From the Argentinian and the Brazilian situations, we may debate a key question: how to change police education composed of a traditional paradigm – guided by criminal law and orthodox positivist criminology and military doctrines – to an orientation that incorporates critical knowledge in law, social sciences and police technologies?

To stimulate these changes, the contribution between the university and police academies and schools should be stimulated, as should the evaluation of the education system. A lot of agreements between police schools and universities exist for undergraduate programmes, the case of Argentina and Brazil.

We can synthesise the previous analysis in terms of five types of police education, which evidently appear mixed in the empirical realities, with predominance of one or the other (Fig. 7.12.).

Fig. 7.12. Types of police education

We could say that the first three types – authoritarian, law dogmatic and militarised – reveal a crisis of police education, since they no longer respond to the realities of the twenty-first century. The following three types – professional, community police and citizen security – appear in different combinations but reveal the new orientations of police education in the age of conflict globalisation.

It seems, therefore, that in several countries, and even in some regions of each country, there is a different orientation in police education: whether it is professionalism or the emphasis on the community police or on the proposal of a citizen security. All affirm respect for human dignity for a new civilising standard. The expansion of a globalised citizenship and the formation of a transnational civil society stimulate a police education concerned with the prevention of crime and the control of violence, guaranteeing citizen security as a fundamental right.

In the conceptual sphere of the "sociology of policing" in police education, there is a theoretical-epistemological tension between the concepts of "training and training" of police officers and the concept of "police education", a tension that permeates police education in Brazil and Argentina.

The purpose of training is to teach a specific method of performing a task or responding to a given situation, with a defined scope. Training is focused on how to carry out a task in a particular goal situation. Police training is a process of acquiring specific knowledge or skills needed for police work, in delimited periods: the purpose of training is to teach a specific method of performing a task or responding to a given situation, with a defined scope.

The objective of the training is "[t]o teach a specific method of performing a task or responding to a given situation. The content taught usually has a limited scope. Training is focused on how to carry out a task in a particular, goal-oriented situation" (Haberfeld 2002, p. 33). Pagon also defines training in the same way: "police training is a process of acquiring particular knowledge or skills necessary for police work, in delimited periods" (Pagon 1996, p. 45).

The former director of the New York Police Academy emphasises that "training, by definition, is teaching a subject at the level of perception. Training is often associated with practical instruction, repetition, and preparation for a skill" (O'Keefe 2004, p. 48).

As a consequence, there is a distinction between training and education, says Haberfeld: "The purpose of training is to teach a specific method of performing a task or responding to a given situation. The subject taught is usually narrow in scope. Education involves the learning of general concepts, terms, policies, practices and theories" (Haberfeld 2002, p. 32).

But education involves the learning of general concepts, terms, policies, practices and theories. Police education is a process of transmitting and acquiring general or specific knowledge related to the police, which lead to the obtaining of a certain degree. Typically, police educational programmes extend over several years. That is, "education, on the other hand, is situated more at the conceptual level and is traditionally associated with preparation for a profession" (O'Keefe 2004, p. 48). Pagon defines police education as a process of transmission of general or specific knowledge related to the police, which lead to the completion of a degree. Typically, police educational programmes last for several years (Pagon 1996, p. 60).

Evoking Paulo Freire, writes Frigotto: "the core of Freire's understanding of education is that it is not training, but a process of formation through which people become able to read reality, to read the world. It is a matter of forming subjects that build their autonomy and in relation to other subjects consciously act in society" (Frigotto 2003, p. 156; see also Frigotto 2009).

Finally, the understanding of social processes is fundamental, since "creating a sensitivity in the police – creating a sociological imagination – is not simply a means of providing information to the police; rather, it is a way of creating a necessary perspective for them to comprehend information widely" (O'Keefe 2004, p. 118). This model was in the core of the transitional process in European police since the 1990s (Kadar 2001).

Conclusions

The police education institutions in Brazil and Argentina present a framework of a legacy of militaristic and law heritage and a corporate segmentation. In Argentina, a national police remains with these cultural heritage.

In Brazil, the military police academies maintain traces of a militarised organisational culture, with the exaltation of discipline, military hierarchy and training in military operations, allied to a pedagogical archaism, with few exceptions. Also in the case of the Civil Police Schools, police training is guided by positive and formal law, leaving little space for disciplines properly related to the exercise of police duties, such as conflict mediation, police performance management and criminal intelligence analysis.

The transition from the military regime to the civil regime, in a process that began in both societies, in the 1880s, implied a set of social and political confrontations around the destiny of public institutions and their roles, in a way that could accomplish the democratisation process.

Meanwhile, the problems of professionalisation of the police are still not concrete: how to guarantee a better working conditions and how to improve police education and training to fabric a competent professional? The real issue is how to perform a public service compatible with the demands of a complex society that presents heavy and complex problems of law and order enforcement.

The issue of police education is based on a difficulty in reducing crime and violence because there has not yet been a break with a model of police training guided by the perspective of army education, guided by the doctrine of national security. Secondly, there is a deep culture resistance to changes inside the police institutions. From the fieldwork research in Brazil and in Argentina, some subjects could be reinforced.

Firstly, the relationship with the universities is a great possibility, but it was not easy due to the need to overcome reciprocal stigmatisations. Therefore, attempts to change the police education system in Brazil started from the reality of a fragmented teaching in which the curricular, democratic and critical proposals coexist with archaic pedagogical practices that give continuity to the old models of police education.

Prominently, the experiences of curricular innovation, of teaching-learning processes, didactic methodologies and institutional integration were an innovative police learning initiatives, within police educational institutions and in agreements with universities in several Brazilian states and in at least three Argentinians Provinces. There was the incorporation of the human sciences, the relativisation of military training, the reduction of the positivist approach in the teaching of law and the absorption of human rights contents. The agreements between police schools and universities are a very unique experiment, and perhaps the collaboration between universities and academies and police schools should be encouraged.

Secondly, the situation of career progression can be seen in all cases analysed by the fact that there is a double pattern. In Argentina, there is a single career in the police, with secondary education being a requirement of selection. The initial training lasts from 6 to 12 months. The contents and their frameworks show the predominance of police technologies and most of the subjects combine theoretical and practical classes.

The initial training is carried out at the premises of the academies or police schools themselves. The progression in the career is made by courses of permanent education, and for the management positions there are usually short-term police management courses. The academic courses have always been carried out in agreements with universities, which certify the degrees (Bachelor and Master). The university plays a role in contributing to the academic qualifications of the police officers, either personally or through the help of scholarships. However, in the case of the specialisation and in the masters, they are always made in agreements with the universities, or exclusively at the universities with recognition of the titles by the police organisations. The programmes contribute to the transition from one position to another in career, plus merit. However, to pass to managerial positions, a graduate degree course is necessary, either inside police academy (the case of Buenos Aires) or in agreements with universities in the form of graduate programmes.

Thirdly, the type of education most valued is internal, a training in the police academy, mainly for the initial level in the career. So, police activity is not classified as a specific higher education area, but it is included in university programmes, undergraduate programmes (the case of Argentina) or post-graduate programmes (Public Security Graduate Programmes, in Brazil). There are also the continuing education courses in Brazil that has been widely used for police officers providing a new reflection on the practices of police work in complex societies marked by the diversity and transformations of our time. Mainly with regard to the use of firearms, there is a theoretical discussion about the deontology of the use of firearms, and in which situations the police officer must use this last resource.

Fourthly, the data provides evidence of the role played by the teaching staff in delivering a good learning. Therefore, it is crucial to have a permanent staff of teachers and to develop teaching and learning methodologies through the dialogue between teachers and students. The big problem is demonstrating teaching training and evidence of regularly updating their teaching skills as the teaching staff has not a permanent commitment with learning, but came under eventual contracts to teach a specific discipline, with no guarantee of permanence. The academies need an improvement of their teaching and learning facilities, mainly to establish libraries and computers laboratories and enough Internet networks. They must seek to overcome a fragmented and only instrumental knowledge, to enable students to experience social situations that favour the formation of content appropriate to police practices. Also, they need to emphasise methodologies of teaching and learning of concepts as instruments of questioning, understanding and transformation of reality. So, the main contributions from the universities could be an idea of collective construction of knowledge with the establishment of connections between theory and practice in the context of interdisciplinary.

Fifthly, how to change the police education of a paradigm composed by positivist criminal law and by militarist doctrines for an orientation that incorporates critical knowledge in law, social sciences and public management? It would also be necessary to develop police training in police technologies that incorporate advances in science and technology. In brief, we observe very few efforts to help police students to learn independently, even if the contemporary university-based orientations learn that directed independent learning is critical to the students future success.

Sixth, the category of diversity began to be incorporated. Still, there is not yet any affirmative action related to ethnicity, which is very important because of the racial diversity in Latin American societies. In Brazil, the real issue is a process to eliminate gender discrimination, sexual, religious or ethnic orientation, inducing a learning guided by respect for human dignity and differences. Law no. 12.711/August 2012, guarantees the reservation of 50% of enrolments per course in the 59 federal universities and 38 federal institutes of education, science and technology to students coming entirely from public high school. The minimum percentage corresponding to the sum of blacks, metis and indigenous people in each state will also be taken into account to guarantee a percentage of these racial minority students. In fact, to accomplish a police community we must have a racial diversity that could include indigenous and black people as policemen and policewomen.

Scholarship, literature and field research in police studies have revealed that there is a recognition that the police officer with the best level of education can be considered the best police officer, provided that the curricular structure incorporates the innovation in science and technology applied to the police service.

There is a worldwide tendency for the insertion of the debate on the schooling of security operators into the public agenda, expressed in several dimensions: valuing pedagogical innovations; the training inserted in the police career; the absorption of students in the School of Police already with university education; or the encouragement to police officers to undertake undergraduate or graduate programmes in universities.

The main issue is to follow the principles of social responsibility of the police education, ensuring all activities are made with respect to human dignity. A contemporary police education must be ethics based and for social responsibility, in the public service in order to develop transparency and inter-institutional accountability, founding the legitimacy of the external control of the police.

The expansion of a globalised citizenship and the formation of a transnational civil society stimulate a police education concerned with the prevention of crime and the control of violence, guaranteeing citizen security as a fundamental right. Hence, the agreements between police schools and universities, as we observe in Argentina and in Brazil, should be encouraged.

In summary, there is a worldwide occurrence of a non-linear process of transformations in police education, full of ambivalence, but with ample civilisational possibilities. It seems, notably, that a new orientation in police education is being outlined in several countries, be it professionalism, or the emphasis on the community police or on the proposal of a citizen security. All assert a respect for human dignity in the fabric of a new civilising process in society.

References

Balestreri, R. B. (Ed.). (2003). *Na inquietude da Paz.* Passo Fundo: CAPEC.

Balieiro, A. (2003). *Avaliação do Processo Ensino-aprendizagem: a concepção dos professores civis e militares da Academia de Polícia Militar Costa Verde – MT. PPG em Educação.* Master Dissertation, Instituto de Educação, Universidade Federal do Mato Grosso – Cuiabá.

Barreira, C., et al. (2004). *Questão de Segurança.* Rio de Janeiro: Relume Dumará.

Brasil, M. G. M. (2000). *A segurança pública no "Governo das Mudanças": moralização, modernização e participação.* Tese (PhD)- Programa de Estudos Pós-Graduados em Serviço Social, Pontifícia Universidade Católica de São Paulo, São Paulo, 323p.

Brasil, G. M., de Almeida, R. O., & de Freitas, G. J. (Eds.). (2015). *Dilemas da "nova" formação policial: experiências e práticas de policiamento.* Campinas: Pontes.

Caruso, H. G. C. (2006). *Polícia Militar do Estado do Rio de Janeiro: da escola de formação à prática policial.* Brasília: SENASP.

Castro, C. (1990). *O espírito militar: um estudo de antropologia social na Academia Militar das Agulhas Negras.* Rio de Janeiro: Jorge Zahar Editor.

Cordeiro, B. M. P., & da Silva, S. S. (2003). *Direitos Humanos: uma perspectiva interdisciplinar e transversal.* Brasília: CICV.

Costa, A. T. M. (2004). *Entre a Lei e a Ordem.* Rio de Janeiro: FGV.

Da Aquino Silva, R. (2010). *Quando os impensáveis entram em cena*. Porto Alegre: CORAG.

da Silva, S. S. (2003). *Teoria e prática da educação em direitos humanos nas instituições policiais brasileiras*. Porto Alegre: Editora CAPEC.

de Albuquerque, C. L., & Machado, E. P. (2001). Sob o signo de Marte: modernização, ensino e ritos da instituição policial militar. *Sociologias* (*Porto Alegre*), 5, 214–236, Jan/Jun.

de Araujo Filho, W. (2003). Ordem Pública ou ordem unida? In: Universidade Federal Fluminense e Instituto de Segurança Pública (Eds.), *Políticas Públicas de Justiça Criminal e Segurança Pública 1*. Niterói: EDUFF.

De Kant Lima, R. (1995). *A polícia da cidade do Rio de Janeiro: seus dilemas e paradoxos*. Rio de Janeiro: Forense.

de Lima, R. S., & de Paula, L. (Eds.). (2006). *Segurança Pública e Violência: o Estado está cumprindo seu papel?* (pp. 125–137). São Paulo: Contexto.

de SÁ, L. D. (2002). *Os filhos do Estado: auto-imagem e disciplina na formação dos oficiais da Policia Militar do Ceará*. Rio de Janeiro: Relume Dumará: Núcleo de Antropologia Política, UFRJ.

de Sousa Santos, B. (2000). *A crítica da razão indolente: contra o desperdício da experiência*. São Paulo: Cortez.

Dias Neto, T. (2000). *Policiamento comunitário e controle sobre a Polícia: a experiência norte-americana*. São Paulo: IBCCRIM.

Fabian Sain, M. (2008). *El Leviatán Azul: Policía y política en Argentina* (Vol. XXI). Buenos Aires: Siglo.

Fernandes, H. (1974). *Política e Segurança*. São Paulo: Alfa – Omega.

Frigotto, G. (2003). Inovação/construção do conhecimento. *Interface. Botucatu, 7*(13), 154–156.

Frigotto, G. (2009). A polissemia da categoria trabalho e a batalha das ideias nas sociedades de classe. *Revista Brasileira de Educação, Rio de Janeiro, 14*(40), 168–194.

Granjeiro, L. H. F., Lima, M. S. L., & de Magalhães, R. C. B. P. (2001). *A academia vai à academia: uma experiência de formação para policiais*. Fortaleza: Demócrito Rocha/UECE.

Haberfeld, M. R. (2002). *Critical Issues in Police Training*. Upper Saddle River: Pearson Education/Prentice Hall.

Jacondino, E. N. (2015). *Saber/Poder e Corpo*. Curitiba: Editora CRV.

Kádár, A. (2001). *Police in Transition (Essays on the Police Forces in Transition Countries)*. Budapest: Central European University Press. (cf. Budapest Helsinki Commission. Polices in Democratic Transition. Budapest, CDROM, 1998).

Kessler, G. (2009). *El sentimiento de inseguridad: sociología del temor al delito.* Siglo XXI: Buenos Aires.

Linhares, C. F. (1999). *Escola de Bravos: cotidiano e currículo numa Academia de Polícia Militar.* Master Dissertation, PPG em Ciências Sociais da Faculdade de Filosofia e Ciências Humanas da Universidade Federal da Bahia.

Mingardi, G. (1992). *Tiras, gansos e trutas.* Scritta: São Paulo.

Neves, P. C., Rique, C., & Freitas, F. (2002). *Polícia e Democracia: desafios à Educação e Direitos Humanos.* Recife: Bagaço.

Nummer, F. V. (2004). *Ser Polícia, ser militar: o curso de formação na socialização do policial militar.* Niterói: Editora da UFF.

O'Keefe, J. (2004). *Protecting the Republic (The Education and Training of American Police Officers – NYPD).* Upper Saddle River: Pearson Education.

Pagon, M. (Ed.). (1996). *Policing in Central and Eastern Europe.* Ljubljana: College of Police and Security Studies. www.ncjrs.org/policing.

Pegoraro, J. (2015). *Los Lazos Sociales del Delito Económico y el Orden Social.* Eudeba: Buenos Aires.

Pinheiro, P. S., et al. (2000). *Democracia, Violência e Injustiça.* Rio de Janeiro: Paz e Terra.

Ponciani, P. (2014). O profissionalismo na formação profissional do policial brasileiro: rupturas, permanências e desdobramentos contemporâneos. *Segurança, Justiça e Cidadania. Ministério da Justiça/Secretaria Nacional de Segurança Pública (SENASP).* Brasilia, ano 4(7), 47–76.

Rondon Filho, E. B. (2011). *Fenomenologia da Educação Jurídica na formação Policial-Militar.* Porto Alegre: Evangraff.

Rudnicki, D. (2007). *A formação social de Oficiais da Polícia Militar: análise do caso da Academia da Brigada Militar do Rio Grande do Sul.* Tese de Doutorado (PhD), PPG – Sociologia, Porto Alegre.

Rudnicki, D. (2014). A Brigada Militar (e a formação do oficial) na contemporaneidade. In: *Segurança, Justiça e Cidadania. Ministério da Justiça/ Secretaria Nacional de Segurança Pública (SENASP).* Brasilia, ano 4(7), 77–130.

Sadek, M. T. (Ed.). (2005). *Delegados de Polícia.* São Paulo: IDESP.

SENASP – Secretaria Nacional de Segurança Pública, Ministério da Justiça, Brasil. 2014. *Pesquisa Perfil das Instituições de Segurança Pública 2013.* Brasilia: SENASP/Ministério da Justiça, http://www.mj.gov.br/senasp.

Soares, L. E. (2000). *O Casaco do General.* São Paulo: Companhia das Letras.

Tavares dos Santos, J. V. (2002). The Worldization of Violence and Injustice. In: *Current Sociology* (Vol. 50(1), pp. 123–134). London: ISA – International Sociological Association/Sage. January.

Tavares dos Santos, J. V. (2004). The World Police Crisis and the Construction of Democratic Policing. In: *International Review of Sociology* (Vol. 14, (1, March), pp. 89–106). Oxfordshire: Taylor & Francis.

Tavares dos Santos, J. V. (2009). *Violências e Conflitualidades*. Porto Alegre: Tomo Editorial.

Tavares dos Santos, J.-V. (2010). The Dialogue between Criminology and the South's Sociology of Violence: The Policing Crisis and Alternatives. In M. Burawoy, C. Mau-Kuei, & M. Fei-Yu Hsieh (Eds.), *Facing an Unequal World: Challenges for a Global Sociology* (Vol. I, pp. 105–125). Taipei: International Sociological Association, Council of National Associations and the Institute of Sociology, Academia Sinica.

Tavares dos Santos, J. V. (2014). Dilemas do Ensino Policial: das heranças às pistas inovadoras. *Segurança, Justiça e Cidadania. Ministério da Justiça/ Secretaria Nacional de Segurança Pública (SENASP)*. Brasilia, ano 4(7), 11–30.

Tavares dos Santos, J.-V., Zaverucha, J., Lima, R. K., Balestreri, R., & Quejada, J. A. J. (2009). Educação policial: limites e possibilidades para a democracia ampliada. In P. H. Martins & R. d. S. Medeiros (Eds.), *América Latina e Brasil em perspectiva* (pp. 379–404). Recife: Editora Universitária.

UFF – Universidade Federal Fluminense E Instituto De Segurança Pública. (2003). *Políticas Públicas de Justiça Criminal e Segurança Pública 1*. Niterói: EDUFF.

Wood, J., & Cardia, N. (2006). Brazil. In T. Jones & T. Newburn (Eds.), *Plural Policing: A Comparative Perspective* (pp. 139–168). London: Routledge.

Zaluar, A. (1999). Violência e Crime. In S. Miceli (Ed.), *O que ler na ciência social brasileira* (pp. 13–107). São Paulo: ANPOCS/Sumaré.

Zaluar, A. (2004). *Integração Perversa: pobreza e tráfico de drogas*. Rio de Janeiro: FGV.

Zaverucha, J. (2003). *Polícia Civil de Pernambuco: o desafio da reforma*. Recife: Editora da UFPE.

8

Higher Police Education in Europe: Surveying Recent Developments

André Konze and Detlef Nogala

Introduction

This chapter aims to shed some light on the recent state of training and education for police and other law enforcement officers in Europe by sharing a set of empirical data that was collected in a small project established by CEPOL – by then called the European Police College[1] – covering the period 2013–2014.[2] The project was set up for upgrading the findings of earlier surveys (CEPOL 2006; Ferreira et al. 2010), which intended to capture the structures and trends of law enforcement training and education in the European Union.

To begin with, it is worth to look back two decades:

> *[I]t is no surprise that the situation regarding European systems of police education and training is an utterly confusing one. One can hear of police colleges that train police officers, police academies that grant university-level degrees,*

A. Konze
European External Action Service (EEAS), Brussels, Belgium

D. Nogala (✉)
European Union Agency for Law Enforcement Training, Budapest, Hungary

© The Author(s) 2018
C. Rogers, B. Frevel (eds.), *Higher Education and Police*,
DOI 10.1007/978-3-319-58386-0_8

schools outside police that exclusively admit police officers, university-level degree granting institutions that prepare for a certain rank within a police hierarchy, etc. (Pagon et al. 1996)

The apparent slight confusion about the state of police education and training systems in Europe in that period can probably be explained by the impact of the monumental shifts in the political landscape and the aftershock affecting the institutional architecture still in process at that time.

Since then, the EU has enlarged from 15 to (currently) 28 member states, the idea of an "Area of Freedom, Security and Justice" had been introduced in the Treaty of Amsterdam (1997), and by the Lisbon Treaty coming into effect (2009), the Stockholm Programme (2010) called, among other things, for fostering "a genuine European judicial and law enforcement culture", where training on Union-related issues would be systematically accessible for judicial staff as well as law enforcement officials (European Council 2010, Article 1.2.6 "Training"). The creation of the "Bologna Process" (since 1999) as a collective effort in modernising the educational system in Europe had also a significant impact on the institutional shaping of police training and education bodies, with harmonising standards and proceedings for the benefit of interoperationability in mind. Last but not least, the establishment of the European Police College (CEPOL) in 2000 has to be considered a relevant element in trying to render the processes and the landscape of police training and educational systems in Europe less "confusing" and more structured.

It is safe to assert, that over the past two decades, essential initiatives on the national as well as the EU level have been taken, in order to modernise and (potentially) harmonise training and education for approximately 2 million police officers[3] on all hierarchical levels.

However, initiating efforts to develop and raise standards and similar procedures to become effective across a multi-national, multi-lingual and multi-organisational environment is not a trivial matter – in particular, not in case of the police and policing, as this is still basically a "national" issue, rooted very much in each countries specific political and legal history.

Thus the Governing Board of the European Police College launched a first stocktaking project in 2005 with the intention to provide a general view on the various national education and training systems in the EU member states. The outcome of the "Survey on European Police Education and Training (SEPE)" was published in November 2006 (CEPOL 2006). Similar to the experience of Pagon et al. (1996), collecting a complete set of data for all countries and educational bodies turned out as being too ambitious, caused mainly by difficulties in regard to identifying authoritative sources or communication issues. While the survey project succeeded in collecting a wide range of data on institutions, structures and content of police training and education in the EU member states, there was little more to conclude than that there was "huge complexity and amplitude of the matter" and that structures of police education and training in the EU were found to be "very different" (CEPOL 2006: 201).

A few years later, in 2009, a follow-up survey was initiated: the focus of the "Survey on European Police Education and Bologna – (SEPEB)" was now on providing an overview of education and training programmes in Europe, which would be "open to foreign police officers, with a focus on the degree of implementation of the Bologna process at national police training institutes in the European Union Member States and at relevant cooperation partners for the period until the end of 2009" (Ferreira et al. 2010: 6). Again, a lot of data were gathered on aspects of, for example, delivering institutions, programmes and topics, even broken down to the national level but more relevant were some of the conclusions:

- that a significant change in police education in Europe had taken place during the first decade of the "twenty-first" century;
- that since the development and introduction of the Bologna agreements, the educational levels for police officers had been raised, especially those aimed at middle and senior ranks;
- that a considerable amount of police curricula had been subject to accreditation processes and comparable degrees and similar credits (i.e. ECTS) had been introduced (ebd.: 9).

Conscious of the dynamics in the field of police training and education, the Governing Board of the European Police College (CEPOL) established in November 2013, the "Working Group for the updating of the survey on the European Law Enforcement Education Systems (ELEES WG)"[4] for the purpose to develop and to implement a follow-up online survey, aiming, once more, at gathering data of and from institutions responsible for the training of law enforcement officials in the member states of the EU as well as Schengen-associated countries.

The chapter will present the main results of this survey project, which intended to collect information valid for the period of the educational years 2013–2014. For the interpretation of the data and the conclusions, it is important to take note that this survey does not claim to represent a comprehensive and absolutely accurate snapshot of police training and education systems for this period for all of the EU member states or the CEPOL-associated countries – the received data were not coherent and complete enough for such an assertion. However, the study represents the latest available set of data on a European level and does allow at least indicative statements about recent trends and tendencies.

Method and Methodology

The Working Group was mandated to develop and to implement an online survey aiming to gather data about institutions responsible for the training of law enforcement officers. In its decision, the Governing Board elaborated the mandate in detail and asked for data about the status and internal organisation of the duly identified institutions, the minimum level of education required for applying for a law enforcement career, the attribution of ECTS (European Credit Transfer System), the involvement in Erasmus programmes, and several other details. While the ELEES project was considered to serve as a follow-up and update of SEPEB (see Ferreira et al. 2010), there would be a few relevant differences:

- ELEES would widen the scope of the survey from "police" to "law enforcement"[5] organisations and institutions.

- In contrast to SEPEB, countries outside the EU, like those who are represented in the Association of European Police Colleges,[6] were not part of the sample anymore.

The ELEES survey eventually covered the 28 current member states of the EU, Iceland, Switzerland and Norway as countries associated via the Schengen agreement, plus a number of EU JHA agencies (CEPOL, Frontex) and Interpol.

Aimed at as being an update exercise of the last survey conducted by CEPOL in 2010, however, being considerate about the differing survey sample, the ELEES Working Group took the various items of the SEPEB questionnaire as a blueprint for developing the ELEES survey, amending and modifying them, where necessary.

Reflecting on the limited time and work capacities, it became evident that the ELEES survey could not become as comprehensive as SEPE (CEPOL 2006) in its scope of questions, but could just deal with particular aspects of law enforcement training systems across Europe.

The members of the ELEES working group had also to consider that the status of police educational institutions could not simply be taken from information provided on the Internet: apart from the issue of translation risks, there would be no coherent set of information ready for analytical takeaway. At the same time, it would be reasonable to assume that police and law enforcement organisations are subject to frequent reforms and organisational change which more often than not would affect structure, form and shape of police training and education systems as well.[7]

As in the SEPE and SEPEB projects, the conclusion was drawn that the most reliable and comprehensive source of information would sit most likely with experts situated on the national level.

Through the network of CEPOL National Contact Points, the countries and organisations of the sample were asked in a first round to identify and appoint experts for becoming the source of best available information. Following the initial contact, 29 out of 31 countries (response rate 94%) appointed (at least one) such an expert responder[8] (Table 8.1).

Table 8.1 Sample of countries and organisations for the first round of the survey

Austria	Belgium	Bulgaria	Croatia	Cyprus	Czech Republic
Denmark	Estonia	Finland	France	Germany	Greece
Hungary	Ireland	Italy	Latvia	Lithuania	Luxembourg
Malta	Netherlands	Poland	Portugal	Romania	Slovak Republic
Slovenia	Spain	Sweden	United Kingdom		
Iceland	*Norway*	*Switzerland*			
EUROJUST	*EUROPOL*	*FRONTEX*	INTERPOL		

Having in mind that, on the practical level, the categories of cooperation, exchange and interoperability are the most important ones for successful working of law enforcement in Europe, the project group decided to depart from two core questions to be asked:

1. "Considering law enforcement education and training in your country, are there any colleges, universities, or other institutions offering programmes and/or courses with reference to the period 2013–2014 that are accredited or in the process of becoming accredited according to the Bologna Process"
2. "Considering law enforcement education and training in your country, are there any colleges, universities or other institutions offering programmes and/or courses with reference to the period 2013–2014 that are open to law enforcement European countries but that are not related to the Bologna Process (CEPOL activities are excluded)?"

The first question clearly aimed at identifying if the process of "Bologna-isation" of police education in Europe, which had been highlighted and demonstrated in the SEPEB-study in 2010, had continued. The second question tried to explore, if there would be channels for cross-border training or education of law enforcement officials, apart from and besides of the more formalised Bologna Process.

In the interest of a lean survey economy, the group went for a three-stage survey process, to avoid unnecessary overload of items in the questionnaires, in case some items were not relevant for the respective institution: Only in case of a positive reply for one of the leading questions in questionnaire 1 (Q1), a second online questionnaire would be sent (Q2), asking for information about the institutions that were indicated as either running Bologna-accredited programmes or courses (or in the process of), or at least would permit attendance of officers from other European countries to their non-Bologna-accredited courses.[9] The third questionnaire (Q3) would invite detailed information about the programmes or courses that would meet one of the two requirements.

The item-sets embraced a wide range of aspects, such as the status and internal organisation of law enforcement training institutions, the attribution/non-attribution of ECTS, the involvement in Erasmus type programmes and/or in other European or international-level law enforcement training activities.

All three questionnaires were sent as tokenised email invitations and the responders would fill in their replies in the online form. Groups of countries were assigned to members of the Working Group in case responses were missing past the deadline of requested submission or returned incomplete.[10] The collected answers were exported into spreadsheet tables, which were in turn taken as the basis for statistical counting and further analysis.

Working with expert respondents from the CEPOL network, using an online tool for gathering and capturing the data, had been a tried-and-tested method for past surveys of the agency. As in earlier projects, there were a few technical issues of compatibility, of which the vast majority could be sorted out swiftly. In general, the method of deploying an online-survey tool worked well and rendered satisfactory response rates at least for stages one and two of the process.

The research process was not perfect though and could thus not yield perfect results, as the ELEES working group encountered a number of difficulties in the course of the project, inviting caution for taking the resulting figures at face value or as precise reflection of the reality regarding the status of law enforcement training and education systems in Europe in the period 2013–2014. The reader should be aware of the project's "package insert":

1. While the overall response rate was good, not all countries and international organisations provided the requested information at all or continuously over the three stages of the research.
2. The expert respondents changed in some cases in the course of the research stages, and there were multiple ones for countries with multiple forces (Germany, France, Portugal, Spain, Switzerland), partly resulting in incomplete or incoherent data.
3. Clarification or verification could not be achieved in each of those cases, as repeated attempts of contact in the later stages of the project failed.
4. The figures are not weighted or set in proportion to factors like the number of forces, the absolute numbers of officers, or the size of a country.
5. Furthermore, some respondent covered law enforcement in the wider sense, while others restricted themselves to inform about police bodies.

Facing these restrictions and impediments, early thoughts about applying more advanced statistical analytics and methods were quickly abandoned. Instead, the authors tried to consolidate the data pool as plausible as possible and left single data sets aside in case the validity was doubtful and could not be verified eventually within reasonable efforts.

In this sense, the results and figures provided in the next section are accurate only as accurate calculations of the consolidated data set. They should not be mistaken as a true, precise or complete snapshot of the topic at hand. With this concession, the authors nevertheless believe that the results are a reasonably meaningful indication of the trends and tendencies that were shaping the landscape of European law enforcement training and education systems in the period 2013–2014.

The outcomes will be presented first as per questionnaire. General trends and conclusions are discussed in the final section.

Results

Q1: "Are there any colleges, universities, or other institutions offering programmes and/or courses..."

Responses were received from all 31 European countries contacted. In the first round, 23 responders indicated that there was at least one Bologna-accredited institution involved in law enforcement training (Figure. 8.1). The European and international organisations were not running any such activities at that time.[11]

Obviously, most European police services follow the trend of innovation through developing their education. Nevertheless, Belgium and the United Kingdom replied they did not have any accredited educational police institution in the surveyed period. The reasons for this vacancy might be different for Belgium and the United Kingdom. It can be assumed that Belgium with its heterogeneous structure of relatively small police services did not found a common agreement yet for one institution to be accredited. But for the United Kingdom, with its well-established police colleges in England and Wales, Scotland respectively, a predestined institution would expectably be available for developing a Bologna-accredited programme/course. Although there are public universities in the country that have accredited programme/courses, the police authorities in the United Kingdom appear to have been reluctant to develop such offerings.[12]

Roughly half of the responding countries (n = 16) countries indicated they would run police training and educational institutions that are not Bologna-accredited but open to be attended by officers from other European countries. The survey counted 40 such institutions – but partly they are the same that were claimed to offer programmes and courses under Bologna accreditation.

There are clear differences in the number of institutions answered for.

Thirteen countries indicated just one – usually the national police college, academy or university. For the other "multiples", there are diverging reasons:

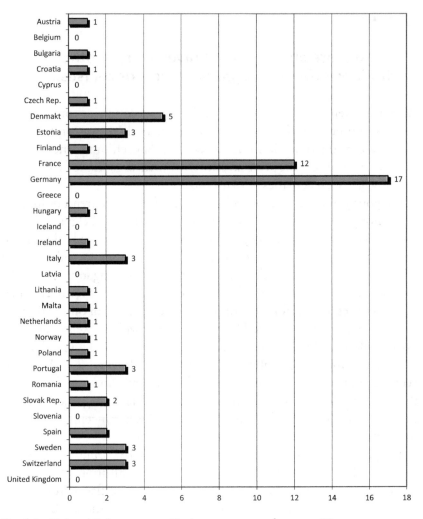

Fig. 8.1 Claimed Bologna-accredited programmes of courses Q1

- due to various locations for the ranks under a single force system (e.g. Sweden),
- due to a multi-force system (e.g. Germany, France, Italy, Spain, Portugal, Switzerland), or
- due to variations how "civil" universities have become integral part of the police education system (Denmark, France, Estonia).

Interestingly, in at least eight countries (roughly a quarter of the sample) universities external to the traditional police education system had become at that time part of training and education schemes (e.g. Estonia, France, Lithuania, Spain).

Q2: The delivering institutions

The answers about the status of the institutions that have been either accredited to the Bologna treaty or are open to Law Enforcement Officers from other European countries show that 36 of 71 institutions claimed university status of some sort.[13] The remaining 45 institutions are claiming academy status (16), college status (10), school status (7) or another status. The fact that the largest group of institutions asserted to have a university status corresponds with the development that has been described in previous paragraphs. A clear majority (23 from 31 countries) declared that there was at least one Bologna-accredited institution per country involved in law enforcement training. The accreditation of a programme/course very often goes hand in hand with the switch from a former police academy turning into a university.[14] Recognising this phenomenon also means to realise that the accreditation of programmes/courses and the development of institutions is not necessarily connected with the aim of the Bologna Process to provide tools to connect with national educational systems. It rather appears that the accreditation is more a means to change the organisational form of an institution.

The answers to the question about the authorities responsible for police education and training indicate that the majority (n = 36) of the 71 institutions are organised under the authority of the respective Ministry of Interior.[15] Only 18 of 71 police training institutions belong to a Ministry of Education. One could wonder if these figures demonstrate the tenacity of law enforcement organisations, as it seems that the Bologna Process affected the governance structure of European law enforcement education systems only partially.

The accumulated figures for the number of bachelor, master, PhD students, and teaching staff provide insight into a number of interesting aspects (Table 8.2).

Table 8.2 Students and teaching staff

	Number of bachelor students (based on 43 institutions)	Number of master students (based on 37 institutions)	Number of PhD students average (based on 25 institutions)	Teaching staff(based on 55 institutions)	Teaching staff with PhD or Doctorate degree (based on 53 institutions)
Total	30.500	5250	351	3936	1330
Average	710	142	14	72	25
Min–Max	20–3.800	20–660	2–84	10–200	1–130
Median	400	40	40	51	12

First, it is obvious that the big majority of Bologna-accredited programmes or courses are tailored towards the bachelor degree. Curiously, the median figure for bachelor, master and PhD students results in a ratio of 10:1:1.

Secondly, there is a large variation in the number of students for the degree programmes: the range is from a pair of PhD students to 3800 in bachelor degree programmes.[16] Again, this variance is a function of the actual size of the force and the respective country.

Even if the combined figures of around 36,000 bachelor, masters and PhD students might appear marginal in the light of the approximately 2 million law enforcement personnel in the EU at first glance, the significance will become more obvious when it is compared to just the age-cohorts of students and cadets who are involved in the law enforcement education systems at a given time.

Finally, and far more interesting from an educational point is the finding on the ratio of students to teaching staff. The average ratio, independently from the size of the services, between these groups is 8:1. Obviously, the modular structure of accredited programmes/course requires such a relatively high number of teaching staff.[17]

Another finding in this regard was that 45% of all surveyed institutions claimed to take part in an Erasmus or Erasmus-style programme at that time.

The same percentage of institutions asserted to include e-learning tools and elements into their programmes/courses, where the open source package Moodle seems to be the favourite. However, indication that software is used for e-learning says little about the scope, quality or impact of its application. The survey data does not reveal anything regarding the value or significance of e-learning software for the learning process, but it is a fair assumption that advanced learning technology has not been implemented or exploited to the full yet across the law enforcement training institutions in Europe.[18]

In the next step, the project group asked their respondents to list the names of institutions, which either deliver Bologna-accredited learning or run courses or programmes that are open for officers from other European countries. Table 8.3 shows the results of this survey-step:

This being a survey round in the middle of the project, the outcome held a few surprises for the project group:

- The count for countries, which positively indicated to run at least one Bologna-accredited programme that would lead to a bachelor's, master's or doctorate degree was 19, increasing to 25, when programmes granting ECTS were accounted for as well.
- Just three countries would offer the whole set of degrees (Bulgaria, Romania and Switzerland). Bulgaria and Romania also reported the highest number of such programmes or courses.[19]
- Judging by the pure figures, it occurs that countries that acceded to the EU at a later stage seem to have put more efforts in and have progressed faster in the "Bologna-isation" of their law enforcement education systems (in particular Bulgaria, Hungary, Portugal and Romania). However, this relatively high figures could likewise be the effect that those countries had included various law enforcement bodies in their survey (including Italy), while the majority of other respondent restricted their figures to police forces.
- After all, eight countries reported on otherwise "open" courses and programmes.

Informed by these results, the project group launched the third and last step of the online survey.

Table 8.3 Listing of delivering institutions

	Bologna-accredited programmes or courses	Doctorate or PhD degree	Master's degree	Bachelor's degree	Other granting ECTS	Non-accredited but open
Austria	5		3	1	1	
Bulgaria	23	9	7	7		
Croatia	2		1	1		
Czech Republic	4			4		
Denmark	1			1		
Estonia	3		1		2	
Finland	2		1	1		
France	15		2	1	12	
Germany	11		3	8		3
Greece	1				1	7
Hungary	15		1	14[a]		
Ireland	1			1		1
Italy	6		1		5	
Latvia	1				1	
Lithuania	2				2	
Malta	2		1	1		
Netherlands	7		5	1	1	
Norway	2		1	1	unspecified	
Poland	2				2	
Portugal	14		6		8	12
Romania	18	1	14	3		1
Slovenia	1				1	
Spain	2		1		1	4
Sweden	1				1	
Switzerland	7	2	4	1		3
U.K.						3
Total	148	12	52	46	38	34

[a]The National University of Public Service in Hungary offers these courses both full- and part-time

Q3: Specific information about programmes and courses

As mentioned earlier, the response rate for the third step of the project survey was significantly lower than for the two forerunners;

Specific information was received for 108 programmes or courses, offered by 53 law enforcement educational institutions from 22 European countries;

**Type of programme or course in the Q3
survey sample**

■ Bologna accredited AND open to police officers from Europe
■ Bologna accredited but NOT open to police officers from Europe
■ not accredited but open to police officers from Europe

Fig. 8.2   Type of programme or course in the Q3 survey sample

Out of those 108 different activities, 40 are depicted as leading to a bachelor's and 33 to a master's degree.

Three quarters of the Q3 sample referred to Bologna-accredited programmes – remarkably 36% are not accessible for officers from other European countries, which could find interpretation in the still resilient national rooting of the police's fabric in the EU member states.

Accreditation is a core element of the Bologna Process and should be a serious process that safeguards that all requirements of the process are fulfilled. All over Europe, the demand to have accredited programmes/courses in the portfolio of an institution is increasing. There is an assumption that external accreditation guarantees a rigorous process. Only 28 programmes/courses have been accredited by external bodies, and in 3 cases external bodies played a part in the accreditation. Moreover, it is noteworthy that institutions with a relatively high number of accredited programmes/courses tend not to use external agencies for the accreditation.[20]

The duration of the vast majority of the bachelor-accredited programmes/courses is three years. Considering the workload and the resulting ECTS points, a three-year bachelor course seems to be considered the best-balanced solution. A two-year master course is the continuation for 12 bachelor programmes/courses. Spain offers a variation of this by applying a four-year bachelor course, followed by a one-year masters course. It can be stated that the Bologna requirements lead to a noticeable harmonisation concerning the length of accredited programmes/courses.

When it comes to the form of delivery of the programme or course, 89% of our sample is organised in residential classroom style. Just in 3 cases, the computer was the medium of delivery and only 13 activities used blended learning.

Only 13 programmes/courses require a foreign language certificate for taking part in the programme. However, 40% of programmes/courses in the sample include foreign language classes, hinting at the requirement to master a foreign language, as a crucial tool for cooperation across borders in Europe, is still not given the high priority it would deserve.

The ECTS was introduced in 1989, within the framework of the Erasmus Program, and later developed into an accumulation system to be implemented at institutional, regional, national and European level, as one of the key objectives of the Bologna Declaration. Credits granted by Bologna-accredited programmes are calculated assuming that the total working time of a student during one study year is equivalent to 60 ECTS. It is also assumed that the student workload of a full-time study programme in Europe amounts, on average, to 36/40 weeks per year and in those cases one credit stands for 24–30 working hours.

The identified and described bachelor programmes are aligned with the ECTS, since almost all of them grant 180 credits, which correspond to three studying years. However, at least one bachelor programme grants only 160 credits (Germany), and another two 183 credits (Italy and Poland), and another one 210 credits (Lithuania), and another one 240 credits (Spain).

The same applies to the Master programmes, since most of them grant 120 credits (equivalent to two studying years). However, also in this case there is significant variations as some programmes, like in France and Spain, grant only 60 credits (equivalent to one studying year). The Netherlands grants just 90 credits (equivalent to one and a half studying years), while Germany grants 160 credits, Poland 183 credits and Portugal grants even 300 credits (equivalent to five studying years).

Credits awarded by PhD programmes also vary, from 60 (Italy, equivalent to two studying years) to 180 (Switzerland, equivalent to three to five studying years). As for other type of programmes, they grant from 3 credits (Portugal) to 180 (Germany), according to the respective total working time.

Discussion of the Results and Tentative Conclusions

The respondents that had been appointed by their countries or organisations were successively faced with three step-by-step explicit questionnaires, requesting to deliver information for the reference period 2013–2014. The first survey simply asked about the existence of educational institutions that offer programmes and/or courses that are accredited or in the process of becoming accredited, according to the Bologna Process. Furthermore, it inquired about institutions that are offering programmes and/or courses that are open to law enforcement officials from other European countries. The second wave of the survey aimed at information about the positively identified training and educational institutions. In stage three, the survey requested detailed information about the actual programmes and courses that were indicated and – inter alia – asked for the degree granted through the programmes/courses, the length, the subject, the ratio between theoretical and practical parts, the delivery types, the number of participants, the requirements, the language and several other information.

The main results of the ELEES surveys, keeping the initial motive for the project in mind – to what degree have law enforcement education systems in Europe moved towards harmonisation, common standards and interoperability? – can be summarised along the following lines:

- Across Europe, at least 71 educational law enforcement institutions offer either a Bologna-accredited degree or are open to law enforcement officials from other European countries.

- Since the last survey (SEPEB), the number of Bologna-accredited programmes/courses increased from 73, which have been identified through the SEPEB survey, to 148 for the period of the years 2013–2014. That is a numerical duplication, which is partially an effect of the extended scope of the survey to cover not just police but law enforcement.
- Fifty-two programmes/courses of the sample grant master's degrees, 46 grant bachelor's degrees and 12 programmes/courses grant doctoral degrees.
- Almost half of the accredited bachelor and master's programmes are obviously not open to non-national police officers or students.

The survey identified 38 programmes (from 13 countries) or courses that grant ECTS and together 8 countries offer 34 courses open for law enforcement officials from other European countries.

As indicated earlier, the data set could not be held consistent across all three main stages of the survey. In respect of the total of 182 programmes and courses indicated in stage two of the survey, only 108 were described in more detail in stage three. Also, the number of respondents of the countries and organisations varied across the survey stages and there was no information for one European country at all. These and other inconsistencies made the project group to desist from claiming full representativeness of the data set or the temptation to apply more sophisticated statistical analytical methods. The authors are aware that the outcome of the ELEES project is not more – but not less as well – than a good approximation for the description of the situation of a part of the law enforcement education systems in Europe in the period 2013–2014.

With this caution assigned to the empirical data presented so far, some conclusions can be drawn nevertheless.

No doubt, the educational level of law enforcement officials rose extraordinarily during the last decades and even since the last survey. This is especially valid for middle- and senior-ranked officials. In this regard, it is fair to say that the Bologna Process had a significant impact on law enforcement training and education systems in Europe. Launched in 1999 by the Ministers of Education and university leaders of 29 countries, the Bologna Process since then aimed to create a

European Higher Education Area (EHEA) by 2010. It has further developed into a major reform encompassing 46 countries. Taking part in the Bologna Process is a voluntary decision made by each country and its higher education community required to endorse the principles underlined in the EHEA. It should be noted though that the Bologna Process does not aim to harmonise national educational systems but rather aims to provide tools to connect them. The intention is – and has always been – to allow the diversity of national systems and universities to be maintained, while the EHEA improves transparency between higher education systems, as well as implements tools to facilitate recognition of degrees and academic qualifications, mobility and exchanges between institutions. The reforms are based on ten simple objectives, which governments and institutions are currently implementing. Most importantly, all participating countries have agreed on a comparable three-cycle degree system for undergraduates (bachelor degrees) and graduates (master's and PhD degrees). Looking at these clarifications, it must be questioned if the current development in police training and education has ever focussed on that. Moving towards a Bologna-accredited police education system should not become an end in itself. Especially, the implementation of tools to facilitate recognition of degrees and academic qualifications, mobility and exchanges between institutions, could not be examined in the ELEES project.

Notwithstanding the fact that the empirical longitudinal observation of the development of law enforcement training and education systems could and shall be improved by including the objective data of accreditation agencies, the outcome of the ELEES survey project confirms the following:

- Police training and education all over Europe has developed extraordinarily since the Bologna Process has been started. Even from the time when the last survey has been conducted, the numbers of institutions and programmes/courses that are accredited have increased significantly.
- The educational requirements for middle- and senior-ranked law enforcement officials have risen since the implementation of the Bologna Process.

- Although educational programmes/courses have been harmonised in terms of using comparable degrees and similar credits all over Europe, the exchangeability of degrees is still very limited.
- The opportunities to participate in another country's training or educational programme are less frequent than the Bologna Process would allow for.

Consequently, it is important to formulate aims for future research. A new set of questions will have to be asked and answered. These questions should focus on the impact of requiring higher educational levels for entering police forces as a low, middle and senior police officer; the impact of implementing the Bologna Process in police and law enforcement education, and especially on the quality of the accreditation process within the European countries. The introduction and intensification of cooperation between higher educational institutions, including joint degrees, and the removal of obstacles to mobility, remain two of the main weaknesses in police high education. While two EU agencies, CEPOL and Frontex, in the meanwhile took their own initiative in this regard by launching their European Master Programmes in 2015, there is still a lot to do. More and more police students enrolled in Bologna-accredited programmes realise that they theoretically could attend similar programmes in other European member states or countries. They may start looking for the most prestigious or interesting ones in Europe. The development documented by the ELEES project made evident that future participants of CEPOL courses will be more and more interested in tertiary education certificates or diplomas. Such certification will became more and more instrumental for their professional careers as police officers. The ability of CEPOL to deliver or help delivering courses granting credits within the European Credit Transfer and Accumulation System will be an essential subject to be undertaken by CEPOL.

As a methodological recommendation, future surveys should be simplified, and the questions must focus more on the actual overarching objectives of higher law enforcement education in Europe. If the survey has different parts, the responding experts must be the same during the entire process. The possibility of online interviews with the respondents from each country needs to be built in. The European Commission Erasmus programme was created to improve the quality and increase the volume of student and teaching staff mobility throughout Europe; the amount of multi-lateral cooperation between higher educational institutions in Europe; the cooperation between higher educational institutions and enterprises; and the spread of innovation and new pedagogical practices and support between universities in Europe. At least for higher police education, it must be stated that the member states could not reach this objective to its full and necessary potential.

The good news for scholars, educators and the public at large, however, is that 20 years onwards, the situation regarding European systems of police education and training is still a bit complicated but certainly not anymore "an utterly confusing one".

Notes

1. The European Police College began as an institutional entity born and financed by the network of national police colleges and academies and converted into an agency of the European Union in 2005. In 2016, the mandate of the agency was expanded to also include border guards, customs officers, prosecutors and other law enforcement personnel and the official name changed to European Union Agency for Law Enforcement Training (CEPOL) (see Regulation (EU) 2015/2219 of the European Parliament and of the Council of 25 November 2015).

2. All responsibility for statements and conclusions presented in this chapter is solely those of the authors. The content of this chapter does neither imply nor reflect endorsement by CEPOL, and shall not be taken in any way as the official position of the agency.

3. Current and exact figures for police officers on the national levels are hard to come by – the figures provided by Eurostat shall be considered as the best available approximation in this regard – see "Personnel in the criminal justice system" (crim_just_job) at http://ec.europa.eu/eurostat/web/crime/database.

4. Appointed members of the ELEES Working Group were André Konze (Germany, chairperson), Gabor Kovacs (Hungary), Joao Cabaco (Portugal) and Renato Raggi (Italy). The group's work was supported by Detlef Nogala (CEPOL).

5. Apart from the police, "law enforcement" would also include customs, border guard or judicial authorities having an investigation mandate.
6. For more information on the AEPC, go to www.aepc.net.
7. For a contemporary account of police reforms in Northern and Western Europe, see Fyfe et al. 2013; for a view from the position of police leadership Caless and Tong 2016.
8. Due to its federal multi-agency set-up, Germany appointed 15 responders.
9. Actually, a follow-up of Q2 was sent out to collect the titles of relevant courses and programmes in order to prepare the principal third stage of the survey.
10. The response rate for questionnaire 1 across all countries and organisations was 85%. For those countries indicating positively such institutions in question in Q1, the response rate in regard to Q2 was 83%. In the case of Q3, the final online questionnaire sent, requesting detailed information on concrete programmes and courses, the response rate halved (41%).
11. CEPOL and Frontex launched their accredited master programmes only in 2015.
12. The ELEES questionnaires did not request reasons for certain developments in the member states or associated countries. It might make sense to give room for such explanations in future surveys.
13. Within that group of 36, there are further differentiations like being a university of applied sciences. Such distinctions have not been further examined or evaluated. It was assumed that these variations are caused by national, historical or cultural reasons.
14. The German Police Academy, for example, became the German Police University simultaneously with the accreditation of its Master's course.
15. The fact that the same number of institutions claims university status is a coincidence. There is an overlap, but there is no dependency between both variables.
16. The state police of North Rhine Westphalia in Germany with almost 45,000 sworn officers accounts for the biggest group of Bologna-students in the ELEES survey.
17. The typical auditor question, if the quality of Bologna-accredited programmes/course justifies the higher costs and efforts, must be answered by the respective institution.
18. A concrete example: The University of Applied Sciences of North Rhine Westphalia, for example, mainly used Ilias© just for administrative issues and for the distribution of material to the students. It might be

worth to observe that development and ask more detailed questions in further CEPOL surveys. This also concerns such institutions, which do not use e-learning programmes at all.

19. Unfortunately, we received no specific information about those programmes in the third step of the survey.
20. However, there is no information available that supports the thesis that there might be a difference in the accreditation quality between internal and external bodies.

References

Caless, B., & Tong, S. (2016). *Leading Policing in Europe: An Empirical Study of Strategic Police Leadership*. Bristol: Policy Press.

CEPOL. (2006). *Survey on European Police Education and Training (SEPE) – Final Report*. Apeldoorn: European Police College.

Ferreira, E., Jaschke, H. G., Peeters, H. & Farina, R. (2010): *Report survey on European police education and Bologna*. CEPOL: Bramshill.

Fyfe, N., Tepstra, J., & Tops, P. (Eds.). (2013). *Centralizing Forces?: Comparative Perspectives on Contemporary Police Reform in Northern and Western Europe*. The Hague: Eleven.

Pagon, M., Virjent-Novak, B., Djuric, M., & Lobnikar, B. (1996). European Systems of Police Education and Training. In M. Pagon (Ed.), *Policing in Central and Eastern Europe: Comparing Firsthand Knowledge with Experience from the West*. Ljubljana: College of Police and Security Studies.

Treaty of Amsterdam Amending the Treaty on European Union, the Treaties Establishing the European Communities and Certain Related Acts. (1997).

Treaty of Lisbon – Amending the Treaty on European Union and the Treaty Establishing the European Community (2007/C 306/01). (2009). *Official Journal of the European Union C 306/1*.

Part III

Application

9

Responding to Needs of Higher Analytical Competence in the Police: Master Programmes at the Norwegian Police University College

Aun Hunsager Andresen and Nina Jon

Introduction

When the Norwegian Police University College offered its first master in police science programme (120 ECTS) in 2006, it was an answer to a perceived need in the police for more analytical skills and competencies among its staff. The goal of the master's degree was to provide more relevant research on policing, analytical competence and strategic work carried out in the police districts. Such competence is an important prerequisite if the police are to develop their knowledge-driven work.

The police have a great need for analytical competence. Benan and Ludvigsen (2013) sharply criticize the police when they conclude that strategic analyses delivered by the country's police districts are more like reports about the police operations than true analyses (Benan and

A.H. Andresen
Agder police precinct, Kristiansand, Norway

N. Jon (✉)
Norwegian Police University College, Oslo, Norway

© The Author(s) 2018
C. Rogers, B. Frevel (eds.), *Higher Education and Police*,
DOI 10.1007/978-3-319-58386-0_9

Ludvigsen 2013). The strategic analyses are descriptive and contain little analysis, and so it is hard to imagine how they can provide a foundation for new ways of acting, which should be created through knowledge-driven policing. Stenbro (2014) shows how documents written about target-oriented management assume that new knowledge will be extracted from these strategic analyses, but if it is the way Benan and Ludvigsen (2013) describe, then it is difficult to envisage how it may be done. They further describe how the local targets are determined on the basis of local prioritizing and experience (Benan and Ludvigsen 2013). Local experience is of course important, and caution is necessary in supposing that all new knowledge has to originate by means of an analysis. Nevertheless, it is hard to see how local experience will end up in knowledge-driven change, which will benefit the whole organization. Such change presumes that knowledge is shared. Tinnholt (2013) has also studied the use of strategic analysis and found that it is little used as a management tool in the police districts, and that in the police sector there is a lack of knowledge about what knowledge-driven policing is about (Tinnholt 2013). Both the "top and the tail" are missing in the strategic work of the organization due to a lack of understanding about what analyses involve. Winsnes (2011) has studied cultural and structural barriers which exist in the fight against organized crime. He shows how commissioning information is regarded as an attack on the personal scope of action, and that this leads to a lost opportunity to analyze the organized crime (Winsnes 2011). If the police are to connect with knowledge-driven policing, then it is also important to be able to relate to analyses as a basis for determining new methods of action.

If requirements for policing activity were to originate from well-educated police leaders and analysts, the policing profession would have much to gain. This argument is also put forward by Gundhus and Bjørkelo (2015), who maintain that top management's understanding will have little effect if there is no trust in other parts of the leadership hierarchy (Gundhus and Bjørkelo 2015, s. 42). If a critical local police leadership with a strong professional culture and good analytical competence could challenge the regulations given, there would be a much better dialogue between the police directorate and the police districts. This is illustrated in a chronicle by Moser m.fl. (2015) where she maintains that well-educated staff in an organization acts as an important driver for innovation and development (Moser m. fl. 2015).

Development of Knowledge-Driven Policing

Upon perusing several of the master theses submitted during the master's programme in police science at the Police University College as well as assignments submitted by students on a master's programme outside PHS, it can be seen that students taking a master's programme acquire perspectives and knowledge, which enable them to identify many of the challenges faced in developing the police into a knowledge-driven and learning organization. We wish to present a few such master theses and show their findings.

Melby's master's thesis (2016) studies the security conversation used by the Norwegian Police Security Agency. Melby sums up by saying that executive officers have little opportunity to take up academic issues. They feel more like individualists than part of an academic fellowship (Melby 2016). The basis for new modes of action is by starting an arena where it is possible to reflect over experiences. Without this, challenges will arise when it comes to initiating knowledge-driven work. In Berge's assignment (2015), there is also a description which can indicate that there are no arenas for sharing experience. The assignment looks at the trust-building work of the police and describes how the work is coincidental and dependent on the person carrying it out, and that greater knowledge is required about which factors impact public confidence (Berge 2015). The fact that the subject is not discussed at police stations shows that there is a lack of reflection over one's own experience, which is the basis for knowledge-driven policing. This will also form the basis for both single-loop and double-loop learning processes (Jacobsen and Thorsvik 2013).

Sporaland's study (2011) of the management group in Rogaland shows that the group is far from being inquisitive, willing to listen and open-minded. It is not interested in asking "why" something works or not. The group is mostly involved in measures for achieving goals, and analyses are omitted. Evaluations are not attempted (Sporaland 2011). Kjærner-Semb (2015) has looked at experiential learning among officers involved in special operations (SO) and technical and tactical surveillance (TTS) and the findings show that there is little sharing and assessment of experiences after assignments. Henriksen (2014) has studied the evaluation of investigative work carried out by the Norwegian police, and the gaps shown are also a clear indication that there does not really exist a culture for assessment in the police. More than half of the informants say that it is not done, or that it is done to a limited extent (Henriksen 2014).

In a knowledge-driven perspective, it is necessary to reflect on experience as well as implement new measures based on analyses. The findings of the master's theses point to the fact that there is a lack of reflection over experience, assessment and analyses. Melby (2016) shows that the security interview is altered individually based on experience, Berge (2015) found that trust-building work was coincidental and dependent on the person involved, Kjærner-Semb (2015) found that there was no system for knowledge-sharing, and Haugland (2014) discovered that there was little sharing of information.

According to Sporaland (2011), the management group in Rogaland used assessment and analysis to very little extent in its work. Winsnes (2011) found cultural resistance to analysis, and Haugland (2014) demonstrates how subjects have been allowed to develop based on assumptions. With regard to assessment as a basis for analyses, Jonassen (2010) points out that there is a lack of assessment after extraordinary incidents. The lack of assessment is also presented in various ways by Kjærner-Semb (2015), Henriksen (2014), and Ørn (2012). These findings have been made at different levels within the organization, but all in all they present a picture of a police service whose work is to little extent knowledge-driven.

A solid finding of the master's theses is that many levels of the police organization experience challenges with double-loop learning where questions are asked about "why" something works, does not work, or about what causes something to be done in a certain way (Støylen 2016; Semb 2015; Haugaland 2014; Ørn 2012; Stenbro 2014; Sporaland 2011; Henriksen 2014; Jonassen 2010; Dyrøy 2010). As the "why" thought is also a major part of systematic thinking (Jacobsen and Thorsvik

2013), this appears as an important finding which has to be considered if the police are to develop as a learning organization. The findings also show that the critical view that the master students have of policing activities is based on critical rationality which the police as an organization can greatly benefit from.

The Learning Organization

If the knowledge-driving force is purely to be found at a strategic level in the organization, there is little connection to the systematic thinking where everyone sees "*entirety and connections within the organization as a whole*" (Jacobsen and Thorsvik 2013, p. 369). In such a case "firewalls of resistance" to new ways of thinking in the organization can also develop more easily (Gundhus 2009, p. 203), which again can inhibit the development of the police as a learning organization. With this term, Gundhus means that when there is an attempt to introduce or try out something new, it is slowed down or halted within the organization itself. When using an analytical approach, signals are sent that the professional judgment of the police officer is undervalued. In addition, ideas about what is regarded as "proper policing" are challenged, and the new working methods are regarded as a work tool for management to keep an eye on the work that is being done (Gundhus 2009, p. 226).

This also shows that culture is a factor to take into account when assessing the police's ability to develop as a learning organization. Dyrøy's findings (2010) also indicate that there is a lack of systematic thinking when it comes to work on strategy. He shows that there is a wish to work in a strategic and preventative manner at a senior level, but that at lower levels cases mostly end up being solved on a criminal law level (Dyrøy 2010). This also confirms that there may be a division in the organization between the operative and the strategic areas. If there is no single approach to the reactive and strategic work being done in the organization, it will be difficult to develop an organization which has common goals.

With regard to Norway, Winnæss and Helland (2014) found out that students at the Police University College are not so interested in theoretical office work. On the contrary, practical outdoor work has positive connotations (Winnæss, P. and Helland, H. 2014, p. 1). Furthermore, they describe how "the police occupation is the sunlight and police education is the shade". This has an impact on the way in which new knowledge and analytical approaches to police operations are assessed. Today's police students are tomorrow's leaders. Aas (2014) has conducted a qualitative study of "the police practitioner's view of police education" in Norway. Several of his findings point to the fact that it is practical knowledge based on experience which takes the focus (Aas 2014, p. 29). He also points to the fact that the informants in the survey regard basic common sense as the source of direction when solving police missions (Aas 2014, s. 31). This contributes to further reinforcing the distance between what is learned through education and what is based on intuition. Knowledge ideals in operative culture can thus contribute to putting a brake on the knowledge-driven approach which is emphasized in higher education. This has been confirmed in international surveys.

The findings of White and Heslop (2012) confirm those of Winnæss and Helland (2014) when they describe how police students take a police education because they wish to become police officers, not because they have a desire for any particular education. Moreover, they point to how the police in England are in a special position compared to other professions with regard to defining the content of the profession based on practical training as well as practical work experience (White, D. and Heslop, R. 2012). Jaschke and Neidhardt (2007) have also drawn a parallel with this from Germany when they underline the fact that there exists cultural resistance to police research. Whereas the police officer is involved in decision-making and dealing with urgent practical tasks, the researcher is engaged in reading, reflecting, asking questions, discussing, conveying insecurity and writing academic texts. These two worlds are not completely compatible (Jaschke and Neidhardt 2007, p. 315).

The lack of higher education in the Norwegian police can contribute to extending the cultural divisions, as well as preserving attitudes which have been engrained in the organization. Those with a higher education can add new perspectives and create a foundation for change, but when this group comprises a small minority, any processes of change are more likely to be halted by the culture. This is also pointed out by Graner and Kronkvist (2014) who write that there have to be enough people in the organization who choose new working methods and ways of thinking (Graner and Kronkvist 2014, p. 75).

Master Programme as an Answer to the Need

Knowledge about policing operations as well as analytical competence will provide the police with better ability to conduct their work in a strategic way. Knowledge-driven policing must be more than just rhetoric. It will also make it easier for the police as a profession to justify their choices. It is also a matter of having people who can come up with new ideas, who possess vision and encourage creativity among the employees. As a response to this need, the Norwegian Police University College is offering master degree programmes.

Education at master's level has a quality which distinguishes it from other education. Not only is new knowledge attained, it is also produced. This requires curiosity, systematics and creativity. It should be possible to ask *why* something is the way it is. The ability to pose the "why" question is a major part of double-loop learning as well as organizational learning (Jacobsen and Torsvik 2013). If one has knowledge about methodology, it will be easier to demand the reason for conclusions that have been reached, and one will be more critical about simple conclusions and "everyday generalizations" (Johannessen, m. fl. 2005), common among all of us. Furthermore, an introduction to research ethics and issues related to the philosophy of science has a major role in the master programmes. There is focus on having a critical and reflected approach to the role as a researcher and to the various views of knowledge existing within police science and investigation.

Currently, the Police University College offers two master's programmes. A third one is being developed. A Nordic master's degree in police management (90 ECTs) is being set up, and the goal is to offer this programme from January 2018. In addition, the Police University College cooperates with NTNU in connection with an experiential master's degree in Digital Forensics and Cybercrime Investigation. This provides specialization in cyber investigation and working practice with regard to forensics, legal protection and the right to privacy.

The two master's degrees already offered at the Police University College are the master's degree in police science and the experiential master's degree in investigation. These will be further presented below.

Master in Police Science

The master's degree in police science has been offered at PHS since 2006. Police Science is an interdisciplinary science which includes research on the police as an institution and on the broader term "policing". Policing is a form of formal control, its main purpose being to uphold law, order and security within society. It can be seen in policing that the police themselves are only one of several players exercising control and surveillance. Police tasks are constantly changing. There is geographical and historical variation with regard to who executes policing tasks. This makes it essential to differentiate between the police as an institution and policing as a process for studying the phenomenon irrespective of time or place.

The purpose of police science is primarily to develop knowledge that the police need in order to understand and carry out their tasks. At the same time police science will contribute to knowledge and critical reflection regarding the tasks of the police in society and the roles and activities of those who conduct policing. A lot of valuable experience-based and silent knowledge is to be found within the ranks of the police, and this has to very little extent been the object of systematic reflection and documentation. The goal of the master's degree in police science is to further develop this knowledge with the help of scientific methods and theory.

The purpose of the master's programme in police science is to raise the level of analytical and research competence in the police. The programmes will contribute to strengthening police competence within knowledge-driven and strategic policing. It provides a qualification applicable to various national and international policing tasks such as analysis, project management and strategic control. The programme is relevant for everyone who wishes to contribute to knowledge-sharing and the development of police science. The main target group of the master's programmes are those with a police education as well as those employed in the police service.

Content and Organization

The programme is organized into nine courses which are interconnected. In total, the courses make up the master's degree in police science which consists of 120 ECT.

Model for the Master's Programme in Police Science

Module 9: Master Thesis (30 ECTS)
Module 8: Project Design (5 ECTS)
Module 7: Depth Studies in Methods (10 ECTS)
7 A: Qualitative Methods **or**
7 B: Quantitative Methods
Module 6: Optional Modules (15 ECTS)
Module 5: Police as Knowledge-based Organization: Intelligence, Analysis and Evaluation (15 ECTS)
Module 4: Research Methods (10 ECTS)
Module 3: Scientific Theory and Research Ethics (5 ECTS)
Module 2: Policing and Practices (15 ECTS)
Module 1: Introduction to Police Science (15 ECTS)

The model illustrates that courses 1, 2, 3, 5 and 9 are specific for the master's programme in police science and are obligatory for all students. Courses 4 and 8 are held simultaneously with corresponding courses in the experiential master's programmes in investigation. In course 6, students take a subject area of their choice. In addition, students in course 7 have to choose between specializations in qualitative or quantitative methodology.

The master's programme is offered on a part-time basis and consists of seminars and independent study. The length of the programme is four years, allowing for average progression.

Learning Outcome

A candidate who completes the programme successfully will have the following total learning outcome defined as knowledge, skills and general competence:

- Knowledge

- The candidate

    - Has advanced knowledge of the basic theories and methods used in police science
    - Has advanced knowledge of research on policing and practice
    - Has thorough knowledge about the police as a knowledge-driven organization
    - Can apply knowledge in new areas
    - Can apply knowledge in planning, designing and implementing professional research and development
    - Can analyze professional problem areas within the framework of police science seen from the perspectives of history, traditions, distinctive character and social position

- Skills

- The candidate can

    - Analyze existing theories, methods and interpretations within police science and work independently with practical and theoretical problem-solving
    - Use relevant scientific methods in research and academic development in an independent manner
    - Analyze and relate critically to various sources of information and apply these to structuring and formulating academic reasoning
    - Carry out an independent, specialized R&D project under supervision and in line with the ethical norms that apply within research

Master's Degree in Criminal Investigation

This master's programme has just recently started up at PHS, and the first students were admitted in spring 2016. Investigation is one of the police's core tasks where quick response and good quality are required at all levels. It is a subject area with long traditions. New knowledge is constantly being developed based on both systematic experience and various branches of knowledge. The ability of the police to conduct successful investigation has an impact on how secure people feel and to what extent they perceive their legal rights as being ensured. Therefore it is of utmost importance that the police possess a high level of investigative competence, and that this is embedded in documented knowledge.

The Police University College offers an experiential master's programmes in investigation to meet the need for knowledge-based, academic specialization and professional management linked to the work practice.

In addition to academic specialization, the programme focuses on critical reflection over ethical dilemmas and roles in investigation work.

Through increased understanding of phenomena within the field and heightened competence in applying knowledge-based methods of investigation, the master's programme will contribute to furthering the theoretical and practical development of investigation as a subject.

The purpose of the master's programme in investigation is to heighten competence among police investigators and staff in civil service departments that collaborate with the police. After completing education, students will possess both broad competence in general investigative tasks and special competence in areas of specific phenomena within the field of investigation. The programme provides a qualification that is applicable to a wide spectrum of tasks and can be implemented both in defined academic positions and in daily operations as investigator, head of section, supervisor and mentor. The programme is relevant for all those who wish to contribute to sharing and developing knowledge within the field of investigation.

The main target group are staff in the police and the prosecuting authorities that have major roles and tasks within various areas of investigation. The programme is open to applicants from the police in other Nordic countries.

Content and Organization

The programme consists of seven integrated and interrelated courses, which in total make up the experiential master's degree in investigation with 90 ECT.

Model for the Experiential Master's Degree in Investigation

Module 7: Master Thesis – 30 ECTS
Module 6: Project Design – 5 ECTS
Module 5A[a]:   Module 5B: Digital evidence
Investigation of Aggravated Assault   and Cybercrime Investigation
and Homicide – 15 ECTS   – 15 ECTS
Module 4:Strategic Leadership and Mentoring for Investigative Work and Studies– 10 ECTS
Module 3: Methodological Topics in Investigation – 10 ECTS
Module 2: Research Methods –10 ECTS
Module 1: Investigation Processes –10 ECTS

[a]Module 5: Elective part in either 5A or 5B

The model shows that courses 1, 3, 4 and 7 are specific for the experiential master's programme in investigation and are compulsory for all students. Courses 2 and 6 coincide with corresponding courses in the disciplinary master's degree in police science at the Police University College. Students are offered two elective courses and need to complete either 5A or 5B.

Organization and Work Methods

The master's programme is part-time and consists of seminars and independent studies. Three years is the nominal length of study. The first three courses are set up during the first and second semesters. Course 4, the elective subject, and course 6 take place in the third and fourth semesters. Independent study connected to the master's thesis is carried out during the final two semesters. Students have a supervisor appointed to provide assistance during this process.

Learning Outcome

The seven subjects in the master's programme will promote a holistic and total learning outcome as described under knowledge, skills and general competence.

• Knowledge

• After completing the master's programme, students have:

- Advanced knowledge about investigation as a subject and field of profession
- Specialized insight into specific cases in investigation and pertaining methods of investigation
- Comprehensive knowledge about the types of knowledge that investigation is embedded in, both experiential knowledge and research-based knowledge and methodology

After completing the Master's programme, students can:

- Apply knowledge in planning, designing and carrying out professional development and projects connected to investigation
- Analyze professional issues from the perspective of investigation as well as its significance for combatting and preventing crime

• Skills

• After completing the master's programme, students can:

- Reflect critically over knowledge and practice in the field of investigation, and the role of investigation in the judicial process
- Analyze theories, concepts and methods to be applied in investigation
- Apply relevant methods for developing knowledge within investigation

- Analyze critically various sources of knowledge and information
- Develop and conduct professional project/development work
- Plan, conduct and assess investigation

Conclusion

By offering master's programmes, the Police University College hopes to contribute to increased academic competence in the police. The general competence provided by a master's degree in police science will enable the candidate to act with professional integrity, to respect the ethical norms of research, as well as to display professional and ethical conduct and critical reflection with regard to established police practice and the role of the police in society. Furthermore, the candidate is able to analyze relevant ethical issues connected to the field, conduct independent, specialized R&D projects and disseminate comprehensive work carried out independently. In addition, the candidate learns to communicate about professional issues, analyses, methodological approaches and conclusions both with specialists and to the general public, as well as applying knowledge and skills in new areas, thus creating innovation and new thinking.

For candidates attending the experiential master's programme in investigation, the general competence involves the students being able to analyze and assess advanced professional issues, as well as apply their knowledge and skills to advanced tasks and projects within the organization and management of investigation. Moreover, they learn how to disseminate independent work and master professional forms of expression used in investigation, communicate professional issues, analyses, methodological approaches and conclusions within a specialized area of investigation. In addition, the candidates learn how to constructively and critically contribute to processes of innovation and new thinking within investigation, and analyze and assess ethical dilemmas when carrying out investigations.

These goals have been established in order to increase the level of competence among police investigators, to raise the analytical and research competence of the police, and to strengthen competence in knowledge-driven and strategic policing.

References

Aas. (2014). *Kvalitetsundersøkelsen: Politiutøverens syn på politiutdanningen* (p. 2). Oslo: PHS Forskning.

Benan, & Ludvigsen K. (2013). *Kunnskapsstyrt politi: Strategiske analyser i praksis* (Masteroppgave, PHS). Hentet fra http://www.nb.no/id tjeneste/URN: NBN: no-bibsys_brage_43575

Berge. (2015). *Et politiblikk på tillit: En studie av politiets publikumsrettede tillitsarbeid* (Masteroppgave, PHS). Hentet fra http://hdl.handle.net/11250/2358418

Bjørkelo, B., & Gundhus, H. I. (2015). Å forbedre en etat. *Magma, 2,* 36–46.

Dyrøy, Å. (2010). *If It's Not a Case It's Not a Problem: A Study of Resource Allocation Within the Norwegian Police* (Masteroppgave, PHS). http://idtjeneste.nb.no/URN:NBN:no-bibsys_brage_18759

Graner og Kronkvist. (2014). *Kontroll av og i politiorganisasjonen I: Innføring i politivitenskap* (Larsson m. fl. 2014). Oslo: Cappelen Damm.

Gundhus. (2009). For sikkerhets skyld: IKT, yrkeskulturer og kunnskapsarbeid i politiet. Oslo: Unipub.

Haugland. (2014). *Hva kan forklare veksten i bevæpningsordrer i politiet?* (Masteroppgave, PHS). Hentet fra http://hdl.handle.net/11250/275157

Henriksen. (2014). *Politiet som lærende organisasjon* (Masteroppgave, UIO).

Jacobsen, D. I., & Thorsvik, J. (2013). *Hvordan organisasjoner fungerer: Innføring i organisasjon og ledelse.* Bergen: Fagbokforlaget.

Jaschke, H.-G., & Neidhardt, K. (2007). A Modern Police Science as an Integrated Academic Discipline: A Contribution to the Debate on Its Fundamentals. *Policing and Society, 17*(4), 303–320.

Johannessen, m. fl. (2005). Samfunnsvitenskapelig metode.

Jonassen. (2010). *Evaluering av ekstraordinære hendelser i politiet som grunnlag for utvikling v ny kunnskap* (Masteroppgave, PHS). Hentet fra http://hdl.handle.net/11250/174767

Kjærner-Semb. (2015). *Å lære seg sivilt politiarbeid: En kvalitativ studie av erfaringslæring ved Spesielle Operasjoner og Teknisk og Taktisk Spaning* (Masteroppgave, PHS). Hentet fra http://hdl.handle.net/11250/2375445

Melby. (2016). *Bruk av sikkerhetssamtalen som metode ved et utvalg klareringsmyndigheter* (Masteroppgave, PHS). Hentet fra http://hdl.handle.net/11250/2389987

Moser, I., Frafjord, A., & Getrang, H. (2015). *Hvorfor er master i helse og sosialfag noe negativt?* Hentet 18 August 2015 fra http://Forskning.no/meninger/kronikk/2015/04/Hvem-har-mastersyken

Ørn M. (2012). *"Den som har begge bena på jorda, står stille": en studie av hvorfor politiet viderefører det straffeforfølgende paradigmet for å redusere distribusjonen av narkotika i Norges tre største byer og hvordan videreføringen påvirker det forebyggende paradigmet* (Masteroppgave, PHS). Hentet fra http://www.nb.no/idtjeneste/URN:NBN:no-bibsys_brage_37733

Sporaland. (2011). *"En for alle, alle for en?": en studie av ledergruppen i Rogaland politidistrikt som en kunnskapsbasert virksomhet!* (Masteroppgave, PHS). Hentet fra http://hdl.handle.net/11250/174769

Stenbro. (2014). *Politiets rasjonale i endring : en diskursanalyse av politi- oglens-mannsetatens styrings- og handlingsbetingelser* (Masteroppgave, PHS). Hentet fra http://hdl.handle.net/11250/191051

Støylen. (2016). *Hemmeligholdets makt: Hvordan konstruerer hemmelighold samarbeidspraksis mellom Politiets sikkerhetstjeneste og Den Kongelige polities-korte?* (Masteroppgave, PHS). Hentet fra http://hdl.handle.net/11250/2382366

Tinholt, L. H. (2013). *Kunnskapsstyrt politiarbeid: i hvilken grad benyttes kunns-kapsgrunnalget i strategiske analyser som styringsverktøy* (Masteroppgave, Politihøgskolen). Hentet fra http://www.nb.no/idtjeneste/URN:NBN:no-bibsys_brage_42830

White, D., & Heslop, R. (2012). Educating, Legitimising or Accessorising? Alternative Conceptions of Professional Training in UK Higher Education: A Comparative Study of Teacher, Nurse and Police Officer Educators. *Police Practice and Research, 13*(4), 342–356.

Winnæss, P., & Helland, H. (2014). Politistudentene: Hvem er de og hvorfor vil de bli politi? *Nordisk politiforskning, 1*(2), 93–123.

Winsnes. (2011). *Kunnskapsstyrt politiarbeid: kulturelle og strukturelle barrierer i bekjempelsen av organisert kriminalitet* (Masteroppgave PHS). Hentet fra http://hdl.handle.net/11250/174779

10

Starting as a *Kommissar*/Inspector? – The State's Career System and Higher Education for Police Officers in Germany

Bernhard Frevel

Since the mid-1970s, police officers in Germany – more or less – enjoyed higher education, when they aimed to become a *Kommissar*, a rank, which is comparable to the inspector in the UK system. So the German police have about 40 years of experience with higher education. The importance of higher education grew over the years, for example, because of factual necessities in the context of social changes (knowledge society, democratisation, etc.), challenging developments in the fields of crime, terrorism, and so forth or the police unions' demands to improve the social situation of officers. This paper discusses the development of higher education for the police against the background of the German framework for public services and the political decisions following a consulting report from the early 1990s. The system of higher education will be presented and explained with the example of North Rhine-Westphalia. A critical view on the acceptance and effects of the system leads to a final discussion about the perspectives of a university-educated police.

B. Frevel (✉)
University of Applied Science for Public Administration North Rhine-Westphalia, Münster, Germany

© The Author(s) 2018
C. Rogers, B. Frevel (eds.), *Higher Education and Police*,
DOI 10.1007/978-3-319-58386-0_10

The Police System and State's Career System in Germany

Since the founding of the Federal Republic of Germany in 1949, the police are in the main responsibility of the member states, the so-called *Länder*. Only in a few fields the federal state has own police competences with the Federal Police (border control, policing the railway and airports, protection of federal property) and the Federal Office for Criminal Investigation.

The 16 *Länder* and the federal state have the right to formulate their own police legislation, their own police organisation and also to decide about the personal matters such as recruitment and education. But all *Länder* and the federal state act in a common framework for the public service, which regulates the rank system and – with chances of specifications – the payment of public servants (Groß and Frevel 2016). A specific of the German system is the differentiation of 'employees' and so-called *Beamte*. All sworn police officers belong to the group of *Beamte*, which means that they have a special binding to the state, are a target group for specific laws, receive a broader social support, but are – on the other hand – not allowed to strike or to negotiate the earnings.

Traditionally, the police had a four-tier career system like also the other career paths of *Beamte* in the public administration, the military and other public sectors.

- The 'simple career path' is for the easiest tasks (pushing files around, conductor in a bus, etc.), which need no intensive education. The growing complexity of public services made it necessary to qualify and to pay the staff better, so the 'simple career path' is nearly dissolved and less than 3 per cent of the *Beamte* in all public services belong to this group.
- The 'middle career path' is for those *Beamte* who have to deal with a bit more responsible tasks, but work under – more or less intensive – guidance and supervision. The individual responsibility is low, while the supervisors are in duty to lead and control the activities. This middle career path needs a professional education of at least two,

mainly three years, which includes practical training (two-thirds of time) and also school-education (one-third).

- The 'upper career path' is for those jobs, which demand individual responsibility, a broad spectrum of knowledge and skills and requires a qualification of a (minimum) three-year university course with the degree of a bachelor (of arts, of science, of laws ...). In the police this would be for the ranks of Inspector and Chief inspector, which are named in Germany Kommissar, Oberkommissar, Hauptkommissar.
- The 'higher career path' is for the senior officers in the rank of superintendent and higher. They have to absolve a master degree (or similar university degrees).

In the German police, the simple career path is dissolved completely. The following figure gives an overview about the German police rank system and the belonging insignia (Fig. 10.1).

Regarding the different police systems in the UK and Germany, a rough comparison would be that the constable and sergeant equate the ranks in the middle career path, the inspector and chief inspector match the upper career path with *Kommissar* up to *Hauptkommissar*, while the *Polizeirat* up to *Leitender Polizeidirektor* are similar to superintendent up to the chief constable.

Until the 1980s, the police in Germany followed the education and training concept of a 'uniform career track' (Groß 2003: 142), which meant that every police recruit started with a vocational training and aimed to become a *Polizeimeister* (similar to constable). Therefore, he (and later also she[1]) underwent a military like training (usually) at formed units of the riot police. After the training, the young officers who worked in the patrol or in the formed units were promoted and about 10 % had the chance to get further education (in the force or later at universities of applied science) and to become a *Kommissar* (similar inspector). Less than 2 % of the police officers visited the Police Leadership Academy and were promoted to *Polizeirat* (superintendent) and got the chance for further career steps.

The philosophy behind this concept was the idea that police work 'on the beat' and on patrol is more handicrafts and requires more experience

Middle career path (blue stars on epaulettes)		Upper career path (silver stars)		Higher career path (golden stars)	
Polizeimeister-anwärter		Polizeikommissar		Polizeirat	
Polizeimeister		Polizeiober-kommissar		Polizeioberrat	
Polizeiobermeister		Polizeihaupt-kommissar		Polizei-direktor	
Polizeihaupt-meister		Polizeihaupt-kommissar		Leitender Polizei-direktor	
Polizeihaupt-meister		Erster Polizeihaupt-kommissar		Vize-Präsident, Präsident and other official ranks	 up to 

Fig. 10.1   Police ranks in Germany

and practical skills than knowledge and science. Only the middle and higher management would need more abstract or even science-based knowledge. The ability 'to kick in the door at half past five in the morning' was considered more important than the reflection of the social background of a conflict or the jurisprudential analysis and legal or ethical discussion of action.

In the 1970s and 1980s, some younger police leaders initiated a quite intensive discussion about police and policing in Germany. They demanded a more civilian than paramilitary-oriented policing, a police that should protect the citizens and society but not primarily the state. They wanted a police reform that, for example, should include more training of communication and de-escalation, the integration of women in the force, a different career track and a better education (Gintzel 2014). The police unions, that saw the chance to improve the social situation of the officers in a reformed force, assisted (some of) these demands.

'Kienbaum Report' and the Consequences

In the early 1990s, the Ministry of Interior of North Rhine-Westphalia asked – inspired by the requests of the police unions – the consultant agency Kienbaum to analyse the work of police officers, their competences and power, for example, regarding the intervention in fundamental rights of people, the range of duties and the needed qualification. The conclusion of the Kienbaum Report (1991) was serious: Being a police officer is challenging and needs so many different qualifications that the job marks the indicators for being categorised for the 'upper career path'. Kienbaum recommended dissolving the middle career path, not to recruit for this path any longer, to qualify the 'sergeants' for being 'inspectors' and to recruit only for the upper career path.

The suggestion of having all police officers in the upper career path would – in the ideal world – mean:

- A longer, science-based police education is leading to,
- better knowledge about law (especially criminal law and traffic law) and social processes in the society,

- higher policing skills and social competences,
- better results of policing (less crime, less accidents, better clear-up rates, higher satisfaction of citizens with the police, less fear of crime, etc.),
- less misbehaviour of police officers,
- trustful relationship between police and public, and
- better, court-proof files leading to efficient trials and fair sentences.

The Kienbaum Report initialised a very intensive discussion about the police, the career paths, the police education and training. The 17 ministries of interior, the chiefs of police, the unions and other stakeholders debated about the consequences. Six German member states (North Rhine-Westphalia, Hessen, Lower Saxony, Bremen, Saarland and Rhineland-Pfalz) decided to follow Kienbaum's suggestions and to initiate a two-tier career system (upper and higher career path), while the other *Länder* and also the Federal Police stick to the traditional three-tier system (by offering a direct access to the upper career path based on a police university degree).

To implement the two-tier career path, new recruits are only employed for the upper career path, while the elder employees were either promoted on a feat-track or had to get a further education at the university.

The conversion of the North Rhine-Westphalia (NRW) police can be shown with some data to illustrate the significant change in their structure of staff (Table 10.1).

Table 10.1 Staff in different career paths

	Medium	Upper	Upper in % of total	Higher	Higher in % of total	Total
1970	30,258	2,714	8.14	366	1.10	33,338
1980	34,731	6,579	15.73	510	1.22	41,820
1990	29,613	9,890	24.69	555	1.39	40,058
1998	8,524	31,944	77.57	714	1.73	41,182
2013	0	39,317	98.21	715	1.79	40,032

Source: 1970–1998: Innenministerium NRW 1999: 2; 2013: Landesregierung NRW 2013: 72

The consequences for the implementation of the two-tier career system are significant:

> Beside fitness and healthiness, law-abiding behaviour, English knowledge, driving licence and a successful assessment every recruit has to prove the qualification for the university entrance (either by subject specified or general Abitur, similar to A-level in UK, or other entrance qualification based on a mixture of school exams, professional education and work experience[2]).

> All (!) police recruits in NRW have to complete a three-year Bachelor course at the University of Applied Science for Public Administration and Management North Rhine-Westphalia, a university, which belongs to the portfolio of the Ministry of Interior.

> The police education is to a large extent based on science, but also includes a lot of practical training (see below).

> The graduates start the career as Kommissar (Inspector), which means that the Inspector delivers the everyday operative duties (patrol, basic investigation, protection of property [embassies, synagogues, ministries etc.], riot police), the Ober- und Hauptkommissar conduct more ambitious processing and middle-management leadership.

Hence, the police in NRW underwent an 'escalator effect' as described by Ulrich Beck (1986: 124, 139; 1992): All ranks are upgraded – but the system of work and also the inequalities of power stay put. The change includes a certain upgrade for the police officers, as the job is seen as especially challenging, and demanding a higher education. On the other hand, it means a degradation of the rank: the *Kommissar, Ober-* and *Hauptkommissar* of the upper career path belonged to the 'top 10' in the 1970s, while now the *Kommissars* are at the bottom of the ladder.

Especially, the police unions belonged to the principal supporters of the two-tier career path, they pointed towards the important role of the police, the everyday challenges of the job, the responsibility of the officers and the rapid changes of the task of fighting crime and securing society. But beneath these arguments, the core duty of the unions gleams: The implementation of the two-tier career path meant a considerable raise of salary and being *Kommissar* is more prestigious and higher valued than *Polizeimeister.*

On the other hand, it implies a reduction of promotion prospects. While in the 1980s, most of the officers had realistic chances to be promoted from *Meister* to *Obermeister* to *Hauptmeister* to *Kommissar* and eventually up to the other ranks in the upper and higher career path, most of the *Kommissars* nowadays have only the chance to become *Hauptkommissar* – and just to go two steps upwards before retirement, and to a large amount still doing the job in the patrol car.

To refinance the costs of this change to the two-tier career path at least rudimentarily, the government put up the working hours per week (now 41), rose the retiring age to 63, created cut backs on extra vacation payment and Christmas bonus. Or simply: *The Lord giveth, the Lord taketh away.*

The Higher Education of Police

Regardless whether a *Land* decided to implement the two-tier career path or sticks to the three-tier model, every Land established and operates a specialised institute for the higher education of police, which qualifies officers for the upper career. Some are named police university, some police academy or university of applied science for public administration. As police are a responsibility of the *Länder* (Groß and Frevel 2016), very different models and curricula can be seen. With the exception of Berlin, the institutes are 'internal' universities belonging to the portfolio and supervision of the Ministry of Interior and not of the Ministry of Education and Science.

The studies are organised in a system of dual university programmes, meaning that they include academic education, practical training and internships with the police. The students get a combination of scientific education, practical/applied science, job skills and knowledge. While in some police academies, education and training are directly linked and offered on the academy premises, other universities appoint the training task to different education partners, which are directly linked to the force.

The dual system has some particular advantages, as the students get a theoretical fundament and practical competences. Dual studies are getting very popular in Germany, not only in the field of police and public administration but also business administration, in technical disciplines and social services (Bär 2016). But they force and challenge the students to live and learn with the contradictory logics of the systems and cultures of police and science.

While **police**...	**science** aims to
are interested in training,	educate,
reduces complexity,	introduce complexity,
want to evolve homogeneity,	point out heterogeneity,
force the officers to accept hierarchy,	irritate hierarchy,
strive legal realisation,	allow social realisation,
follow a technical approach to deal with practical problems efficiently,	favour a methodical approach to analyse problems of knowledge systematically,
needs rapid action in interaction with object,	support reflection and consideration with distance to object,
have to act fast and efficient with the objects,	analyse calm and with distance to the object.

Inspired by Ohlemacher 2016: 16; Bornewasser 2002: 17.

The tension between police and science becomes obvious when a curriculum has to be developed, the learning goals to be described and the shares of learning time to be distributed. Every discipline points out its importance for the successful education.

The Example: Studying Police in North Rhine-Westphalia

The police force in North Rhine-Westphalia employs about 40,000 police officers plus administration staff. This force grew in the 1970s and 1980s, and a large amount of officers is going to retire in the next years. The average age in the NRW police force is 44.90 years, but especially in rural parts of NRW some forces have an average age of about 50 (MIK 2014: 7). Therefore, the police have to 'renew' the personnel. In 2013 and 2014 about 1500 and in 2015 and 2016 about 2000 new recruits joined the force and began to study at the University of Applied Science for Public Administration (*Fachhochschule für öffentliche Verwaltung NRW – FHöV*). The Ministry of Interior plans to increase this high numbers from 2017 to 2022 up to 2.300. This degree course is one of the largest courses in the German university system.

The interest persons apply at the police, have to do an online precheck, are invited to an assessment of three days (tests, interviews, medical check) and eventually employed as a '*Beamte auf Probe*' (probationary officer). They are paid during the study/education and earn (in 2016) 1140 Euro, which is about 950 British Pounds a month. Being employed and paid means that the students are not free in their decision to attend or miss a lecture: the attendance is compulsory.

This course is delivered not only by the university at its eight locations in the different parts of the country but also its partners, which are the State Office for Education, Training and Personnel Matters of the Police NRW (LAFP) and the 47 regional police forces.

The recruits study the theory at the FHöV (72 weeks +7 weeks writing bachelor thesis), learn practical policing in a training atmosphere at the LAFP (25 weeks) and have to gain experience during internships at a police department (36 weeks) as well in matters of deployment, criminal investigation and traffic.

As it would be too extensive to describe the educational system in depth, it should be enough to list the titles of the modules in an overview.

- Police in state and society: scientific work and learning, political science, sociology, psychology, public services law, ethics
- Deployment law and state's law: constitution and fundamental rights, framework of policing, legal basis of police power
- Deployment: basics of tactic, surveillance and operation with small units
- Criminal law: basics, crime against persons and property
- Crime control: criminalistics, forensics, first actions at a crime scene and filing charges
- Road safety: basics of traffic policing, traffic offences

- Training: operational standards, crime control, traffic control, acquisition of accident data
- Delinquency in the public space and domestic violence: law, tactics and criminology
- Fighting petty crime and medium crime: operational service, forensics
- Causes of delinquency and planning of police action: criminology, dealing with offenders, victims and witnesses, crime analysis and crime prevention, collaboration and leadership
- Seminar I
- Training: every day deployment, crime scene activities, traffic control
- Deployment and operative services in cases of special crime: crime control, offender – victim and prognosis, urban sociology, sociology of violence and force
- Legal classification of police operations: criminal law, personal freedom and participation, traffic accidents, traffic crime
- Police operation with high risks of conflict and danger: accidents, demonstrations, stress – burden, emergency psychology, victim support, threats against own and other life; English
- Seminar II
- Training: operations with high risks of conflict in everyday tasks, case processing of criminal investigation, operations in special settings (large groups of persons, Amok, special organisation), traffic accidents
- Internship: patrol, criminal investigation
- Current challenges of (international) police work: outstanding and current operations, outstanding and current types of crime, foreigners in traffic, crimes against the state and malpractice/abuse of office, police in historical change, Europeanization of internal security, rights to intervene in international collaboration, technical English
- Elective module/current developments
- Training: police operation in dangerous situation, operation by particular crime, acquisition of data in cases of complex accidents
- Practical training: shooting – not-shooting, techniques of intervention, driving training, first aid, communication systems, photography, sports, deployment training, fire-fighting,
- Training of social competences

- Reflection of professional role and experiences
- Thesis (*Source*: FHöV NRW: Modulhandbuch Bachelorstudiengang PVD, 2016: I f)

This list of modules reveals a lot of information about the job profile of police officers and the self-perception of the police in Germany, here North Rhine-Westphalia. Dealing with crime and difficult situations, like accidents, are the main tasks of police. This requires special skills and must be lawful. Police work concentrates on the specific situation and has to understand this in the social context. In the words of the module-handbook, this is described as followed:

'Professional competence:
The students

- *plan and fulfil the core tasks in the fields of threat aversion/deployment, crime fighting and road safety during the beat duties and response under estimation of the social, societal and juristic frame conditions,*
- *integrate themselves in the deployment organisation during operations of special causes and decide about measures in the beginning phase under consideration of the particularities of the single case,*
- *process cases of simple and medium crime and analyse preliminary pro-ceedings of criminal investigation.'* (Fachhochschule für öffentliche Verwaltung NRW, 2016: 2)

Rules and theory of policing, law and social sciences are taught at the university. The lecturers are experienced police officers (mainly belonging to the higher career path), which are employed at the university or more often deputed for about five years from the force, or professors and lec-turers with an academic background. Hourly paid lecturers, doing this in a sideline job beside their tasks as police officers or scientists, deliver about 40 % of the lectures. This mixture should guarantee a nearness to the actual practice as well as theory-based knowledge transfer. The recruits learn in classes of about 30 students.

The training at the LAFP happens in smaller groups of about 12 to 15 students and is guided by experienced police officers of the upper career path. Role-plays, exercises and tutorials belong to this part of the education.

During the internships, each student is assigned to a personal tutor, who is a qualified police officer and coaches the student during the everyday practice either on patrol or processing criminal investigation.

An Accepted Concept?

The *Fachhochschule* evaluates continuously the teaching and the programme. The students are asked to give feedback on each module and the lecturers, and the programme in a whole. Beside an online questionnaire, which is regularly used, also group interviews with students, lecturers, trainers and tutors were conducted (Drees 2015). Some important findings of Drees are:

- Overall the police students in North Rhine-Westphalia are very or quite satisfied with the course, its content and the organisation.
- The basic studies in the first year are estimated very differently. The students would wish to extend the 'major subjects', including law, with the direct reference to policing and would accept reduction in the 'minors' such as sociology and scientific methods. The amount of study matter and the level of difficulty of exams are seen critically.
- These critics are also mentioned in the evaluation of the main study 1 (beginning of second year): The study load would be too high, the examination requirements opaque and the assessment criteria would be heterogeneous. In main study 2 (end of second year) the workload for the exams was criticised.
- Continuous opinion of 30 to 50 % of the students is that the different social sciences would have too much space in the course, could not prove their job relevance sufficiently, and would be too academic.
- The preparation for the internships would be better delivered in the trainings than in the theory at university.
- The idea of the dual study is, in total, highly esteemed. But often the students criticise that the teaching content would not be coordinated enough between university, training centre and practice. Also some lecturers, trainers and tutors would disagree with the content taught by the partners (motto: 'Forget everything you have learnt at the university, this is the real policing' resp. 'What you have learnt from your tutor is not state of the art and even wrong/illicit').

Put in a nutshell, the students (and also some practitioners, who work with the graduates), the critics concentrate on

- too much/wrong theory
- too much academic skills
- too few practical relevance

for the competencies required for 'duties on the street'.

This critic is not shared by all students as there is a broad range of attitudes and student-characters. Bernhardt and Christe-Zeyse (2016: 25) tried to categorise the students at the Police University of Brandenburg and differed three types:

- Group A: competent and interested students, who enjoy discussion, reflection and scientific topics and see a study as a good fundament for the oncoming job in the police;
- Group B: students, who study because it is required as an entry to the upper career path of police. They are more interested in practical aspects of policing but have difficulties with theory and science;
- Group C: students, who are neither motivated nor able to study and often are even unsure, whether they want to become officers.

The authors estimate – without valid empirical facts and rather from watching the students through the days – that group A share 20 to 30 %, B about 50 to 60 %, and C about 10 % (and increasing) of the students. Especially, members of group B and C are supporters of the critic.

Hence, the vast majority of the police students (not only) in North Rhine-Westphalia are mainly satisfied with their education but long for a more coherent curriculum with a stronger emphasis on the practical policing and less academic stuff (as long as they cannot prove practical relevance, which the legal science do better than social science). This opinion stays in continuity with former studies, like, for example, from Ohlemacher et al. 2007.

Unfortunately, the evaluation in NRW didn't ask the students the crucial question whether they would prefer a vocational training to study.

But scientists from the Hessian University for Police and Public Administration asked this to their students. About 20% said a vocational training would be better, 40% preferred study and 40% did not make up their mind. Nearly 60% said that the practice during the study would be too little and only about 15% disagreed with this position (Groß and Schmidt 2016: 113, Groß 2011, 2015).

It is a unique selling point of the Universities of Applied Science and their dual studies to integrate theory and practice, and with this they address especially those students, who are not particularly interested in complex theory, scientific models and the academic discourse, but prefer (science-based) application knowledge. So the main objectives to study at a Police University are not orientated on higher education as an end in itself, but on the aim to become a police officer. Several studies on the study and career motives show the importance of 'law and order, action and [social] security' (Rabitz-Suhr 2016: 70, see also Groß and Schmidt 2014) – and academic motives, like research, new findings, critical discussion are not ranked.

Therefore, the mentioned critics cannot really surprise. But it is necessary not to look only into the students' view and their personal wants, but also the needs – at least how they are seen by the highest ranked police officers, the minister of interior, the members of parliament or other stakeholders.

These positions are not collected systematically as it would be appropriate in an evaluation (which is still missing; see below), so they can only be extracted from other sources, like speeches, statements or parliamentary protocols.

Already in 2001, the Ministry of Interior presented a concept for the further development of higher education at the *Fachhochschule* and pointed out the necessity to base professional policing on higher education and research:

The police can only complete their tasks professionally, if the policing relevant disciplines have a scientifically valid fundament and develop this continuously with applied research [...] which contributes to critical analysis, to problem solving and to the development of concepts. (Innenministerium NRW 2001: 8)

During a parliamentary hearing, a representative of the police union GdP, Volker Huß, said:

> We see the university study as a form of education and also professional qualification. It should not be reduced to impart handicraft training. It is a matter in the university course to impart competences for life long learning. Therefore methodical expertise and key competences should be gained. (Landtag NRW 2015: 6)

This can be read as a plea for academic education and not for vocational training. And the Minister of Interior of North Rhine-Westphalia, Ralf Jäger, wrote enthusiastically in a congratulatory note on the 40th anniversary of the *Fachhochschule*:

> She [the university] readies [the students] for the work in public administration by application-oriented teaching and studies. With this balancing act she ensures both: a substantiated, academic demanding higher education and a practical oriented training regarding the needs of the everyday activity in the public authorities. A dual-study at the University of Applied Science for Public Administration of North Rhine-Westphalia therefor is the best of both worlds. (Jäger 2016)

The university course for the police is not just 'to entertain' and satisfy students, but is – so the collective opinion of stakeholders – to deliver a broad spectrum of knowledge, abilities and competencies, even garnished with complicated theory.

Assessment of the 'Post-Kienbaum'-Situation

Especially in comparison to the career system, and the length and content of police education in the UK or USA, the German situation might seem strange or even odd. But there is a broad consensus of society, politics, police and police unions that police officers need a long and good education. The citizens expect a professional behaviour, which should be based on education – and they honour the police with a high trust into the institution (GfK 2013, 2014) and appreciate the police officer (IfD Allensbach 2016). The expectations towards highly professional police forces are also shown in distrust in private security and as well in voluntary police (like special constables; existing only in Hessen, Baden-Wurttemberg and Saxony) or services with fewer competences (like PCSOs; existing only in Hessen). A profound vocational training of at least 2 ½ years and/or a bachelor course of 3 years are seen as a guarantee for good policing and legitimated police.

Hence, there is no discussion in Germany about going beyond the education and payment standards of the status quo, but rather some discussion in some *Länder* about the implementation of the two-tier career path, for example, in Hamburg[3] or Baden-Wuerttemberg.[4]

After the Kienbaum Report, all 16 *Länder* and the two federal police forces had to decide about their career systems, and – as described above – six *Länder* implemented a system with a two-tier career path, which meant to have higher education as an entry qualification to the police, while the other forces kept the three-tier career path, with a combination of vocational training for the middle career path, and the university degree for the achievers from the middle career path and also for a direct entry to the upper career path for A-level students.

The expectations were high, that a higher education would improve police and policing significantly. Were these expectations fulfilled? Is it worth to implement the two-tier career path despite of the higher wages, the longer and more expensive education?

It seems ridiculous that in the days of new public management, austerity and changing challenges to policing, there is still no evaluation of the higher education and the policing performance in *Länder* with two- versus three-tier systems. There are (or more prudent, might be) political reasons that none of the 17 Minister of Interior in Germany wants this evaluation and would be happy or at least willing to give access to internal data, would allow scientists to interview officers and other stakeholders and to agree in a benchmark. What would happen, if the two-tier system proves to be more successful? The 11 Ministers of Interior, who had not implemented the system, would have difficulties to explain, why they put their citizens on risks – caused by poor policing and not enough education. What would happen, if the three-tier system would be sufficient to guarantee good police service? How could the six ministers explain, why they spent money for not needed qualification?

There would be a wonderful opportunity for an evaluation – but the political will, the funding and the field access won't be given. What a pity!

As there is no opportunity to design a complex mix-method research design to evaluate the career systems, one has to use data, which are accessible but not really valid. Such data are the crime statistics and also road accident statistics. Both statistics are related to police work – but of course also dependent on many other influence factors. For the comparison, the figures of five indicators were extracted from official statistics and the data were ranked. The chosen figures are about

- Traffic accidents:

    – injured people per 100,000 inhabitants
    – killed people per one million inhabitants

- Crime:

    – crime rates per 100,000 inhabitants
    – offence rate German juveniles
    – clearance rate

To condense the ranking, the five ranks of the indicators were summed and divided by five to get a total rank. The result is shown in Table 10.2.

To make complex things short: There is no clear evidence that the two-tier career path (2 tcp) produces better results than the states with the three-tier system – at least not with the selected indicators. In each column, forces with and without the two-tier system are in the top and the bottom ranks. Hessen, with the two-tier system, achieves rank 1 – based on good figures in all categories, Bavaria (3 tcp) is on rank 4, because of bad date concerning the road accidents, but is on rank 1 in all three crime categories. North Rhine-Westphalia (2 tcp) is on the 6th position, getting quite good results in the traffic, but has only rank 12 and 13 in the crime rates and the clearance rate. The chosen performance data are not sufficient to answer the question. It would need a multivariate analysis of the statistics and also some other quantitative

Table 10.2 Selected data of road accident and crime statistics as indicators of police performance

	Traffic injured p. 100.000 inhab.	accidents rank	Traffic killed p. mio. inhab.	accidents rank	Crime p. 100.000 inhab.	rates rank	Offence rate Juveniles German	rank	Clearance rate	rank	Sum Ranks/5	rank
Germany	469		41		7530		5010		54,9			
Baden-Württemberg	436	6	44	8	5592	2	4411	3	58,9	7	5,2	2
Bayern	555	15	54	13	5164	1	3847	1	64,4	1	6,2	4
Berlin	485	10	11	1	15873	16	7412	13	44,9	15	11	13
Brandenburg	427	5	69	16	8004	10	6582	11	52,4	11	10,6	12
Bremen	896	16	12	2	12744	14	7443	15	45,8	14	12,2	15
Hamburg	545	13	15	3	13743	15	8107	16	43,9	16	12,6	16
Hessen	461	8	36	5	6566	3	4190	2	59,3	6	4,8	1
Mecklenburg-Vorpommern	420	4	50	11	7304	8	7260	12	60,4	5	8	7
Niedersachsen	524	12	53	12	7095	6	5410	8	60,6	4	8,4	10
Nordrhein-Westfalen	414	3	27	4	8543	12	5193	6	49,8	13	7,6	6
Rheinland-Pfalz	469	9	44	8	6623	5	5150	5	61,9	3	6	3
Saarland	508	11	37	6	7642	9	5039	4	53,3	10	8	7
Sachsen	404	2	47	10	8086	11	5852	9	54,8	9	8,2	9
Sachsen-Anhalt	456	7	62	15	8665	13	7439	14	57,1	8	11,4	14
Schleswig-Holstein	548	14	37	6	7184	7	5235	7	51,2	12	9,8	11
Thüringen	374	1	56	14	6574	4	6486	10	63,9	2	6,2	5

Länder with a two-tier career system are marked grey

Statistisches Bundesamt (2014) Verkehr. Verkehrsunfälle 2013 Fachserie 8 Reihe 7, S. 51. Bundeskriminalamt: Polizeiliche Kriminalstatistik – Jahrbuch 2014, S. 21, 29. 123

and qualitative research to evaluate the advantages and results of the qualification and the career systems, for example, measuring the citizens' (also of members' of ethnic minorities) trust and satisfaction with the police, data about misbehaviour of officers, job satisfaction, self-estimation of officers about their qualification and education needs, estimations of prosecutors and judges, recruitment and assessment results, and so on. This would bring interesting results – and the ministers should not be so frightened.

A different approach to analyse the effects of higher education for the police was followed by Carsten Dübbers (2015), a senior police officer, who wrote a sociological PhD on the changes of the police culture in which higher education contrasted the 'state-oriented' and the 'citizen-oriented' attitudes of police officers with and without academic qualification. His results are mainly based on a case study in Cologne, where he interviewed officers of different age and different qualification levels about attitudes and competences, for example, in the fields of tasks of police, esprit de corps and values. His findings are also not entirely stringent that a university course would 'produce' better officers – in the sense of culture, work orientation and performance. But he sees significant indicators that the implementation of the two-tier career path changes the police for the better – but only step by step.

Summary and Perspectives

The police in Germany have a good tradition to train and educate the police. Striving for a professional police, the paramilitary training was suspended in about the 1970s, and a more civilian, citizen-oriented, rule-of-law inspired and to the democratic principles dedicated police should be built with well-educated officers. Following the German common framework for the public service officers have to do a vocational training of 2 ½ years or a 3-year university course.

After an assessment of the police tasks by the consultant agency Kienbaum, some *Länder* implemented a two-tier career system and transferred the now compulsory higher education from the police schools to

Universities of Applied Science, which offer – since the 2010s – bachelor courses. The graduates start into the police career as *Kommissars* (equals inspector in the UK system), while there are no lower-ranked officers (which would be comparable to constables and sergeants).

The courses are designed as dual studies with theory at the university/ academy and practical training, which is either offered at the university/ academy or delivered in co-operation with police institutes and/or regional forces. While the 'political' stakeholders estimate the university course as useful and necessary for good policing, some students wish a more practical orientation and less 'academic stuff'.

A proper evaluation of the effects of the higher education for the police in Germany and especially regarding the two-tier career system is for different reasons still missing. The few studies on it, which are mainly restricted to a specific *Land* or selected aspects, do not prove a significant advance. But there are serious indicators that the ongoing professionalisation of police by higher education alters the police as an organisation, the police culture and the work habits of the officers towards a modern, professional, citizen-oriented and adaptive force.

The police – not only in Germany – often saw the job more as a handicraft and were reluctant towards science and academics. But slowly since the 1990s implemented and increased higher education changed this picture. A growing number of graduates from police universities continue their studies at other universities, become masters and even write their PhD. With this a new normality of academics and academic thinking within the force emerges. This opens the police towards new ways of planning and action, towards evidence-based policing and more reflective attitudes, for example, regarding ethnic minorities, social problems and other professions like street work. With this the often-problematic cop culture might break up.

The 'trickling down' of academic education opens the force to accept scientific insights, to use studies to evaluate police activities, and to develop concepts and strategies based on theory, models and data. This evolves professional expertise and expands the range of action and behaviour. And it also strengthens the resonance body for (applied) police science and police research.

On the other hand, policing cannot and will not be an academic discipline. It still demands action, needs physical skills and takes place in the public space (and not in the library or study room). So the education is well positioned at Universities of Applied Science and is best delivered in a dual study system.

Higher education of the police enhances their position in a (Western, industrialised, by globalization influenced) society, which undergoes a process towards a knowledge society. Police cannot afford to stay behind and has to keep up with the times.

Notes

1. Females were not allowed to the uniformed police until late 1970s, and Bavaria was the last state offering women the access in 1990, see Werdes 2003: 200.
2. See http://www.hochschulkompass.de/en/degree-programmes/prerequisites-for-studying.html (accessed: 21.7.2014).
3. See http://www.dpolg-hamburg.de/2012/08/zweigeteilte-laufbahn-ja-aber-richtig/ (14.8.2014), http://www.hamburg.de/contentblob/5090372/920b78235d85c6f079a462e1874b18de/data/hpj-ausgabe-01-2016-do.pdf, p. 14.
4. See http://www.baden-wuerttemberg.de/de/service/presse/pressemitteilung/pid/weichen-fuer-schrittweise-einfuehrung-der-zweigeteilten-laufbahn-in-der-polizei-gestellt/ (14.8.2014). After the election in 2016 and a new coalition of the Green party with the CDU the discussion seems suspended for the ongoing legislature period.

References

Bär, B. (2016). *Was Sie über das duale Studium wissen sollten. Süddeutsche Zeitung*. Available at http://www.sueddeutsche.de/bildung/duales-studium-bueffeln-und-basteln-1.2897094. Accessed 30 Sept 2016.

Beck, U. (1986). *Risikogesellschaft. Auf dem Weg in eine andere Moderne*. Frankfurt am Main: Suhrkamp.

Beck, U. (1992). *Risk Society. Towards a New Modernity*. London: Sage Publications.

Bernhardt, M., & Christe-Zeyse, J. (2016). Von reflektierten Praktikern und handlungssicheren Akademikern. Szenario für eine didaktische Synthese von Wissenschaft und Praxis in der Polizeiausbildung. In B. Frevel & H. Groß (Eds.), *Empirische Polizeiforschung XIX: Bologna und die Folgen für die Polizeiausbildung* (pp. 24–42). Frankfurt am Main: Verlag für Polizeiwissenschaft.

Bornewasser, M. (2002). Kooperation trotz Abgrenzung der Institutionen: Über einige Schwierigkeiten, die die Zusammenarbeit von Wissenschaft und Polizei zu einem Wagnis werden lassen. In M. Bornewasser (Ed.), *Empirische Polizeiforschung III* (pp. 13–27). Herbolzheim: Centaurus.

Drees, P. (2015). *Evaluation des Studiengangs Polizeivollzugsdienst. Zusammenfassung zentraler Evaluationsergebnisse.* Gelsenkirchen: FHöV NRW (Internal, Not Published Paper).

Dübbers, C. (2015). *Von der Staats- zur Bürgerpolizei? Empirische Studien zur Kultur der Polizei im Wandel.* Frankfurt am Main: Verlag für Polizeiwissenschaft.

Fachhochschule für öffentliche Verwaltung NRW (Hrsg). (2016). Modulbeschreibung Bachelorstudiengang PVD ab EJ 2016. Gelsenkirchen: FHöV NRW.

GfK – Gesellschaft für Konsumforschung. (2013). *Global Trusts Report 2015.* Press release. Available at http://www.gfk-verein.org/sites/default/files/medien/359/dokumente/pm_global_trust_2015_final_dt.pdf. Accessed 30 Sept 2016.

GfK – Gesellschaft für Konsumforschung. (2014). *Trust in Professions 2016.* Press release. Available at http://www.gfk-verein.org/sites/default/files/medien/359/dokumente/pm_gfk_verein_trust_in_professions_2016_de.pdf. Accessed 30 Sept 2016.

Gintzel, K. (2014). Polizeigeschichte. Zu zeigen, was eigentlich gewesen ist – zugleich eine Ergänzung der Forschungsergebnisse zur Nachkriegspolizei in Nordrhein-Westfalen und Niedersachsen. *Deutsche Polizei, 63*(12), 27–31.

Groß, H. (2003). Fachhochschulausbildung in der Polizei: Lehrgang oder Studium. In H. J. Lange (Ed.), *Die Polizei der Gesellschaft. Zur Soziologie der Inneren Sicherheit* (pp. 141–156). Opladen: Leske + Budrich.

Groß, H. (2011). Wer wird Polizist? Berufswahl und Studienmotivation in Hessen. *Polizei & Wissenschaft, 2*, 47–61.

Groß, H. (2015). Sicherheit und Thrill. Veränderungen der Berufs- und Studienmotivation von hessischen Polizeistudierenden 2009-2013. In C. Stark (Ed.), *Soziologie und Polizei. Zur soziologischen Beschäftigung mit und für die Polizei* (pp. 19–33). Norderstedt: Books on Demand.

Groß, H., & Frevel, B. (2016). Polizei ist Ländersache! – Polizeipolitik unter den Bedingungen des deutschen Föderalismus. In A. Hildebrandt & F. Wolf (Eds.), *Die Politik der Bundesländer. Staatstätigkeit im Vergleich* (pp. 61–86). Wiesbaden: Springer.

Groß, H., & Schmidt, P. (2014). Das Polizeistudium: Veränderungen der Berufs- und Studienmotivation von hessischen Polizeistudierenden 2009–2013. In K. Liebl et al. (Eds.), *Forschung zu Sicherheit und Sicherheitsgewährung. Festschrift für Manfred Bornewasser* (pp. 181–194). Frankfurt am Main: Verlag für Polizeiwissenschaft.

Groß, H., & Schmidt, P. (2016). Kriminalpolizeiliche Studiengänge in Deutschland. Notwendige Spezialisierung oder überflüssige Elitenbildung? In B. Frevel & H. Groß (Eds.), *Empirische Polizeiforschung XIX: Bologna und die Folgen für die Polizeiausbildung* (pp. 103–115). Frankfurt am Main: Verlag für Polizeiwissenschaft.

IfD Allensbach: *Allensbacher Berufsprestige-Skala 2013*. Available at www.ifd-allensbach.de/uploads/tx_reportsndocs/PD_2013_05.pdf. Accessed 30 Sept 2016.

Innenministerium NRW. (Ed.) (2001). *Konzept der Landesregierung des Landes Nordrhein-Westfalen zur Weiterentwicklung der Ausbildung für Verwaltung und Polizei an der Fachhochschule für öffentliche Verwaltung des Landes Nordrhein-Westfalen.* Decree II B 4, 9.7.2001.

Innenministerium NRW. (1999). Antwort der Landesregierung auf die Große Anfrage 14, Drs. 12/3504, Situation der Polizei NRW. Landtag NRW, Drs. 12/3776 v. 8.3.1999. Düsseldorf: Landtag

Jäger, R. (2016). 40 Jahre Fachhochschule für öffentliche Verwaltung in Nordrhein-Westfalen. *DVP – Deutsche Verwaltungspraxis, 67*(9), 353.

Kienbaum Unternehmensberatung GmbH. (1991). *Funktionsbewertung der Schutzpolizei. Studie im Auftrag des Innenministers des Landes Nordrhein-Westfalen.* Gummersbach: Kienbaum.

Landesregierung NRW. (2013). *Haushaltsplan für den Geschäftsbereich des Ministeriums für Inneres und Kommunales für das Haushaltsjahr 2013.* Düsseldorf: Landesregierung.

Landtag NRW (Ed.) (2015). *Innenausschuss. 70. Sitzung – Sachverständigengespräch „Polizeiausbildung verbessern: Schwerpunktstudiengänge ,Kriminalpolizei" und ,Schutzpolizei' einführen.* LT-Drs. Apr 16/1054 v. 29.10.2015.

MIK – Ministerium für Inneres und Kommunales NRW: *Demografischer Wandel und Polizei – Teil 3. Antwort auf die Kleine Anfrage 2327 vom 13.6.2013,* Landtag NRW – Drs. 16/6068.

Ohlemacher, T. (2016). Polizei und Wissenschaft an polizeilichen (Aus-) Bildungseinrichtungen. In B. Frevel & H. Groß (Eds.), *Empirische Polizeiforschung XIX. Bologna und die Folgen für die Polizeiausbildung* (pp. 13–23). Frankfurt am Main: Verlag für Polizeiwissenschaft.

Ohlemacher, T., Weiß, H., & Aust, N. (2007). Zweigeteilte Laufbahn in Niedersachsen. Ergebnisse des Projekts Ausbildungsprofil Fakultät Polizei der Niedersächsischen HFVR. In B. Frevel & K. Liebl (Eds.), *Empirische Polizeiforschung IX: Stand und Perspektiven der Polizeiausbildung* (pp. 74–97). Frankfurt am Main: Verlag für Polizeiwissenschaft.

Rabitz-Suhr, S. (2016). Wer wird heute warum Polizist? Dien Anwärterbefragung der Polizei Hamburg. In B. Frevel & H. Groß (Eds.), *Empirische Polizeiforschung XIX: Bologna und die Folgen für die Polizeiausbildung* (pp. S. 61–S. 78). Frankfurt am Main: Verlag für Polizeiwissenschaft.

Statistisches Bundesamt. (Ed.) (2016). *Personal des öffentlichen Dienstes 2015.* Wiesbaden: Statistisches Bundesamt. Available at https://www.destatis.de/ DE/Publikationen/Thematisch/FinanzenSteuern/OeffentlicherDienst/ PersonaloeffentlicherDienst2140600157004.pdf?__blob=publicationFile. Accessed 30 Sept 2016.

Werdes, B. (2003). Frauen in der Polizei. Einbruch in eine Männerdomäne. In H. J. Lange (Ed.), *Die Polizei der Gesellschaft. Zur Soziologie der Inneren Sicherheit* (pp. 195–212). Opladen: Leske + Budrich.

11

Higher Police Education in the Netherlands

Jan Heinen and Harry Peeters

Introduction

The Police Academy of the Netherlands was founded in 1992. Ten years later, a radical metamorphosis of police education has been enacted (Grotendorst et al. 2002) of which the occupational profiles have been recalibrated in 2011 (Nijhof et al. 2011). Since 2006, the Police Academy has the status of University of Applied Sciences, granted by the Ministry of Education,[1] which is required in the Netherlands to be allowed to award (accredited) bachelor and master degrees and to establish research chairs (called lectorates). In January 2017, the Police Academy will become part of the Dutch National Police[2] on which behalf it is the selection and recruitment centre for training, knowledge and research. So far, almost 2000 students accomplished initial training programmes, that is, the vocational curricula and the Bachelor of Policing. More than 25,000

J. Heinen (✉)
Police Academy of the Netherlands, Apeldoorn, The Netherlands

H. Peeters
Canterbury Christ Church University, Canterbury, UK

© The Author(s) 2018
C. Rogers, B. Frevel (eds.), *Higher Education and Police*,
DOI 10.1007/978-3-319-58386-0_11

students attended post-initial training programmes with respect to five master programmes[3] and detective, commander and specific police tasks.

Whatever adjustments have been made during the past 15 years, they never corroded the renewed educational quintessence. Societal changes were, are and will be the driving forces that affect the demands for policing, that is, regarding the professionalism of the organisation as well as the competencies of police officers, who are required to respond to complex changes in a flexible way and to be on a continuous learning curve (Stam et al. 2007).

To be more specific: it's about the multicultural nature of society, the exacerbation in violence among citizens and towards the police, the diminishing respect for the police, the growing impact of social problems and the fact that the police must be more accountable to society (Stam et al. 2007). Of late, the police have to cope with new criminal phenomena like cybercrime, terrorism and human trafficking. Against this backdrop, the essential principles of the Dutch (higher) police education reform are still valid, namely, occupational and qualification profiles that are based on core tasks of policing, a coherent system of (higher) police education, diploma-equivalence of policing and non-policing degrees, accreditation of bachelor and master degrees, a so-called dual training system and lectorates that are supportive to both policing tasks and police training (Peeters 2010). These principles were initially laid down in the Law on the Police Academy and Police Education[4] and have been confirmed in an Amendment of the Police Law[5] (into force from January 2017). The main difference is that the Police Academy's position as an Independent Governing Body (ZBO[6]) will cease as soon as the Academy will become part of the National Police, but except for matters referring to conducting research (a new item) and external diploma-equivalence of accredited bachelor and master degrees. For these objectives, the Police Education Council[7] (POR) still has a prominent place in both laws.

In the following sections, we will elaborate on the points raised in the introduction in terms of a generalisation of the prevailing similarities during the educational and institutional changes and by pointing to recent adjustments.

Police Education Council

Since 2013, the Police Education Council (POR) is an independent governmental advisory body advising, both solicited and unsolicited, the Minister of Safety & Justice on matters of police education – to which applied research has been added (www.politieonderwijsraad.nl). In addition, the council is a dialogue platform for stakeholders of Dutch police education, which consists of independent academic members and representatives of the National Police, Police Trade Unions, the Public Prosecution, the Police Academy and educational partners from vocational schools and universities (of an academic or applied nature). The tasks and formal position of the POR are described in Acts of the former and present police laws. These Acts regulate police education (and currently applied research) in terms of structure and functioning, tasks and responsibilities of the Police Academy, the police organisation and institutions of vocational and higher education, contributing to police education. The Police Education Act assigns the following tasks to the Council:

- contributing to the development and maintenance of a consistent, national qualification structure for police education;
- contributing to an adequate match between the supply of police education and the needs of police forces, reckoning with developments in police practice, labour market perspectives of students and relevant developments from an international perspective;
- formulating competence based exit qualifications, indicating what students should be able to do in actual practise, in addition to what students already should have learned in prior education;
- ensuring diploma equivalence of police education in relation to regular vocational and higher education (also in an international context);
- advising on quality criteria for dual education (learning at the workplace);
- advising on the government funding of police education and training, in order to contribute to an efficient and effective use of governmental financial means;

- ensuring that police education and the research and knowledge function ties in more closely with police tasks and the remit of the National Police (added goal).

Occupational and Qualification Profiles

In order to gear policing requirements to police education, the joint development of occupational profiles by academia and police professionals, already in 2000/2001, was vital (Peeters 2010). The first profiles have been legitimised by Police Councils and have been decreed by the Ministers of Justice and the Interior. In terms of acknowledged diploma-equivalence, it is important that they also received the consent of the Ministry of Education (den Boer and Peeters 2007).

In 2011, the POR published a thorough recalibration of the occupational profiles based on a digital questionnaire amongst sworn police officers and six two-day conferences for them, directed at core processes of policing: emergency response, law enforcement, criminal investigation and police leadership (Nijhof et al. 2011). The report distinguishes occupational profiles from qualification profiles: the former refer to the particular responsibilities and tasks of the professionals in question, the latter to the corresponding learning and examination requirements. To guarantee the link between both profiles, they have been structured identically, namely, consisting of a division in four complementary categories of competencies: professional, contextual, social and individual ones.[8] The focus is on the profession and on the context that affects the performance of the professional in terms of interactions and personal input (Peeters 2014).

The required competencies are divided into four categories as to ensure that all aspects of policing and the underlying academic concepts are taken into account (Peeters 2010):

- *Professional* competencies are at the core of the profession and enable the police officer to deliver products and services in an adequate and systematic way.

- *Contextual* competencies enable the police officer to plan and co-ordinate his/her daily activities within the societal context and the policy framework of the organisation.
- *Social* competencies enable the police officer to function and co-operate in a multicultural and multidisciplinary environment.
- *Individual* competencies enable the police officer to reflect on and contribute to his/her own development, the profession and the organisation s/he works for.

Derived from the recalibration of the occupational profiles by the POR, the competency structure has been developed in a more systematic way for the sake of comparable levels of qualification profiles as laid down in Qualification Dossiers issued by the POR on its website (www.politieonderwijsraad.nl) (POR 2016). Each of the aforementioned categories consists of four competencies, each of which refers to a specific aspect of policing as to enable a comparison of higher or lower qualification levels and of less or more complex content of curricula *on the same dimension,* also in relation to distinctive EQF standards.[9]

It is based on a template that can be used irrespective of the type of occupation or education, whilst it allows for an elaboration for the particular profession that can be further specified along the lines of the distinctive core processes in question, in this case those of policing (Peeters 2014).

To give an example of the first dimension of the first category: "the degree of complexity of a situation" within the police profession regarding law enforcement. At a bachelor level of policing (EQF6), the competency could be described as "being able to develop, conduct and evaluate a plan for a high-risk operation", which compared to a master level of policing (EQF7) on the same dimension could be "being able to draft policing strategies based on information of traditional and new media". In EQF terms, the bachelor competency equates to the corresponding generic EQF6 standard of disposing of "advanced innovative skills to solve complex and unpredictable problems", whilst the master competency equates to the generic EQF7 standard of disposing of "specialised problem-solving skills to develop and integrate (new) knowledge".

Another example with respect to the fourth dimension of the fourth category: "the scope of results of own input" within the police profession regarding criminal investigation (Peeters 2014). At a bachelor level of policing (EQF6), the competency could be described as "being able to assess the relevance and sensitivity of sharing intelligence", which compared to a master level of policing (EQF7) on the same dimension could be "being able to contribute to a body of knowledge of crime science". In EQF terms, the bachelor competency equates to the corresponding generic EQF6 standard of having "advanced knowledge, involving a critical understanding of theories and principles", whilst the master competency equates to the generic EQF7 standard of having "highly specialised knowledge as the basis for original thinking and/or research".

These characteristics apply to all curricula of the Police Academy of which the higher levels, that is, from EQF level 5 up to EQF level 7, are highlighted in the following overview.

Coherent System of (Higher) Police Education

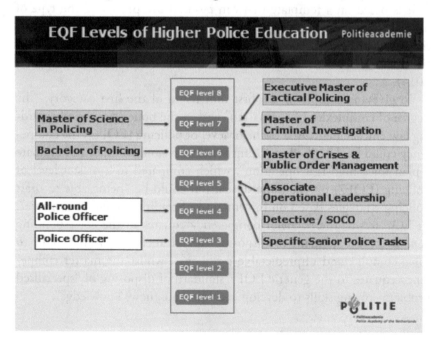

The Dutch system of Police Education is coherent in the sense that the competency structure of occupational profiles and qualification profiles is specified in the design of curricula and modules in terms of core tasks; that there is no overlap between the various modules within or between curricula and that similar competencies will become more complex and more difficult to perform if one progresses to a programme with a higher EQF level of policing. This holds for moving on within the initial programmes (as presented on the left side of the picture) or from initial to post-initial programmes (as presented on the right side).

The flexibility of the coherent system of police educations is designed to promote the mobility of police officers as well as their career possibilities, not only in order to attain management positions but even more to grow as a police expert or specialist (Grotendorst et al. 2002). Throughout the years, this objective has been repeated in important police documents: "Employers' Vision, an Inspiring Foundation" (Council of Chief Constables 2008); "Switching in Responsibility: Police Occupations Recalibrated", a publication from the Police Education Council (Nijhof et al. 2011); "Development Plan National Police" (Ministry of Safety & Justice 2012). The first document advocates that career opportunities and salaries for police specialists should be comparable to those of police managers. The second one advises that the vocational training for All-round Police Officer, situated at EQF level 4, should be the minimal level of police education and that there is an obvious need for launching a Bachelor of Criminal Investigation. The third one emphasises that for the National Police *operational* leadership will become the starting point" as to diminish the distance between police leaders and police officers and to enable police leaders to become more occupied with steering and supporting daily police work. All these observations and the aforementioned societal challenges to safety and security point to the necessity of a higher level of policing. The study programmes that are situated at the EQF levels 5, 6 and 7 can potentially address these concerns.

Before we present the outlines of these programmes based on the Qualification Dossiers, published by the POR (www.politieonderwijs-raad.nl), we will briefly describe the new Function Structure of the National Police (LFNP),[10] because the programmes are now directly or indirectly linked to a reduced set of 92 police functions that are divided into three categories: management, implementation and support. With regard to management functions the top-down hierarchy is chief constable (now only one!), police chief, director, sector head, team chief C, B and A. Concerning implementation, 11 policing disciplines are listed in combination with the function of assistant, fellow worker, generalist, senior, operational expert or operational specialist (potentially related to EQF 2, 3, 4, 5, 6 or 7 in educational terms). Some disciplines have a generic character (community policing, tactical investigation, forensic investigation); some are of a more specific nature (control room, intake and service, protection, aviation) or of a specialist nature (intervention, observation, running informants, intelligence). With respect to support the LFNP functions, teacher A to D, researcher A to C and lector are relevant in this context.

Curricula for Specific Senior Police Tasks

These post-initial curricula or set of modules refer to a great variety of policing tasks ranging from all-round community policing and specialist (leading) functions in the field of crisis and conflict control or public order management to specific law enforcement or criminal investigation tasks concerning environmental policing (fire work offences, pollution) or traffic control (accidents, driving expertise). The LFNP-function of *Senior* is tasked with the coordination of cases, which is related to EQF level 5.

Curricula for Detectives and Scene of Crime Officers (SOCO)

There are extensive post-initial programmes for detectives with regard to leading a team large-scale investigation, possibly to be followed by specialisations in fighting crimes in the field of vice, finance, drugs, weapons, youth problems and domestic violence. There are also courses in interview specialisms, human trafficking, digital investigation and special or covert investigation tactics. For scene of crime officers, there are two basic training tracks, either for a generic forensic investigator or a generic forensic digital investigator. The first track enables them to specialise in several forensic areas, for instance, concerning vice, violence, arson, traffic accidents, biological traces, explosives, victims of calamities, documents, finger prints and all kinds of material objects. The second track can be continued in terms of specialising in hacking investigation, windows forensics or other operating systems.

Those tasks are also situated at EQF level 5, so in line with the LFNP function of *Senior*.

Associate Operational Leadership

This curriculum is meant for the operational commander who in relation to the LFNP will be deployable as *Team Chief A*, or in a case-coordinating function of a *Senior* or even an *Operational Expert*. The graduate will get an Associate Degree (AD) situated at EQF level 5. The introduction of the LFNP and the implementation of a national police force has led to a substantial reduction in leadership positions in terms of people management in favour of investing in the coordination of police tasks and pertaining networks. This ideological shift is clearly visible in the new curriculum. To give a few examples of required competencies, respectively of a professional, contextual, social and individual nature:

- "… resolve impasses during the daily steering of an operational (project) team"
- "… translate developments in society and the police profession into own activities…"
- "… stimulate colleagues to take responsibility for achieving results …"
- "… reconsider one's own way of leading operations after an evaluation …"

Bachelor of Policing

The Bachelor of Policing is an EQF level 6 programme, whose graduates are eligible for developing to the LFNP-position of *operational expert* after a career start as a *senior* or a widely deployable *generalist*. An operational expert is supposed to be in charge of interventions, being able to deal with complex, risky or unexpected situations. The POR-report "Police Occupations Recalibrated" (Nijhof et al. 2011) attributes the necessity of a bachelor programme on policing to the increasing complexity of society (international, multicultural, technological) and the increasing ingenuity of criminals, which in itself requires a structural upgrading of police work, a strong analytical capability and intensive cooperation with internal and external partners. "As an all-round operational expert and representative of the monopoly on force the Bachelor of Policing is fully authorised to be deployed in all core tasks of policing and criminal investigation as well as in mobilising, organising or coordinating the linkage to the responsibilities of similar chain partners.

Under changing and hectic circumstances s/he is responsible for his/her own broad performance and an adequate referral to specialists or effective cooperation with chain partners. S/he takes care of sustainable safety arrangements and a proactive approach to criminality on the basis of analysing and evaluating societal developments, scenarios and the combination of local and nodal intelligence. The broad and at the same time differentiated area of responsibility as well as the operational position in a particular chain of law enforcement or criminal investigation requires cognitive flexibility, i.e. the capacity to switch continuously between perspectives, options, approaches, performers and legal areas, whilst policing both internally and externally. Police work at this level poses high demands to balancing between street wise and science wise, answering to and realising the responsibility question and gaining authority."

If it comes to higher education, the Bachelor of Policing is a key programme in the educational system of the Police Academy, as this diploma provides access to its four master programmes: the Master of Science in Policing (MSc in Policing), the Executive Master of Tactical Policing (EMTP, a leadership master), the Master of Criminal Investigation (MCI) and the Master of Crisis & Public Order Management (MCPM).

The Bachelor of Policing programme is divided along the lines of core processes of policing (emergency response, law enforcement, criminal investigation) extended with issues of interagency policing. To mention the key tasks within each of these fields of policing:

- Emergency Response: managing interventions with regard to cases of violence, accidents, incidents, nuisance, anti-social behaviour; involving partners on the basis of control room information; dealing with critical incidents in terms of planning, participation and evaluation; capacity management.
- Law Enforcement: management and coordination of policing events, traffic safety, environment offences; mapping, analysing and prioritising high-risk areas; switching between different jurisdictions; briefing and debriefing.
- Criminal Investigation: conducting and coordinating a comprehensive investigation; cooperating with other investigation services and the public prosecutor; scene of crime management; scenario development.
- Interagency Policing: creating effective (multicultural) networks with public and private partners; considering public expectations towards the police; relating intelligence to neighbourhood policing; translating societal developments into policing strategies.

The body of knowledge is based on police science, political science, sociology and social psychology, methodology, penal law, civil law, administrative law and constitution law. The Bachelor of Policing must also be able to (re)consider the legitimacy of applying policing skills.

Master of Science in Policing

The MSc in Policing, an EQF7 programme. The MSc graduate is in principle deployable for the LFNP functions of *Operational Specialist, Teacher* or *Researcher*, dependent of their personal career path or experience, and possibly related to the aforementioned 11 disciplines of the LFNP.

A profile description can be based on findings of the POR-report "Police Occupations Recalibrated" (Nijhof et al. 2011). "The Master of Science in Policing is able to engage in academic research in support of strategies, tactics and operational policies for daily and special police work, criminal investigation and international cooperation in this field. Vice versa s/he is able to deduce long-term police perspectives or concepts from thorough evaluations of common and incidental policing operations, leading to efficient improvements of a future approach to law enforcement in case of large-scale events, the control of unpredictable or dangerous situations and the way of organising criminal investigation.

S/he is able to deploy intelligence methods for the purpose of predicting trends in crime and to match the findings with the intelligence produced by analysts, with information from community policing and with analyses of relevant societal developments. Due to his/her academic way of thinking the Master of Science in Policing is able to produce policy reports for the Public Prosecutor or Police Authorities and to contribute to the development of police science. If s/he disposes of police powers, s/he will also be able to fulfill an eminent generic or specialist operational role."

The MSc in Policing is delivered and examined in English in cooperation with Canterbury Christ Church University, whose professors and lecturers take care of about 20% of the curriculum and the assessments. The content has a strong overarching and international focus which comes to the fore in the title of the modules: Policing Models (re criminality and law enforcement strategies), Police and Society (re diversity and legitimacy issues), International Policing (re theoretical, strategic and legal models of international policing and security in an international context as well as re transnational control of terrorism and organised crime). The programme is concluded by an extensive master thesis (dissertation) on any policing topic that represents one-third of the credits.

Executive Master of Tactical Policing

The EMTP is a leadership master at EQF level 7 with a Major in Criminal Investigation. In relation to the LFNP, the most likely function could either be *Team Chief (B/C)* or *Operational Specialist (A/B/C/D)*. Police leaders at a tactical level perform a hinge function between the operational and strategic level.

The programme has to be geared to the consequences of the transformation from regional police forces to the national police organisation.

With this caveat, a renewed profile of the EMTP probably sticks to the main characteristics of a tactical position, that is, mid-term decision making, directing police tactics, conferring with chain partners, leading main processes of policing (in a geographic or functional sense), being in charge of the operational commanders. But it must also take heed of recent or conceivable developments, that require the ability to manage public expectations of police behaviour or police performances; the ability to cooperate effectively with special or private investigation services, or the ability to balance professional discretion of operational commanders with the remit that has been bestowed upon them (Nijhof et al. 2011).

Master of Criminal Investigation

The MCI is also a master at EQF level 7 that consists of a generic track and several different majors, that is, on financial investigation, forensic investigation, digital investigation, environmental investigation, tactical investigation and analysis. Corresponding functions of the LFNP are either *operational expert* or the function layers of an *operational specialist*. The particular function will be based on this diploma, most likely on the major in question, on another relevant diploma, or on particular experience – in all cases related to the specific disciplinary field of the LFNP.

A Master of Criminal Investigation is, for instance, able to:

- gear criminal investigation competencies to policing in general or competencies in law matter;
- gear criminological strategies to forensic strategies;
- handle the tension between his/her professional know-how and the hierarchic responsibility of his/her superior;
- analyse and assess social developments that are relevant to criminal investigation and crime control;
- cooperate with different disciplines of criminal investigation inside or outside the police force;
- project him/herself into social backgrounds of a delinquency;
- apply and anticipate new information and intelligence;
- pass and receive criticism with regard to an approach of a criminal offence.

Each couple of lines refers respectively to professional, contextual, social and individual competencies.

Master of Crisis & Public Order Management

Again, as each master programme, the MCPM is situated at EQF level 7. In terms of the LFNP, a graduate is deployable in the function layers of the *operational specialist A–F*. The occupational profile of the MCPM shows the characteristics of the partnership between the Police Academy and the Dutch Institute for Physical Safety (NIFV), as illustrated by a few headings of a set of competencies: functioning in a multidisciplinary team and in a complex, multidisciplinary context; performing on the basis of different perspectives; operating in a political and administrative field of influences. Furthermore, required competencies refer to linking work to theories and science, applying information management or scenario thinking; dealing with media or with evaluations.

Diploma-Equivalence

In order to gain societal acceptance of policing degrees, which also fosters the recruitment and mobility of police officers, the equivalence of these degrees to other academic degrees is very important. Therefore, it is part of the remit of the Police Education Council (POR) "to ensure diploma equivalence of police education in relation to regular vocational and higher education, also in an international context" (www.politieonderwijsraad.nl). And that is why, from the outset, it was a crucial objective of the Police Academy "to tie-up with the qualification structure of regular vocational education" as to guarantee the mutual access to each other's programmes (Grotendorst et al. 2002). For these reasons, the intended diploma-equivalence was acknowledged by a former Minister of Education, Culture and Sciences[11] (already in 1999) and has been confirmed by the Council for Universities of Applied Sciences ("HBO-raad")[12] in 2007 with regard to the matter of "mutual access" to each other's programmes. The "HBO-raad" declares in a letter, sent to all Universities of Applied Sciences (UAS) in the Netherlands, that the

Police Academy's curriculum for All-Round Police Officer is situated at EQF level 4, which is the entry requirement for a bachelor study at any institution with an UAS status.

Accreditation of Bachelor and Master Degrees

In line with the Declaration of Bologna, the Police Academy strives to get its bachelor and master degrees accredited by submitting the programmes to the NVAO, the Dutch-Flemish Accreditation Organisation, which in the Netherlands is a prerequisite to get such programmes funded by the Ministry of Education for those Universities (of an academic or applied nature) that offer regular programmes. Although this is not applicable to the Police Academy as it is funded by the Ministry of Safety & Justice, the importance of accreditation and thus national and international recognition is a conclusive argument for the Police Academy to engage in accreditations. All programmes have now been accredited twice on the basis of a self-evaluation report and a visit of an independent panel that advises the NVAO on the basis of both the report and discussions with internal and external stakeholders during their visit. The Master of Science in Policing is also validated, twice too, by Canterbury Christ Church University because of a Memorandum of Agreement with the Police Academy. Although the accreditation/validation procedures differ between the UK and the Netherlands, the assessment standards are more or less identical as they are based on the guidelines of the ENQA, the European Association for Quality Assurance in Higher Education, of which UK's Quality Assurance Agency (QAA) for Higher Education and the NVAO are members.

Core Tasks

In order to bridge the gap between theory and practice "to the extent that the professional norm [before 2002] was to forget what one had learned at the Police Academy" (den Boer and Peeters 2007), the new education became competence-oriented as to focus on acts and results and the integration of knowledge and skills; the courses became context-bound as to guarantee that modules reflect core tasks of policing and the training system became complementary, that is, a dual system of learning, meaning that learning takes place alternately at school and in the police force (Peeters 2013).

During the start of the renewed police education, core tasks of policing have been formulated in sessions of police professionals and academics. "They had to answer the following questions in relation to the particular level of education" (Peeters 2010):

- Which critical and authentic situations confront a police officer?
- Which activities belong to these situations?
- Which crucial decisions have to be made in these circumstances?
- And finally: when is this police officer competent, that is, what does he or she need in order to be able to perform these activities and make the appropriate decisions?

This approach of formulating modules in terms of core tasks and competencies makes the way of learning more or less identical to what can be expected on the spot. As said before, these competencies are divided into four categories and have been elaborated more systematically later on.

Dual Training System

The philosophy behind the dual training system is not only to reduce the cleavage between theory and practice but also to integrate these approaches. Training on-the-job takes place in combination with practice-oriented police training at the Police Academy or a partner's institute. The knowledge that has been gained in a period at school can be used, implemented and reflected upon in a subsequent period in the police force (den Boer and Peeters 2007).

The dual training system is embedded in a supervisory structure which is anchored both within the police force and the Police Academy. Within the Police Academy, a learning process supervisor monitors the student's general progress. In the force, the student is assisted by an on-the-job coach and a route supervisor, who is normally a line manager who has already gained plenty of experience in his or her career within the police force, but who at the same time is not used to intensive involvement in education (den Boer and Peeters 2007).

One can imagine that the higher or more specific the level of education is, the more difficult it becomes to find a qualified on-the-job coach. On the other hand, this potential problem is diminishing since more and more police officers did attend a higher level of police education.

The learning process supervisor and the route supervisor have to consult each other because of their complementary responsibilities. In addition, the police trainee who studies at one level may study or perform together with a fellow-trainee of another level or a non-police trainee of the same level, if the profession (i.e. the managing authority within the relevant police force) demands such a particular form of cooperation (den Boer and Peeters 2007).

An interesting challenge which is produced by the dual training system is that a police force has to resist the temptation to regard the trainee as an ordinary employee with full-time availability. Therefore, formerly the regional Police Forces and now the National Police, have to be committed to the dual training.

A consequence of the competency nature of the dual training system is that many performances of students have to be assessed on the basis of competency tests (Peeters 2013). Four types of tests can be distinguished, as presented in the following typology:

Work sample	Simulation	Authentic task	Written exam
Characteristics	*Characteristics*	*Characteristics*	*Characteristics*
Judgement of behaviour, process and product	Emphasis on correct behaviour	Emphasis on judgement of product	Measures only fraction of a competence
Applications	*Applications*	*Applications*	*Applications*
Most realistic assessment	Performance of skills under simulation	In predominantly cognitive processes	Isolated knowledge and understanding
Modes	*Modes*	*Modes*	*Modes*
Performance under normal working conditions	Re actor Re equipment Re computer	Practical products re problematic and complex cases	Open questions Closed questions

Lectorates (Knowledge and Research)[13]

Within the Police Academy, knowledge and research are aimed at improving and strengthening the police profession. This is knowledge about the police, owned by the police and developed and made accessible in cooperation with the police. All activities are aimed at improving police practices and enhancing training and education.

Implementing knowledge is at the forefront. To achieve this goal, the academy is in continuous contact with educational institutes and police forces. Other knowledge institutes and partners in the security sector develop knowledge which is also relevant to the policing profession. To ensure an optimum development of the police force, the Police Academy is part of this knowledge infrastructure and cooperates with these institutes. It distinguishes itself by validating and enabling the implementation of developed and acquired knowledge.

Universities of Applied Sciences, such as the Police Academy, have the possibility to install research chairs, which are called lectorates. The research of the lectors and colleague-researchers is directed at enlarging policing knowledge relevant for police practice and at reinforcing the connection between theory, police practice and police education. Questions that arise from police practice are the starting point for the research projects. The researchers are closely linked to police practice, but they also distance themselves from the topic and commissioners on time in order to provide critical and independent conclusions. They will explain the findings and will give advice on their application in practice and in education. They teach, contribute to educational innovations and assist in the validation of the core tasks. They monitor the research projects and bachelor and master theses, whereas teachers take part in research projects of a lectorate.

Research topics are deduced from the Strategic Research Agenda for the police as established by the Minister of Safety & Justice in order to bring coherence and focus into what will be researched and to improve the impact on policies, education and the police profession. The research framework, called "A more effective police and a safer society" consists of four categories: current developments and police interventions, the police officer, the police in its environment and the police organisation.

Presently, there are nine lectorates: Criminality Control & Criminal Investigation Science, Forensic Investigation, Neighbourhood Policing, Public Order & Danger Control, Police History, Intelligence, Valuable Practice Development, Resilience and Cyber-safety. Because of shifting priorities, some lectorates ceased to exist (Traffic & Environment Policing, the Learning Police Organisation, Crisis Management, Police Leadership & Multicultural Issues) and new lectorates have been launched, for instance, on Resilience and Cyber-Safety.

International Contacts

The Police Academy contributes actively to conferences and programmes of CEPOL,[14] the organisation of European Police Colleges. To give a few examples of the Police Academy's participation in the development of programmes with regard to higher education:

- The EMJP (2014), European Joint Master of Policing. Also participation in teaching in collaboration with Canterbury Christ Church University (CCCU).
- Policing in Europe (2011), partially the predecessor of the EMJP. It is a multi-modular course at an academic level that deals with legal and operational aspects of international police cooperation.
- Survey on European Police Education and Bologna (2010). The aim of the SEPEB survey was to find out to what degree countries in Europe structure their police curricula according to the guidelines of the Declaration of Bologna.
- A Competency Profile for Senior Police Officers in the Field of International Police Cooperation (2005).

Apart from CEPOL the Police Academy cooperated or cooperates with partners abroad:

- With Canterbury Christ Church University (CCCU) concerning its MSc in Policing Programme.

- With University College Dublin (UCD) concerning its MSc FCCI (MSc in Forensic Computing & Cybercrime Investigation). The Police Academy is allowed to offer this MSc degree. UCD is the Centre for Cybersecurity and Cybercrime Investigation. Both parties are involved in delivering the online and residential part of the programme.
- With the Police Academy of Lower Saxony (Germany) and the Hungarian National Public Service University concerning ComPHEE (2011–2014), a EU funded programme that was directed at exchanging modules of international relevance, that is, Mobile Banditry, Virtual Worlds & Criminality, and Hate Crime.
- With the Police Forces of Belgium and Germany concerning a Gold Commander Course on the premises of the Police Academy in Ossendrecht.

Conclusion

The Police Academy has constantly adjusted its coherent system of police education and research objectives and keeps on doing so, be it due to external factors, that is, decisions of Ministries or the changes in the Police Organisation, be it as a result of advice of the Police Education Council to the Minister in question, be it driven by own initiatives.

This applies to the review of occupational and qualifications, to the structure of the programmes, to the elaboration of the competency structure, to the establishment of research chairs (lectorates), to the selection of partnerships. In spite of all necessary adjustments that have been made, the innovative principles that led to a completely different approach of police education and research 15 years ago, have not been messed with. The Police Academy still sticks to:

- the importance of diploma-equivalence between policing and regular degrees and the accreditation of its bachelor and master programmes as to ensure mutual societal and international acceptance;
- the competency approach, the dual training system and the formulation of modules in terms of core tasks as to minimise the cleavage between police theories and police practice;

- the engagement in applied research as to stimulate that enquiries into policing matters impacts both policing theories and the practice of policing, both advantages for updating police education and policies at a ministerial or organisational level that affect policing strategies.

Notes

1. The Status of University of Applied Sciences is based on a regulation (BVH 2006/128011 U) issued by the Ministry of Education, Culture & Sciences (11–10, 2006), by which the Police Academy of the Netherlands became an Institution for Higher Professional Education (Institution Number 28 DP) under Article 6.9 of the Law on Higher Education and Scientific Research.
2. Amendment of Police Law 2012 in view of the incorporation of the Police Academy into the new police organisation, First Chamber of the States General, 16 February 2016.
3. Presently, there are four master programmes. The Executive Master of Police Management (EMPM) for police leaders at a strategic level is not delivered for the time being, because the content and need of it have to be discussed as a result of an altered view on leadership within the National Police.
4. The Law (from 2003) refers to the former name of the Police Academy: LSOP, a Dutch abbreviation. The name LSOP changed into Police Academy in 2014.
5. Several articles of the Amendment to the Police Law refer to the confirmation of the original principles of the educational innovation.
6. ZBO means "Zelfstandig Bestuursorgaan", a Dutch acronym for Independent Governing Body.
7. POR stands for "Politieonderwijsraad", a Dutch acronym for Police Education Council.
8. CEPOL also uses this competency structure, the particular division of competencies into four categories, for the profile of Senior Police Officers. Refer to: Brekelmans, T., Tomkowa, H., Vossen, B., and Peeters, H. (2005) *A Competency Profile for Senior Police Officers in the Field of International Cooperation.*, CEPOL: Bramshill, UK.
9. EQF stands for European Qualifications Framework.

10. LFNP stands for the Dutch acronym "Landelijk Functiegebouw Nederlandse Politie" (Independent Governing Body). The process of giving police officers and police leaders a new LFNP function is still going on, not in the least because of a great number of personal objections.

11. The diploma-equivalence was not only signed by the Minister of Education, Culture and Sciences but also by the Minister of Justice and the Minister of the Interior, in a joint letter to the MPs of the Second Chamber, 8 April 1999.

12. 'HBO-raad' is a Dutch acronym that stands for "Hoger Beroepsonderwijs Raad', Council for Higher Professional Education, nowadays internationally referred to as Universities of Applied Sciences.

13. Text partly derived or paraphrased from Website Politieacademie (open source); available at: www.politieacademie.nl (accessed 08-11-2016)

14. CEPOL is the European Union Agency for Law Enforcement Training, see http://www.cepol.europa.eu. Since 1 July 2016, the date of CEPOL's new legal mandate, the official name of CEPOL is "The European Union Agency for Law Enforcement Training".

References

Council of Chief Constables. (2008). *Employers' Vision, an Inspiring Foundation* ['*Werkgeversvisie, een inspirerend fundament*']. De Bilt: Landelijk Programma HRM [National HRM Programme].

Den Boer, M., & Peeters, H. (2007). A View Across the Border: Higher Police Education in the Netherlands. In B. Frevel & K. Liebl. (Eds.), *Empirische Polizeiforschung IX: Stand und Perspektiven der Polizeiausbildung* [Empirical Police Research IX: State and Perspectives of Police Education] (pp. 115–130). Frankfurt: Verlag für Polizeiwissenschaft.

Grotendorst, A., Jellema, M., Stam, L., Van Der Vegt, M., & Zandbergen, C. (2002). *Leren in Veiligheid, het nieuwe politieonderwijs in maatschappelijk perspectief* [Learning in Safety, the New Police Education from a Societal Perspective]. Apeldoorn: Politie LSOP.

Ministry of Safety & Justice. (2012). *Development Plan National Police* [*Inrichtingsplan Nationale Politie*]. Available at L-www.rijksoverheid.nl. Accessed 8-11-2016.

Nijhof, W., Beukhof, G., Geerligs, J., Kicken, A., Peeters, H., Van De Pol, R., & Wijngaarden, R. (2011). *Schakelen in Verantwoordelijkheid, beroepen van de politie herijkt* [Switching between Responsibilities, Police Occupations Recalibrated]. The Hague: Politieonderwijsraad [Police Education Council, POR].

Peeters, H. (2010). Ten Ways to Blend Academic Learning within Professional Police Training. *Policing, A Journal of Policy and Practice*, 4(1), 47–55. Oxford: Oxford University Press.

Peeters H. (2013). *Power Point: Generic Presentation Politieacademie*.

Peeters, H. (2014). Constructing Comparative Competency Profiles: The Netherlands Experience. In P. Stanislas (Ed.), *International Perspectives on Police Education and Training* (pp. 90–113). London/New York: Routledge.

POR: Qualification Dossiers [Kwalificatiedossiers]. Available at: www.politieonderwijsraad.nl. Accessed 8-11-2016.

Stam, J. G., Grotendorst, A., Prins, B. A., & Peeters, M. H. A. (2007). New Look, Reforms in Police Training. In P. C. Kratcoski & D. K. Das (Eds.), *Police Education and Training in a Global Society* (pp. 199–211). Lanham: Lexington Books.

12

Down Under: Police Education at the Charles Sturt University, Australia

Tracey Green

Overview

Policing and Higher Education in Australia have a long-standing and complex history. Whilst progress towards a full professional model has been made, levels of resistance are still evident in some quarters. This chapter focuses on the progress which has been made towards policing achieving a professional status and discusses some of the changes and enduring partnership which have evolved 'down under'. In particular, the authors describe the collaborative recruit programme between the New South Wales Police Service and Charles Sturt University which has endured for over 15 years with a new 10-year contract recently signed. This programme has stood the test of time whilst other such initiatives have failed to thrive. This chapter explores the features of the collaboration in an effort to identify the factors that may have led to the ongoing resilience and success of this model for police recruitment within a higher

T. Green (✉)
Charles Sturt University, Port Macquarie, Australia

© The Author(s) 2018
C. Rogers, B. Frevel (eds.), *Higher Education and Police*,
DOI 10.1007/978-3-319-58386-0_12

education programme. In addition, the author explores the patterns and trends of serving officers engaging in continual professional development within higher education throughout Australia.

Policing in Australia

Emerging as a direct result of the colonial history, Australia has a strongly centralised and largely bureaucratic policing style (Findlay 2004; Wilson 2009). Influenced by the introduction of appointed constables in the UK, settlers of British origin brought with them experience of the 'new police' in London and attempted to re-create a similar force to retain law and order in Australia (Findlay 2004; Wilson 2009). With the original constables appointed by the governor of the day, Australian policing originated with strong political links and was 'surrounded by acute political conflict' (Reiner 2000; Green 2015).

Many of the early constables were appointed from the Irish convict heritage and were frequently dismissed for drunken or violent behaviour (Stobbs 2009; Wilson 2009). As the colony grew so did the need for public order to be maintained. Colonial issues emerged including mass migration to the numerous gold fields, frequent attacks by bush rangers and resistance to colonisation by Indigenous Australians. All of these issues reinforced the arguments for centralised control as settlers urged the colonial government to provide them protection (Findlay 2004; Wilson 2009). The significance of this colonial history is still evident in so much as policing in Australia today, despite being based on Peelian Principles (Manning 2005), remains a matter for the state rather than the direct responsibility of the local community (Finnane 1994; Stobbs 2009; Wilson 2009). In addition, the police in Australia evolved as an armed force based on a military-style training and background as opposed to the unarmed civilians introduced by Peel to form the 'new police' in the UK (Corns 1988).

Australian policing remained organised at the State level for almost 70 years until 1979 when in response to the Hilton Hotel bombing, Sir Robert Mark was commissioned to conduct a review of the Australian police which became known as the Mark Report (1978). The implementation of the review saw the establishment of the Australian Federal Police (AFP) who were a dedicated national response for crimes against the Commonwealth and were also charged with the responsibility of policing the Australian Capital Territory (Stobbs 2009). In addition to the AFP, there are currently six State Police Forces, New South Wales, Queensland, South Australia, Tasmania, Victoria and Western Australia, and two territories: the Australian Capital Territory (ACT) and the Northern Territory (Dean and Thorne 2009). Each State and Territory also shares a range of national responsibilities and a limited range of common services. Most of these initiatives were brought under the one organisation in 2007 with the establishment of the Australian New Zealand Police Advisory Agency (ANZPAA). ANZPAA 'is a joint initiative of the Australian and New Zealand Police Ministers and Commissioners' (ANZPAA 2014a, b), which replaced a large number of previous ad hoc arrangements. ANZPAA seeks to develop common standards for training, promotion and professional behaviour as well as co-ordination of joint standing committees (ANZPAA 2014a, b).

Police Recruitment in Australia

A range of inquiries and Royal Commissions have criticised the recruitment practices of Australian police leading to a number of experiments with alternate training and education programme (Fitzgerald 1989; Wood 1997; Kennedy 2004; Rush 2012). Following the Fitzgerald Inquiry (1989) into police corruption in Queensland, the Queensland Police formed a partnership with Griffith University to deliver a broader curriculum to new police recruits in an effort to provide a higher level of education and help reduce corruption amongst officers (Wimshurst and Ransley 2007). This programme was short lived with the police reverting back to an 'in-house' delivery model with claims that the new officers were not being adequately prepared for policing (Wimshurst and Ransley 2007).

Likewise, the Wood Royal Commission (1997) into the New South Wales Police Service determined that the internalised and insular training of new recruits was responsible for the recreation of police culture and bred an atmosphere in which corruption and inappropriate behaviour amongst police could thrive. Wood (1997) recommended that all new recruits should attend university to study a generic, higher education programme and socialise with a broader group of the community in a university setting in preparation for the police force (Wood 1997). The New South Wales Police in response to the Commissions criticisms established a collaborative university partnership with Charles Sturt University whereby, the university jointly delivers an associate degree in policing practice recruit programme within the police academy, in what was considered by some a compromise situation (Bradley 1996; Wimshurst and Ransley 2007; Green and Woolston 2013). This approach has, however, endured and remains the compulsory programme for police recruitment to the New South Wales Police (Corboy 2008; Green and Woolston 2013). This collaborative program is discussed in detail later in this chapter. The Tasmanian Police Force has also similarly engaged the University of Tasmania to be involved in their recruit programme; however, this programme is post recruitment and not compulsory (Tasmania Police 2016).

Between 1973 and 2006 (Pitman 2009), Australian policing was subject to a total of 25 public inquiries, many of which recommended sweeping change to police minimum education levels for recruitment and the internalised training which dominates the preparation for the role (Fitzgerald 1989; Wood 1997; Kennedy 2004; Rush 2012). Despite these recommendations, the minimum academic entry level for recruits to Australian Policing remains low and the minimum qualification following approximately two years of training is generally situated at the diploma level. Each jurisdiction makes its own determination as to the minimum standards for recruitment and the training or education that they are required to undertake. ANZPAA as a national advisory body recommends the minimum standards which are currently located in the vocational education sector for the rank of constable (ANZPAA 2014a, b). Many of the jurisdictions have increased the number of women, graduates and minority groups but there remains a disparity similar to that seen in the UK (Accenture 2013; Brown 2013; Green and Woolston 2013; Prenzler and Sinclair 2013; Silvestri et al. 2013).

Table 12.1 is a summary of the current (2016) minimum entry requirement, qualifications and training and salary on being sworn in as a probationary constable for police throughout Australia.

Table 12.1 Qualifications and training for Australian police (Green 2015)

	Minimum pre-entry qualification	Entry-level training/education	Length of time to complete	Salary on commencement ($)
New South Wales	Completion of University Certificate in Workforce Essentials	Associate Degree Policing Practice	1 year and 32 weeks (including probation)	61,000
Tasmania	Year 10 education + literacy numeracy test	Includes subjects towards Bachelor's Degree	29 weeks plus probation	55,865
West Australia	Year 10 education + literacy numeracy test	Diploma Public Safety (Policing)	28 weeks plus probation	66,960
Queensland	Year 12 education or 3 years paid employment + literacy and numeracy test	Diploma Public Safety (Policing)	25 weeks plus probation	52,823
South Australia	Year 12 education preferable + literacy, numeracy test	Diploma Public Safety (Policing) *NB About to change to an internal police qualification*	29 weeks plus probation	57,680
Northern Territory	Year 12 education	Diploma Public Safety (Policing)	30 weeks plus probation	58,392
Victoria	Victorian Certificate of Education and literacy, numeracy test	Diploma Public Safety	23 weeks plus probation	58,176
Australian Federal Police	Year 12 education	Diploma Public Safety (Policing)	25 weeks training programme plus probation	54,893

Ref: Recruitment web sites of each jurisdiction as accessed on 1.9.2015
- http://www.police.nsw.gov.au/recruitment/being_a_police_officer
- http://www.policerecruit.qld.gov.au/academyLife/Recruit+Information.htm
- http://www.police.wa.gov.au/Aboutus/Recruitment/tabid/980/Default.aspx
- http://www.police.tas.gov.au/join-us/about-the-role/
- http://www.achievemore.com.au/officer/the-process.html
- http://www.pfes.nt.gov.au/Police/Careers-in-policing.aspx
- http://www.policecareer.vic.gov.au/police
- http://www.afp.gov.au/jobs.aspx

It is clear that with the exception of New South Wales Police Force and to a lesser degree Tasmania Police Force (Tasmania Police 2016), recruit level preparation for policing in Australia remains entrenched in a practitioner-focused, skills-based, training environment.

Police Training and Specialisation

As a sworn police officer and having successfully completed probationary requirements, the future career trajectory of the individual is a highly personal and self-directed path. Promotion is regarded as the primary recognition of good work and reward, with increased pay and responsibility attributed to successful application for promotion (Green 2015). Similarly, transfers into specialist departments are seen as advancement and offer a range of pathways for officers to diversify and forge a rewarding career path. It should be noted however, that all such transfers, be it to an area of specialisation or a promotion, are highly competitive and not necessarily attractive for everyone. Kennedy (2004) noted in the Royal Commission into the Western Australia Police that for those who are content to remain at the constable rank, staff development or training requirements are minimal:

> It would appear that officers as a rule only undertake training courses if they are seeking information. It is a matter of particular significance because of the large number of senior constables who spend many years at that rank, and on present figures, may remain senior constables until retirement. Apart from being obliged to update their shooting skills, there is little obligation to undertake any regular training or professional development. (Kennedy 2004)

Police can, therefore, spend a great deal of their service without continuing professional development other than minimum mandatory training such as updates on new legislation or in Australia, firearms certification.

In Australia, there is a range of national guidelines for police training and recommendations regarding the appropriate skills, knowledge and qualification framework for certain specialist roles ANZPAA (2014a, b). A more consolidated approach to national standards has recently resulted in the development of the Australia New Zealand Police Professionalisation Strategy 2013–2018 (ANZPAA 2014a, b); however, participation in the new strategy on behalf of the police jurisdictions also remains voluntary.

Training for specialist policing tasks areas generally remains 'in house', while some areas of police specialisation and leadership have formed partnerships and linkages with tertiary providers to develop specific skills and knowledge such as forensic science, counter-terrorism or cyber-crime (Neyroud 2011). Higher education leadership development programmes have also been offered for senior police officers for many years (AIPM 2014; College of Policing 2014), but the vast majority of police training remains internally delivered and based within the vocational education frameworks, if accredited at all (Green 2015).

The Issue of Professionalisation

While there is a general acceptance by both the community and the police themselves that police should behave 'professionally' (Wood 1997; Lanyon 2007), professional behaviour is not the only requirement of an occupation wishing to be regarded as a 'profession'. Despite many years of debate and consideration in Australia, there is not a clear professional pathway as yet established for policing to achieve professional status (Gates and Green 2014). There are many higher education programme which 'inform' or build upon the underlying disciplines of policing, the defined 'discipline area' (knowledge base) of policing is still emerging (Rojek et al. 2012). Many including the Police Federation of Australia stand firm on the need to develop enabling structures of national membership and registration (Neyroud 2011; Police Federation of Australia 2016), "there is as yet no consensus in Australia regarding the need to embrace full professional status" (Gates and Green 2014, p. 74).

The many definitions of a profession can be summarised as the transformation of an occupation into a profession (Higgs et al. 2009). 'Definitions of what constitutes a "profession" within the literature are diverse, contested and constantly evolving' (Gates and Green 2014, p. 75). However, from the literature, the group of characteristics provided in Fig. 12.1 can be derived.

Fig. 12.1 Entry requirement, qualifications and training and salary for probationary constables (Gates and Green 2014, p. 75)

It is evident that the occupation of policing reflects some of the characteristics of a profession as identified above; yet despite the common practice of practitioners identifying policing as a profession (ANZPAA 2014a, b; College of Policing 2016), there remain characteristics commonly adopted by other professions which are yet to be fully embraced by policing in Australia: in particular, the commitment to higher education and lifelong learning, self-regulation and self-organising system of rewards.

Explanations for the reluctance of police to fully engage with the full range of characteristics of a profession are numerous (Gates and Green 2014) but despite years of agreement by the most senior of police in

Australia (Lanyon 2007) that a fully developed profession of policing would best serve the community, the road blocks remain in place. For example, the issue of the establishment of a "National Police Registration Scheme" remains the second highest priority on the key national issues for the Police Federation of Australia (Police Federation of Australia 2016). Recent moves in the UK to formalise the requirements for relevant tertiary education for recruitment, specialisation and promotion of police (College of Policing 2016) are echoed in Australia but not implemented on a national basis. There is no common approach or adoption of policing educational standards despite the development and agreement by the Commissioners of Police to the Australian, New Zealand Professionalisation Strategy 2013–2018 (ANZPAA 2014a, b) which scopes the practice standards required at the point of recruitment, promotion or specialisation as well as strategies for continuous professional development, mobility and national registration. All of the States and Territories send a limited number of officers to the Australian Institute of Police Management (AIPM) to participate in the only common programmes that lead to post graduate tertiary awards but this is a staff development opportunity and is not directly linked to promotion. Each state and territory has their own priorities and arrangements for the development of their staff and while some are beginning to mirror the recent announcements in the UK to adopt a higher education framework (College of Policing 2016) this is by no means the common practice for many reasons, including

- Concerns regarding the ability to be able to recruit sufficient police to rural and remote areas
- loss of control of industrial issues
- terms of employment
- loss of ability to directly respond to the political environment within the state at any given time (see, Gates and Green 2014).

Current Status of Police Education

Changes to both the higher education system during the past decade and the requirements of policing to be technologically adept and sophisticated have unconsciously collided to bring about a shift in the cultures of both universities and policing (Rogers 2010; Gates and Green 2014; Christopher 2015). Once the bastions of the elite and privileged (Barnett 2011; Blass and Hayward 2014; Norton 2014) universities in Australia (and the UK) find themselves facing a very different landscape. Government changes have introduced funding cuts, open competition and drastically increased targets for the number of people accessing higher education (Norton 2014). These changes are compounded by the large number of private providers now able to issue higher education qualifications. Universities have been forced to engage in a much more business-like approach to ensure the survival of their institutions and have therefore in many cases embraced new and emerging professional areas such as social worker, para-medicine and policing. This diversion from the traditional academic profile of the university has not been universally welcomed but is seen by some as essential in a dynamic and evolving educational landscape (Blass and Hayward 2014; Norton 2014). Likewise, policing has been forced to accept that the role of policing has developed beyond recognition. At the release of the policing education reforms in the UK, Chief Constable Alex Marshall stated:

> *The nature of police work has changed significantly. Cyber-enabled crime has increased. So has the need for officers and staff to investigate and gather intelligence online and via information technology. Protecting vulnerable people has rightly become a high priority for policing. Officers and staff now spend more of their time working to prevent domestic abuse, monitor high-risk sex offenders and protect at-risk children.* (College of Policing 2016)

While there is no doubt that some remain unconvinced in both institutions that there are benefits to be gained by co-existence, it seems that there is a substantial shift in the culture and attitude of individual officers. Many officers are now engaging in their own higher education and building the body of knowledge from a practitioner basis (Heslop 2011; Lanyon 2007; Ratcliffe 2002; Rossmo 2009; Selfox 2009; Wilkinson 2010). These practitioners are gradually beginning to influence their own environment and professional identity (Gates and Green 2014). Despite the rhetoric that some police will only undertake higher education qualifications to improve their promotion prospects (Baro and Burlingame

1999; Chan and Doran 2009), this is negated by the number of officers engaging well beyond their own professional development requirements. 'It seems from the emerging body of knowledge that police practitioners—both serving and retired officers—are invading the higher education sector. This body of knowledge is practice based and applied to the discipline of policing. It details and contests the professional practice of policing and engages practitioners that are keen to enhance their own performance by researching police practice' (Gates and Green 2014, p. 85).

In Australia, a brief scan of the executive staff of every one of the state and territory police agencies demonstrates that they have all had some level of engagement with higher education all holding a wide range of postgraduate tertiary qualifications. Whilst it is difficult to obtain exact data from each of the jurisdictions regarding the level of graduate entry, the rapid growth and popularity of university programmes designed to enhance the skills and abilities of serving officers are testament to the engagement of police in higher education. There is little doubt that individual officers see the benefits for their own development and are increasingly prepared to invest both financially and intellectually in their own future (Green 2015). Evidence of the change in culture and expectation can be seen in the case study outlined below which clearly demonstrates a shift in the experience of police recruitment in Australia.

Case Study, the New South Wales Police Force and Charles Sturt University Collaboration

By way of profile, Charles Sturt University (CSU) is a public university in the State of New South Wales, Australia. The University has eight regional campuses located across the state, which to put into geographical perspective, is approximately the combined size of France and Germany or the state of Texas. The diversity of the state is extreme with the bulk of the population located in Sydney and other east coast cities. However, both the University and the New South Wales Police Force (NSWPF) are required to provide services across the entire state.

NSWPF is one of the largest Police Forces in the English-speaking world with over 16,000 sworn officer serving a population of 7 million people spread over 801,600 square kilometres housing over 500 police stations (see https://www.police.nsw.gov.au/__data/assets/pdf_file/0007/435868/Internet_Figures_31102016.pdf).

The University offers approximately 400 courses to over 38,000 students across Australia and the world through multiple campuses in NSW and by online education. An extensive professional course profile, and emphasis on workplace learning and practicum components, means CSU has a reputation for being the University for the Professions. Roughly one in seven of the University's students are in police or law enforcement (see http://www.csu.edu.au/).

The University committed itself in 1992 to work with policing to develop policing as a professional field of study at university level. CSU now employs a strong cohort of policing academics, including senior academics with strong practitioner roots in policing. During the 22 years lifetime of the partnership between NSWPF and CSU (including the programme which predated the ADPP), they have enrolled more than 66 intakes of policing students and produced in excess of 32,000 graduates. The University and NSWPF share the longest sustained police and academic institution partnership in the world.

The origins of the current programme, the associate degree in policing practice (ADPP) as explained earlier in this chapter, arose as a result of the Wood Royal Commission (Wood 1997) into Corruption within the NSWPF. Acknowledging the claims of some commentators that the NSWPF/CSU model is a compromise on Woods original recommendations (Wimshurst and Ransley 2007), the success of the programme is largely dependent on that very factor for its ongoing success. Determined not to be forced into a 'non-police specific' degree entry pathway for the NSWPF as recommended by Wood (1997), the Police recognised the need to embrace change but chose to co-develop a collaborative partnership between themselves and a university partner. CSU were successful in tendering to co-deliver the recruit level programme and so began the work of developing a partnership approach which could meet the needs of the NSWPF, whilst embedding the change which could be brought by exposure to higher education. Several key elements combined to allow for the collaboration:

- NSWPF had to be seen to acknowledge the findings of the Wood Royal Commission, which targeted the initial recruitment and training of new officers as a particular factor which encouraged the replication of corrupt and unethical behaviours (Wood 1997).
- CSU were engaged in professional education and had experience of working in partnership arrangements with curriculum designed to meet the needs of new and emerging professions.
- The NSWPF Association at the time acknowledged the requirements for change and saw the opportunity for a step towards a 'professional status' for policing and the subsequent status and salary increase this could demand (Chambers 2004).
- The availability of a flexible funding mechanism on which the programme could be based.
- Visionary leadership on all sides to ensure that the collaborative model that was established would meet the recruitment needs of the NSWPF including a diverse workforce.

Central to the programme has been the collaborative approach between the University and the NSWPF. The ADPP is the only recruitment pathway into the NSWPF therefore mandatory for all new recruits (other than a very small number of re-joinee officers). It is therefore the joint responsibility of CSU and the NSWPF to oversee every step of the process from initial recruitment to graduation and confirmation in the role of police constable. The number of students allowed to be admitted into the ADPP is totally controlled by the recruitment requirements of NSWPF; therefore, only the number required for employment will be allowed to commence study ensuring (allowing for some attrition) there is no backlog of fully qualified students waiting to be employed. This important measure was seen as an essential element of the programme development to ensure currency of learning and ethical recruitment to both the University and the NSWPF.

Beyond the determination of recruitment numbers, the entire development of the ADPP is a shared exercise. The NSWPF Academy is also home to the CSU School of Policing Studies and all teaching and administrate teams are collocated to ensure the maximum level of collaboration. The design of the programme is based on the entry-level requirements of police officers and focuses on the foundational studies and applied skills of a modern policing profession. The curriculum builds on firm academic principles which are applied in the policing context in a programme designed to prepare police officers for the role they are about to undertake. This level of specific professional preparation, rather than the acquisition of a generic tertiary education, as recommended by Wood (1997) and others (Chan 1997, Punch 2007) is far more reflective of other emerging and long-standing traditions of preparatory professional university education. Punch (2007) also argued the benefits of exposure to a broader university environment as being potentially beneficial to new police recruits. However, the average age of the students entering the ADPP has remained around 27 years of age therefore expelling the myth that NSWPF recruits have little experience or exposure to a diverse range of life skills.

Delivery of the ADPP is also a collaborative exercise with both police and university staff each delivering half of the curriculum. The only area not co-delivered is the officer safety component involving the use of weapons and self-defence.

Phases 1 and 2 of the ADPP are effectively two 16-week trimesters that require full-time attendance at the NSWPF Academy. Throughout these first two phases, all students (potential recruits) are university students; they are not in receipt of a salary and have not been employed by NSWPF. They have undergone the full screening process for employment and must have met the full medical, fitness and selection requirements (largely at their own expense) for entry into the NSWPF before being offered entry to the ADPP. All students are then effectively undertaking a 32-week selection process whereby they are required to meet all of the physical, behavioural and educational requirements of the programme before being offered employment by NSWPF. Students are in receipt of assistance with living costs and some qualify for a means tested scholarship; however, none are employed prior to the point of attestation at the successful completion of Phase 2. Clearly, this provides savings in salary for the NSWPF but also allows for both the police and the student to determine if the police force is in fact the best career choice for them.

Diversity

One consistent ambition of policing in Australia is to increase diversity in their recruitment practices (ANZPAA 2012). The introduction of the ADPP as a compulsory requirement for recruitment into the NSWPF determined that the inclusion of a tertiary partner, and the award of an academic qualification for completion of recruit training, encourages a more diverse group of applicants and increased applications from people who had previously not considered policing a career option (Corboy 2008; Green and Woolston 2013). The number of applications from students of ethnically diverse background has remained high and the overall application numbers for the programme far exceed the recruitment numbers required. This is not common across the country with some states struggling to recruit particularly in the states with strong mining employment.

Flexible delivery pathways have been developed for the first stage of the programme (16-week full-time equivalent) including an option for 'online' delivery (which extends the duration to 32 weeks). This option was designed to encourage more mature students or those with financial or family commitments to be able to undertake Phase 1 of the ADPP in a part-time mode, whilst still working or living at home. The online pathway has now been available for over ten years and has assisted in retaining a very diverse group of applicants for the programme in terms of gender, ethnicity, education and experience.

Pathways have been developed and introduced to ensure recruitment from all areas of the community. One example is the IPROWD programme, designed to assist Indigenous students to prepare for the physical tests and the study requirements of the ADPP, which recently won the prestigious national AHRI Award for Indigenous Employment recognising the success of the programme in attracting and retaining Indigenous recruits and increasing engagement and employment within NSWPF (AHRI Awards 2016).

Funding

As mentioned, this model of police recruitment provides savings in salary for the NSWPF but also allows for a period of preparation for the role during which the student can demonstrate that they are suitable for the role prior to being employed. Students who fail to meet the employment standards can transfer into appropriate CSU programme with credit for any subjects successfully undertaken. The fees are established under an 'employer reserved model', which in effect means that the employer provides half of the training, while the student funds the remainder. The University delivers half of the programme, which is funded by the student fees representing a cost saving in the number of police staff required to deliver training. Students are able to repay student fees in instalments once employed by the police and may be in receipt of student allowances during Phases 1 and 2 of the programme.

The Curriculum

The curriculum ensures the practice standards for the role of constable as agreed by the Australian New Zealand Council of Police Professionalisation (ANZCoPP) and managed by ANZPAA are met (ANZPAA 2014a, b). Mapping of the ADPP curriculum against the practice standards demonstrates the additional learning undertaken within the programme (Davies and Rogers 2015; Chilvers 2016). This includes development in the areas which were strongly criticised by the Wood Royal Commission (Wood 1997) and other critics of police nepotism and cultural blindness (Westmarland 2005). The curriculum is delivered in an integrated model which reinforces learning and develops critical thinking, decision-making, ethical behaviour and provides ample opportunity for 'practice'. The entire second year (Phases 3, 4 and 5) is spent as a probationary constable, learning on the job with a clear developmental pathway to take the recruit through stages of competency acquisition to the point where they are able to operate automatously in the role of a constable. This practice acquisition is combined with a requirement for them to demonstrate that they are developing as a reflective practitioner, able to consider their own performance and further refine and develop their learning. CSU staff work with NSWPF teaching staff to ensure the educational relevance and applicability of the curriculum in preparing students for the role of early career police officers in New South Wales.

The ADPP has been reviewed on numerous occasions for a variety of reasons but generally to determine the level of preparedness of probationary constables and to evaluate the effectiveness of the programme. Given the size and variability of the NSWPF footprint, it is challenging to prepare probationary constables for deployment throughout the region, but recent reviews of the ADPP by Davies and Rogers (Davies and Rogers 2015) and Chilvers (2016) have found that local commanders are confident in the quality of the probationary constables. A process of constant evaluation has assisted in guiding staff performance, curriculum delivery methodology and consistency in the workplace learning. Because the ADPP is an award of the University, the Australian Quality Assurance Framework also has to be adhered to. The programme, because of the collaboration between higher education and industry and the somewhat unusual approach, has been audited regularly to ensure university standards are adhered to. Again, the results were positive with the partnership between NSWPF and CSU being awarded a gold star rating for a collaborative university/professional model in the most recent partnership review by the Australian Tertiary Education Quality and Standards Agency (TEQSA).

The completion of the ADPP is mandatory, therefore, not an 'optional extra' as some other programme have been designed. Successful completion of the ADPP is also aligned with confirmation of employment and appointment to the rank of constable at the end of the probationary period, therefore, all inclusions and, importantly, exclusions in the curriculum do come under scrutiny in a variety of legal arenas including the Industrial and Coroners Courts. It is paramount that the curriculum is managed, maintained and reviewed to ensure that both CSU and the NSWPF can confidently provide evidence as to the level of preparation of all probationary constables.

Challenges

One of the greatest challenges is the fluctuation of the student numbers, which are directly linked to the number of vacancies, held within the NSWPF. This number tends to be fluid and can be influenced by pending state elections or an amendment in the legislation, which creates a change in employment conditions triggering a period of high attrition. The programme currently has a rolling trimester design with three new intakes a year, which then continue through the next five trimesters as is the practice for normal university progression. However, in the case of the ADPP, this can mean very differing intake numbers varying from as low as 40 up to 870 in a single intake, depending on the numbers required. This creates numerous challenges including the physical resources required as well as resourcing the qualified teaching staff and suitable placements for the students once they are sworn in as probationers.

The physical location of the Police Academy in a rural town approximately 200 km inland from Sydney also creates challenges, as it is difficult to attract both police and academic staff to a location so far from the coast and within a small community. Employment for family and partners is not easy to find and the choices for education of children are limited compared to the larger cities on the coast. This same factor is also unhelpful in staff renewal because both academic and police staff who do relocate find it very expensive to return to the coastal cities. Currency and quality of teaching staff is therefore a constant risk, which requires ongoing attention. The issues involved in assisting the transition of police practitioners to enable them to become successful police educators are also complex and may have varying degrees of success. A full debate of the challenges faced by practitioners transitioning into higher education is beyond the scope of this chapter (see Green 2015).

The obvious differences between the two bureaucratic organisations and their different approaches have now largely been overcome however should not be understated. This has required flexibility on both sides but some of the issues that have been overcome relate to the following:

- employment of university staff and police staff essentially on very different terms and conditions,

- requirements of the university to meet AQF requirements, whilst including the practice elements of the programme in the curriculum,
- NSWPF need to meet constantly changing policy and legal challenges,
- sharing of student information and privacy,
- workplace learning and occupational health and safety requirements between students and police officers,
- entry requirements,
- English language, literacy,
- physical disabilities,
- a critical mass of students to ensure the viability of such a collaboration and allow for the programme to survive during the times of low recruitment.

The list is extensive and seems to throw up new and emerging debates between what is essentially an inherent requirement to be a police officer versus the right to be a student. Many lessons have been learned!

Conclusion

The ADPP is not being presented in this chapter as a 'perfect model' and will continue to have a process of constant renewal to ensure it is fit for purpose and meeting the needs of NSWPF and the community. It does, however, have a strong and durable history that has served the numerous parties well. In examining this model as suggested above, there are lessons to be learned.

To succeed, it appears that essentially there needs to be a very strong and genuine commitment to work in collaboration. No one party to a partnership should be reluctant or unwilling to flex to solve the many challenges that will inevitably emerge.

Lessons learned in this collaboration can be echoed through the landscape of policing and higher education. The benefits of engagement are unlikely to be achieved without a common respect for the benefits that both sides can bring. This requires flexibility, respect and understanding by both the universities and policing as a foundation upon which to build. If either party believes they have a superior or dominant role the relationship is likely to be unproductive and short lived and those who have for many years stated that higher education has no place in policing will continue to gloat (Green 2015).

References

Accenture. (2013). *Preparing Police Services for the Future: Six Steps Toward Transformation.* Accenture. From https://www.accenture.com/us-en/insight-preparing-police-service-future-six-steps-toward-transformation

AHRI Awards. (2016). *NSW Police Force, AHRI Award for Indigenous Employment Finalist.* Retrieved January 1, 2017, from https://www.tafewestern.edu.au/news/prestigious-award-for-iprowd

AIPM. (2014). *Australian Institute of Police Management.* Retrieved April 8, 2014, from http://www.aipm.gov.au/

ANZPAA. (2012). *Directions in Australia New Zealand Policing 2012–2015* (p. 16). Melbourne: Australian New Zealand Police Advisory Agency.

ANZPAA. (2014a). *Australia New Zealand Police Professionalisation Strategy 2013–2018* (p. 20).

ANZPAA. (2014b). *Australian New Zealand Police Advisory Agency Home Page.* Retrieved February 28, 2014, from https://www.anzpaa.org.au/about-us

Barnett, R. (2011). *Being a University.* New York: Routledge.

Baro, A. L., & Burlingame, D. (1999). Law Enforcement and Higher Education: Is There an Impasse? *Journal of Criminal Justice Education, 10*(1), 57–73.

Blass, E., & Hayward, P. (2014). Innovation in Higher Education; Will There Be a Role for "The Academe/University" in 2025? *European Journal of Futures Research, 2*(1), 1–9.

Bradley, D. (1996). In D. Chappell & P. Wilson (Eds.), *Contemporary Police Education in Australia. Australian Policing: Contemporary Issues* (pp. 85–110). Sydney: Butterworths.

Brown, J. M. (2013). *The Future of Policing.* Hoboken: Taylor and Francis.

Chambers, R. (2004). *Collaborative Police Education – A Report.* Rotterdam: World Association for Collaborative Education.

Chan, J. B. (1997). *Changing Police Culture: Policing in a Multicultural Society.* Cambridge: Cambridge University Press.

Chan, J., & Doran, S. (2009). Staying in the Job: Job Satisfaction among Mid-career Police Officers. *Policing: A Journal of Policy and Practice, 3*(1), 66–77.

Chilvers, G. (2016). *External Examination and Quality Audit of the ADPP Course Provision* (p. 40). Goulburn: NSWPF.

Christopher, S. (2015). The Quantum Leap: Police Recruit Training and the Case for Mandating Higher Education Pre-entry Schemes. *Policing, 9*(4), 388–404.

College of Policing. (2014). *College of Policing.* Retrieved February 23, 2014, from http://www.college.police.uk/en/home.htm

College of Policing. (2016). *Developing and Delivering an Education Qualification Framework for Policing.* 1: 44. London: College of Policing. From http://www.college.police.uk/What-we-do/Learning/Policing-Education-Qualifications-Framework/Documents/PEQF_2016.pdf

Corboy, M. (2008). *Operation Viente: A Review of the New South Wales Police Education and Training Command.* Unpublished Paper/Internal Report, Parramatta, Sydney.

Corns, C. (1988). Policing and Social Change. *Australian and New Zealand Journal of Sociology, 24*(1), 32–46.

Davies, A., & Rogers, C. (2015). *Evaluation of the Pre Attestation Phases of the ADPP for Preparing Probationary Constables for Operational Duty.* CSU and NSWPF: Goulburn.

Dean, G., & Thorne, C. (2009). In R. Broadhurst & S. Davies (Eds.), *Organisation and Management of Police. Policing in Context: An Introduction to Police Work in Australia* (pp. 49–67). Melbourne: Oxford University Press.

Findlay, M. (2004). *Introducing Policing: Challenges for Police and Australian Communities.* Sydney: Oxford Press.

Finnane, M. (1994). *Police and Government: Histories of Policing in Australia Melbourne.* Melbourne: Oxford University Press.

Fitzgerald, G. (1989). *Report of a Commission of Inquiry Pursuant to Orders in Council.* Brisbane. From www.ccc.qld.gov.au/research-and-publications/publications/police/the-fitzgerald-inquiry-report-1987201389.pdf

Gates, A., & Green, T. (2014). Understanding the Process of Professionalisation in the Police Organisation. *Police Journal: Theory, Practice and Principles, 87*, 75–91.

Green, T. (2015). *Becoming a Police Academic: From Practitioner to Educator.* Faculty of Arts, Charles Sturt University, Australia. PHD.

Green, T., & Woolston, R. (2013). In P. Stanislas (Ed.), *Police Training and Education- Collaboration in Australia International Perspectives on Police Education and Training* (pp. 42–57). Oxon: Routledge.

Heslop, R. (2011). Reproducing Police Culture in a British University: Findings from an Exploratory Case Study of Police Foundation Degrees. *Police Practice and Research, 12*(4), 298–312.

Higgs, J., McAllister, L., & Whiteford, G. (2009). The Practice and Praxis of Professional Decision Making. In B. Green (Ed.), *The Practice and Praxis of Professional Decision Making* (pp. 101–120). Rotterdam: Sense Publishing.

Kennedy, G. A. (2004). *Royal Commission Into Whether or Not There Has Been Corrupt or Criminal Conduct by Any Western Australian Police Officer* (Final Report, Vol. II, p. 235). Perth: Police Royal Commission.

Lanyon, I. (2007). In M. Mitchell & J. Casey (Eds.), *Professionalisation of Policing in Australia: The Implications for Police Managers. Police Leadership and Management.* Sydney: Federation.

Manning, P. (2005). The Study of Policing. *Police Quarterly, 8*(1), 23–43.

Mark, R. (1978). *Report to the Minister for Administrative Services on the Organisation of Police Resources in the Commonwealth Area and Other Related Matters.* Canberra: AGPS.

Neyroud, P. (2011). *Review of Police Leadership and Training. Home Office Research* (Vol. 1, pp. 1–196). London: Home Office.

Norton, A. (2014). *Mapping Australia Higher Education 2014–15* (p. 104). Melbourne: Grattan Institute.

Pitman, G. (2009). Think About It! Police Education, Training and Professional Development. In R. Broadhurst & S. Davies (Eds.), *Policing in Context: An Introduction to Police Work in Australia.* Melbourne: Oxford University Press.

Police Federation of Australia. (2016). *Key National Issues.* Retrieved January 1, 2017, from http://www.pfa.org.au/key_national_issues.

Prenzler, T., & Sinclair, G. (2013). The Status of Women Police Officers: An International Review. *International Journal of Law, Crime and Justice, 41*(2), 115–131.

Punch, M. (2007). Cops with honours: University Education and Police Culture. In M. O'Neill, M. Marks, & A. Singh (Eds.), *Police Occupational Culture* (Vol. 8, pp. 105–128). Oxford: JAI Press.

Ratcliffe, J. (2002). Intelligence-led Policing and the Problems of Turning Rhetoric into Practice. *Policing and Society, 12*(1), 53–66.

Reiner, R. (2000). *The Politics of the Police.* Oxford: Oxford University Press.

Rogers, C. (2010). Professionalising the Police- The South Wales Approach. In *Contemporary Wales* (Vol. 23). Cardiff: University of Wales Press.

Rojek, J., et al. (2012). The Utilization of Research by the Police. *Police Practice and Research, 13,* 1–13.

Rossmo, D. K. (Ed.). (2009). *Criminal Investigative Failures.* London: CRC Press.

Rush, J. (2012). *Inquiry into the Command, Management and Functions of the Senior Structure of Victoria Police*. State Service Authority. Melbourne, State Government Victoria.

Selfox, P. (2009). *Criminal Investigation: An Introduction to Principles and Practice*. Cullompton: Willan Publishing.

Silvestri, M., et al. (2013). Gender and Police Leadership: Time for a Paradigm Shift? *International Journal of Police Science & Management, 15*(1), 61–73.

Stobbs, N. (2009). In R. Broadhurst & S. Davies (Eds.), *Police Powers and Duties. Policing in Context: An Introduction to Police Work in Australia* (p. 6981). Melbourne: Oxford University Press.

Tasmania Police. (2016). Tasmania Police Recruitment. Retrieved January 8, 2017, from http://www.police.tas.gov.au/join-us/.

Westmarland, L. (2005). Police Ethics and Integrity: Breaking the Blue Code of Silence. *Policing and Society, 15*(2), 145–165.

Wilkinson, S. (2010). The Modern Policing Environment. In G. Bammer (Ed.), *Dealing with Uncertainties in Policing Serious Crime* (pp. 15–25). Canberra: Australian National University E Press.

Wilson, D. (2009). In R. Broadhurst & S. Davies (Eds.), *Histories of Policing. Policing in Context: An Introduction to Police Work in Australia* (pp. 18–31). Melbourne: Oxford University Press.

Wimshurst, K., & Ransley, J. (2007). Police Education and the University Sector: Contrasting Models from the Australian Experience. *Journal of Criminal Justice Education., 18*(1), 106–122.

Wood, J. R. T. (1997). *Royal Commission into the New South Wales Police Service: Final report, Volume 1: Corruption*. The Government of New South Wales: Sydney.

Index

© The Author(s) 2018
C. Rogers, B. Frevel (eds.), *Higher Education and Police*,
DOI 10.1007/978-3-319-58386-0